ɩ

"Babe Ruth, Ty Cobb, Willie Mays, and Barry Bonds are all names mentioned when fans and historians create lists of baseball's all-time greats. Lincoln Mitchell takes on a journey through baseball's past and present by shifting our focus from thinking about the greatest of all time to the most important players in the modern game. Entries offer distinct insights into players and events of the modern game. Superstars and lesser accomplished players are looked at in new light, enhancing our appreciation for baseball's history from the perspective of the narratives that mean the most to us and explain the modern game's evolution, good and bad. Bryce Harper's importance thus emerges not just from his being a superstar but of how his path to Major League Baseball unveils the talent development pipeline that evolved in the early 21st century in the United States. A thought-provoking read for baseball enthusiasts."

Adrian Burgos, Jr., Professor at University of Illinois and author of *Playing America's Game: Baseball, Latinos, and the Color Line*

"No sport has had a greater impact on American social and political culture than baseball and no one has a greater grasp of that impact than Lincoln Mitchell. The One Hundred Most Important Players in Baseball History is essential reading for anyone who wishes to truly understand the relationship between America and its National Pastime and for anyone whose love of baseball extends beyond the mere appreciation of numbers in a box score."

Craig Calcaterra, Cup of Coffee Baseball Newsletter and author of *Rethinking Fandom: How to Beat the Sports-Industrial Complex at Its Own Game.*

"Lincoln Mitchell has done us a great service by taking the discussion of 'greatest players in history' away from statistics and reframing it around social impact, thereby giving us a list not of the batters with the most homers or the pitchers with the most wins, but of the men and women who made the most significant contributions to the American story that is both reflected in and embodied by our national game. In short, here is the intersectionality of baseball recognized and indispensably codified."

Steven Goldman, host of the Infinite Inning podcast and author of *Baseball's Brief Lives*.

"Lincoln Mitchell has done it again! In his latest book, the prolific political analyst and baseball historian revises the 'best ever player' genre of sportswriting by providing novel insights on the impact of baseball on American society. A fascinating and engaging read."

Frank A. Guridy, Professor of African American and African Diaspora Studies, Columbia University and author of *The Sports Revolution: How Texas Changed the Culture of American Athletics*

"Lincoln Mitchell delivers an outstanding comprehensive overview of the history of baseball in a unique way in this wonderful book. Mitchell discusses the great players, the great moments, and baseball's great history while also making astute observations on the many struggles the game has faced since its inception. This book pulls no punches. Lincoln Mitchell shares the stories of baseball's past while also using his deep knowledge of American history and the political world and to bring this compelling book together. Baseball fans will want to read, discuss, and debate the conclusions in this original and compelling book. The player biographies are concise, but extremely thought-provoking. This is bound to become a baseball classic."

Dr. Paul Semendinger, author of *Roy White: From Compton to the Bronx*, *The Least Among Them*, and *Scattering the Ashes*.

"Mitchell's...assessments of the player are informed and perceptive...This is the essence of baseball."

Greg Proops, Comedian and Social Critic.

"By the luck of the alphabet, the first two entries in this affectionately assembled compendium of the 100 most influential players in baseball history are Henry Aaron and Dick Allen, whose impact on the game extends far beyond mere stats and acronyms. Lincoln Mitchell's fresh approach to enumerating the best of the best sets his book apart from a crowded field, and includes some eye-openers - women! little people! spies! - that will spark heated debate while inspiring a deeper appreciation of many of the players about whom we thought we knew a lot, but find out in these pages that we still have much to learn."

Perry Barber, umpire, Jeopardy! champion, inaugural winner of The Dorothy, SABR's Women In Baseball Lifetime Achievement Award

The One Hundred
Most Important Players
in Baseball History

by

Lincoln A. Mitchell

**Artemesia
Publishing**

ISBN: 9781951122669 (paperback) / 9781951122676 (ebook)
LCCN: 2023938622
Copyright © 2023 by Lincoln A. Mitchell
Cover Photo: Shutterstock image 182628029 by Blulz60
Cover Design: Geoff Habiger

Printed in the United States of America.

Artemesia Publishing
9 Mockingbird Hill Rd
Tijeras, New Mexico 87059
info@artemesiapublishing.com
www.apbooks.net

Introduction

For decades baseball fans have enjoyed debating questions such as who was the best player, catcher, left-handed pitcher and the like. Another variation on that is the who is better debate-who was better Willie, Mickey or the Duke? Schmidt or Brett? Mathewson, Seaver, or Maddux? Harper, Judge or Trout? The most elevated version of these debates is to list, in order, the 100 greatest players of All-Time. MLB does this on their website from time to time while baseball writers as different, and accomplished, as Maury Allen, Bill James and Joe Posnanski have written entire books, or large sections of books, on the greatest one hundred players.

Although I enjoy these books and the question of who the best 100 players ever were, my interest in baseball, as well as my background as a political scientist with a keen interest in baseball's place in American history and society, has taken me in a different direction, focusing on a different group of one hundred players. One of the things that has made baseball so compelling for so many people over the years is that baseball is always about the game itself while simultaneously being about something bigger. The story of baseball for the last 125 years or so is a saga that is filled with great drama, heroes, blunders, stories, humor and a pre-history from before 1900, that taken together are what lead many fans to love the game, while also making it possible for us to discuss and write about baseball in great depth and with a passion that seems downright weird to non-baseball fans. The story of baseball is also deeply intertwined with labor conflicts, America's long struggle with racism and other forms of discrimination, globalization and the broader journey of America.

Lists of the best 100 players can capture some of this because many of the game's great players like Babe Ruth, Jackie Robinson, Willie Mays or Roberto Clemente are central to the larger story and context of baseball and indeed of American history, but ultimately these lists are focused on the game on the field and exclude many of the lesser players, some still very good, who have played a large role in either the development of the game, baseball's role in American and global culture or in the larger sweep of American history.

In some respects, the idea of metaphorically walling off baseball from the rest of society, culture and politics is appealing. Keeping baseball as a safe space where the divisions, ugliness and politics that dominate the rest of American life do not creep in is a very seductive idea, but it is also impossible. Baseball has always been a portal into the larger culture and cannot be disaggregated from the rest of America. Some of this is obvious. Jackie Robinson was much more than a baseball hero, but was a civil rights, and indeed an American, hero. There is nobody else quite like Jackie Robinson in baseball, or American, history, but there are other players who were similarly important to other groups. For example, Felipe Alou, Roberto Clemente, Joe DiMaggio, Hank Greenberg, Stan Musial and Fernando Valenzuela are central figures to Dominican American, Puerto Rican, Italian American, Jewish American, Polish American and Mexican American history.

The interaction between baseball, politics and culture is sometimes more subtle than groundbreaking ballplayers. It includes the work of ballplayers like Curt Flood who fought to shift the balance of power in baseball away from the owners and towards the players, as well as players whose baseball skills have elevated them almost to the level of folk hero or national symbol. During the turmoil of the 1960s, Paul Simon and Art Garfunkel asked where Joe DiMaggio had gone. A few decades later, Willie Mays, the finest player of the postwar era, reminisced with a clearly awed President Barack Obama about his days growing up in segregated Alabama. Yogi Berra's malapropisms, real or invented, are now embedded in the culture and have been repeated in classrooms, boardrooms and living rooms for decades, but the great Yankees catcher was also the son of hard-working immigrants and a war hero who in a very real way lived the American Dream. On the other hand, the experiences of players like Barry Bonds and Sammy Sosa reflect the complicated relationship between race, substance abuse and selective justice in our country.

There have been baseball players who have gone on to become prominent, if too frequently reactionary, political figures as well as participants in spycraft at the highest level and with the highest stakes. The race to develop the atomic bomb was central to the outcome of the World War II and thus to the future of humanity. A peripheral player in that struggle was a good field no hit catcher.

The baseball historian Steven Goldman frequently comments that "baseball is everything and everything is baseball." This book embraces that view, seeing baseball as both an end unto itself and a window into, well everything. That is the spirit with which I approached this book and sought to identify the one hundred players whose contributions to baseball, America or both, were most significant.

Before that list can be assembled, it is essential to define some terms. First, it is useful to explain what I mean by baseball players. Baseball players, for the purpose of this book, are people who played big league baseball either in the American or National League or in leagues of comparable skill level. That latter category includes Negro Leagues in the US, various Caribbean leagues, the Nippon Professional Baseball (NPB) league in Japan and the All American Girls Professional Baseball League (AAGPBL), a women's baseball league that lasted from 1943-1954. Excluded from this group are people who played in the minor leagues or in college, but never made it to the big leagues. Mario Cuomo, who served three terms as governor of New York, and almost ran for president at least once, for example, played one year of minor league ball in the Pittsburgh Pirates system, but did not appear in a single big league game, so did not make the list. George H. W. Bush was a light-hitting first baseman for Yale University in the 1940s, but does not qualify as a baseball player for this book. I also decided to treat the old Pacific Coast League (PCL) as a minor league, so players who only played there did not make the list. This did not have much of an impact on the book because many great and important PCL players, like Joe DiMaggio or Ted Williams, also played in the Major Leagues.

The only exceptions I made were for women who played either before or after the AAGPBL. Women have been almost completely excluded from organized baseball, but there have been many women who played the game, were very good at it and have either had an impact on the game's past or have been trailblazers that will likely influence the game's future. Several of these women are on the list because to leave them off the list would be to blame the victims of sexism for their exclusion.

I also only included those who played after 1900. In doing that I eliminated important figures from baseball's pre-history, like Cap Anson, who was an excellent 19th century first baseman and was instrumental in segregating big league baseball, Albert Spalding, a pitcher from the 1870s, who was an early promoter of the game and the founder of the sporting goods company that still bears his name or Moses Fleetwood Walker, the first African American to play in the Major Leagues. This was a somewhat arbitrary decision, but baseball in the 19th century was such a different game, and very poorly documented. While there are undoubtedly very important players from the 19th century, their histories and even the game they played are much less likely to be accessible or of interest to the 21st century fan. However, I found something of a compromise by including several players whose careers spanned the 19th and 20th century, such as Cy Young and Honus Wagner.

Some players who had very brief playing careers are included in the book either because of other ways in which they contributed to the game—like Branch Rickey—or because of the unusual but significant role they played in baseball history-like Eddie Gaedel. However, because this is a book of players only, many people who were extremely important to the development of Major League Baseball, for example Marvin Miller, Effa Manley, and Walter O'Malley, did not make the list because they never played in the big leagues.

The question of who was an important player is complicated

because it depends a lot on what is meant by important, while raising questions of importance to what or to whom. The players in this book were important in different ways. Some were important largely because of how great they were on the field. Henry Aaron, Ted Williams, Willie Mays and Babe Ruth are examples of this. However, all these great players were important for other reasons as well. Therefore, while there is overlap between my list and most lists of the one hundred greatest players, there are many great players, like Tris Speaker, Johnny Bench, Rogers Hornsby, or Mike Schmidt that are not included.

Baseball as a folk tradition or in the corporate form of Major League Baseball (MLB) is a powerful and influential institution in the US and globally. Individual players who helped that institution evolve are thus important in their own right. Branch Rickey who both helped create the system of affiliated minor leagues and signed Jackie Robinson to a contract with the Dodgers, Curt Flood and Andy Messersmith who helped forge free agency and Ichiro Suzuki who was instrumental to making the game more global in this century are all on the list for this reason. There are also a handful of players whose contributions outside of baseball landed them on the list, such as Jim Bunning. Bunning was an excellent pitcher who became an influential member of congress.

Some players are almost unknown outside of baseball and had careers that were somewhere between undistinguished and excellent, but whose impact on the game, or on the history of the game was enormous. These players, like Tommy John, Fred Merkle or Bobby Thomson make up a portion of the list. One way to think of these players is that although they were not always among the best in the game-although some, like John, were, the history of baseball since 1900 cannot be told well without mentioning their contributions. The surgery named for Tommy John has saved hundreds of pitching careers and helped usher in the strikeout-oriented game we see today. Merkle's failure to touch second base in a key game between the Giants and Cubs in 1908 was one of the most famous moments of baseball's earliest days and Thomson's "shot heard 'round the world" in 1951 remains the most famous moment in baseball history.

Rather than rank the players in order, which, given the breadth of reasons why players made it into the book, would have been extremely difficult, I decided to present them in alphabetical order. This approach deemphasizes the question who was more important than whom while keeping the attention on the players, their stories and their impact on baseball and society. After all, questions like who was more important, Catfish Hunter, who was the first star to be a free agent and was the subject of a song by Bob Dylan, or Hideo Nomo, the second Japanese player, and first Japanese star, in the big league, are entirely subjective and impossible to answer with any certainty.

A Few Words on Statistics:

This is not a book of baseball statistics and no graduate training in quantitative methods is needed to fully understand this work. Nonetheless, any book that discusses one hundred baseball players is going to use some data. The statistics in this book fall into one of two categories. The first are conventional measures such as wins, losses, strikeouts, Earned Run Average (ERA), batting average, home runs, Runs Batted In (RBIs) and stolen bases that will be familiar to even the most casual of fans.

The second category includes some slightly advanced metrics. In the interest of making the book more accessible, I have limited my use of these indicators. However, there are a few that I use throughout the book. Importantly, these metrics as well as the conventional ones are most useful in evaluating players who spent their careers in the American or National Leagues and where schedules were more consistent and historical data is more accessible. What follows is a quick primer on the advanced metrics you will find in the book.

Wins Above Replacement (WAR) - WAR is based on a formula, actually two formulas one for pitchers and one for position players, that seeks to reflect the overall value of the player. There are several different WAR formulas, but I use the data from Baseball Reference, an online baseball encyclopedia that can be found at https://www.baseball-reference.com. The formula itself can be found on that site, but the easiest way to understand WAR is that it seeks to measure how much better, or worse, a player is than a replacement level player. A replacement level player is the kind of player who is more or less freely available to most teams most of the time. Replacement players are below average, but still reasonably competent, big leaguers.

Less than zero WAR in a season is a very bad year, two to three WAR is a solid position player or mid-rotation starter. Five or more WAR is a probable all-star. Eight or more WAR is an MVP or Cy Young candidate and ten or more WAR is an exceptionally standout season. For a career, 30 or more WAR is a very solid big leaguer; 60 or more WAR is a potential Hall of Famer, 70 or more WAR is a likely Hall of Famer and 100 or more WAR is an all-time great. Babe Ruth has 182.6 career WAR, the most of any player ever, while Walter Johnson's 165.1 WAR is the most of any pitcher.

ERA+ - ERA+ seeks to normalize Earned Run Average across eras and ballparks. An ERA+ of 100 is average in any given season or career. This measure helps us see that players with similar conventional numbers may have had very different seasons. For example, Pedro Martinez in 2000, Ron Guidry in 1978, Hippo Vaughn in 1918 and Sandy Koufax in 1964 all had ERAs of 1.74. Vaughn and Koufax did that in relatively low offense eras and Guidry in a more or less average offense. However, Martinez posted his 1.74 ERA at the height of the PED era while pitching in a hitters' park. For that reason, Martinez's ERA+ was an astounding 291, while Guidry's was 208, Koufax's 186 and Vaughn's was 156. In this example, ERA+ shows us that Martinez 1.74 ERA was by far the most impressive of the four.

Fielding Independent Pitching (FIP) - FIP seeks to evaluate a pitcher based on the things the pitcher can control such walks, strikeouts and home runs give up. FIP is similar to ERA, but less dependent on things like the defense behind the pitcher. FIP is expressed similarly to ERA, so, for example a FIP of under 3.00 is very good, but a FIP of over 4.00 is not great.

On base plus slugging (OPS) - OPS is simply the sum of a player's on base percentage and slugging percentage. An OPS of .700 is generally a solid regular; .800 or better a possible all-star, .900 or better is a standout offensive season. A variation on OPS is to present a player's batting average, on base percentage and slugging percentage separated by slash marks. These are referred to as a player's slash lines. For example, in 1965 Willie Mays slashed .317/.398/.645 for an OPS of 1.043. Mays also won a Gold Glove for his defense and won the MVP award for his outstanding season.

OPS+ - Like ERA+, OPS+ seeks to normalize a player's offense over ballpark and era. Again, 100 is league average. 120 or better is a solid starter and potential all-star. 140 or better is an MVP candidate and a potential Hall of Famer. An OPS+ of 150 or better is a standout season and an almost certain Hall of Famer. For example, Mays's 1965 OPS of 1.043, because he did that in a low offense era playing his home games in Candlestick Park, meant that his OPS+ for the season was 185. Thirty-four years later, Jeff Bagwell had a slightly higher OPS of 1.045, but because 1999 was in the middle of a very high offense era, his OPS+ for that season was only 164, a great year with the bat, but not as good as what Mays did in 1965.

The Players

One
Henry Aaron

Henry Aaron began his career in 1952 as an eighteen-year-old middle infielder for the Indianapolis Clowns, a Negro League franchise that was trying to survive as the integration of the American and National Leagues was devastating the Negro Leagues. Aaron's career wrapped up 24 years later when he was a designated hitter for the Milwaukee Brewers who were then in the American League.

The long career of Henry Aaron was central to the history of baseball in the postwar era. Aaron's brief time with the Clowns meant that when he retired following

Photo 120060737 / Baseball © Sports Images | Dreamstime.com

the 1976 season, he was the last Negro Leaguer to play in the American or National League. In that regard, Aaron was the last link between the baseball of Oscar Charleston and Josh Gibson with that of modern MLB. Aaron remained sufficiently famous into his late 80s that his vaccination against Covid-19 in January of 2021 was covered in the national media.

Henry Aaron was one of the greatest players ever. By the time he made it to the National League and the Milwaukee Braves in 1954, Aaron was no longer an infielder and had moved to the

11

outfield, but he could do everything on the ball field. He was a solid defender with a strong arm who was fast enough to steal 20 or more bases six times, but his true value was as a hitter, particularly because he was so consistent. Aaron had an OPS+ of at least 140 every season from 1955-1973 a period where he averaged 37 home runs and 150 games played every season. National League teams played only 154 games until 1962.

Aaron's 143 WAR is seventh on the all-time list, but Aaron is most known for breaking Babe Ruth's all-time home run record in 1974. Aaron ended the 1973 season with 713 home runs, one short of Ruth's career total of 714, so as the 1974 season approached Aaron was poised to tie and then break the record early in that season. This was a much bigger deal in those years than it would be today. Baseball in the early 1970s was in its waning days as the national pastime, but still played a major role in American culture. Babe Ruth had been dead for more than a quarter century by then, but he was still an American hero and, unlike today, there were still many baseball fans around who had seen Ruth play. This meant that Aaron's home run chase was a major national story. I was just becoming aware of baseball at the time and remember people saying that Aaron only was able to break the record because of the longer seasons since expansion, that Ruth has spent the first few years of his career as a pitcher, or even, absurdly, that Aaron traveled by plane while Ruth had to endure long train rides. However, Aaron also played in an integrated league, thus ensuring better competition, had to play many games at night and, towards the end of his career, had to bat against fresh relievers in the late innings rather than exhausted starting pitchers.

The home run record chase also occurred at a time, like so many others in American history, when race and civil rights were at the center of national politics. As he closed in on Ruth's record Aaron was bombarded with racist letters and threats of the ugliest nature. Many white fans were furious that one of baseball's most important records—and for the previous forty years, no record had been as important as Ruth's 714 home runs—was going to be broken by an African American. These fans did not hesitate to share their anger with Aaron. Additionally, Aaron was playing for the Atlanta Braves, in the heart of the deep south. When Aaron finally broke the record on April 8th, 1974 against Dodgers hurler Al Downing, it was covered as a story of racial triumph. Vin Scully, who was calling the game for the Dodgers captured this sentiment "What a marvelous moment for baseball. What a marvelous moment for Atlanta and the state of Georgia. What a marvelous moment for the country and the world. A black man is getting a standing ovation in the deep south for breaking a record of an all-time baseball idol. And it's a great moment for all of us." Unfortunately, despite Scully's inspiring words, Aaron's path to the home run record was one that revealed, rather than redeemed, racism in baseball.

Aaron's record lasted 34 years, almost as long as Ruth's record had stood, before it was broken by Barry Bonds whose prodigious power numbers have been tainted by the strong likelihood that he was using performance enhancing drugs (PEDs). Many, including Bud Selig, who served as Commissioner of Baseball from 1998-2015, still view Aaron as the all-time home run leader.

The sheer longevity of Henry Aaron's career in baseball—he served as an executive for the Braves well into the 21st century—is extraordinary. He is one of the few inner circle all-time greats who worked in baseball well after his playing days. Towards the end of his playing years, Aaron was known for mentoring young African American players, particularly if they were outfielders. Among those for whom he played this role was a young Dusty Baker, who later played a similar role in the career of a young Glenn Burke. Both Baker and Burke will be discussed later in this book. Aaron died in 2021 a few days before what would have been his 87th birthday. Shortly before his death, Aaron was vaccinated against the Corona virus as part of an effort to encourage African Americans to trust the vaccines.

Henry Aaron's impact on baseball was enormous. In addition to being one of the greatest players ever, and a longtime executive, and facing terrible racism simply because he was an African American man who broke one of the game's sacred records, Aaron was a role model and mentor to many players.

Two
Dick Allen

The exclusion of African Americans from the American and National Leagues until 1947 meant that great players like Josh Gibson, Cool Papa Bell and Oscar Charleston, never had the chance to compete against the top white players of their era in a formal league setting. Most baseball fans are aware of that, but there is another later generation of players who had the chance to play in the integrated big leagues, but due to racism and related

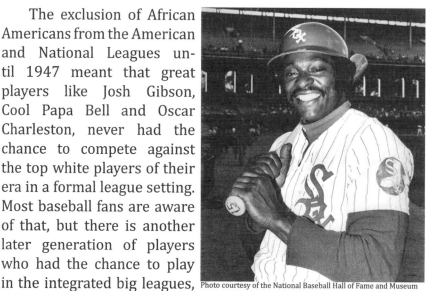

Photo courtesy of the National Baseball Hall of Fame and Museum (Allen Richie 5090.72_HS_NBL)

pressures did not achieve what they might have on the ballfield. No player is a better example of that than Dick Allen.

Dick Allen was primarily a first and third baseman, who played a little left field as well. During his career from 1963-1977, he was mostly known as a slugger. He hit thirty or more home runs, back when thirty home runs meant something, six times, and led his league in slugging percentage three times. His career OPS+ of 156 is tied for 23rd with Frank Thomas and is just ahead of Henry Aaron, Joe DiMaggio, Willie Mays, and Mel Ott's 155. Despite his extraordinary offensive numbers, during his career Allen was seen as never quite reaching his potential and, in the racially coded language of the time, was frequently described as controversial or difficult.

Allen grew up in Wampum, Pennsylvania a small town in the northwest part of the state, not far from Ohio. Two of his brothers, Hank and Ron, also played briefly in the Major Leagues. Fans of 1970s baseball may remember that in 1977, while playing for the A's in the last year of his career, Allen briefly wore the word "Wampum" on the back of his jersey instead of his name.

Allen signed with the Phillies as a fifteen-year-old, but league rules prohibited him from joining the organization until he graduated from Wampum High School shortly after he turned eighteen years old. From 1960-1962, Allen played in the low minors for the Phillies and hit wherever he went. In 1963 he was promoted to the Phillies' AAA affiliate, the Arkansas Travelers. Allen had never experienced the deep south before and was the first African American to play for the Travelers.

The racism aimed at Allen in Arkansas was intense and Allen, rightly, felt the Phillies organization did little to protect him from the worst of it. One way that Allen responded was by dominating the league with his bat. He slashed .289/.341/.550 and was called up to the big league team at the end of the year. By 1964, Allen was in the Phillies Opening Day lineup batting third and playing third base. He got two hits that day and ended the season with a 162 OPS+. He easily won Rookie of the Year honors and finished seventh in the MVP balloting, but the Phillies collapsed at the end of the season, narrowly losing the pennant to the Cardinals.

Despite his great rookie season, Allen's relationship with the team and the fans was not good. He was the first African American Phillies star and whenever he slumped or did not get a hit in a clutch situation he was booed and became the subject of racist jeers. He was a young African American man who had to put up with a lot, but was not the kind of person who kept his anger and frustration bottled up. Allen made little effort to conceal his dissatisfaction, but he just kept hitting. In his six years with the Phillies, from 1964-1969, he posted an OPS+ of 164 while averaging 30 home runs a year. He spent the 1970s with the Cardinals, Dodgers and White Sox and hit wherever he went. He returned to the Phillies in 1975; and in 1976, as part time first baseman and pinch hitter, helped the team back to the post-season for the first time since 1950. Allen ended his career with the A's the following season.

Allen died in late 2020 and in the years since his retirement has been the subject of a campaign to get him elected to the Hall of Fame. Allen is a border-line Hall of Fame candidate, but there are several Hall of Famers who were not as good on the ballfield as Dick Allen. His reputation has also changed as what 60 years ago was seen as anger and controversy on Allen's part is now understood as the actions a proud young man who had no tolerance for racism. Due to his good looks, seventies hairstyles and panache, Allen has also become something of a symbol of 1970s cool on the baseball diamond.

More importantly, Dick Allen's career forces us to reckon more deeply with the integration of the American and National Leagues. While the racism confronted by Jackie Robinson, Larry Doby and other players of that era is relatively well known, as is the apartheid system in what was then known as Organized Baseball until 1947, the difficulties faced by the next generation is overlooked. These men, including Allen, Bobby Bonds, Dock Ellis, Reggie Jackson, and many others, grew up in the Civil Rights Era and found themselves part of an institution that was still run by white people, many of whom had very little understanding of race in America. Allen bounced around the big leagues, was all but run out of Philadelphia early in his career, and never fully appreciated for his extraordinary baseball abilities and performance because of that dynamic.

Three
Felipe Alou

One of the most signif-
icant, and best, changes in
MLB over the last 65 years or
so has been that it has become
much more international.
There are now players from
Venezuela, Cuba, Mexico,
Japan, Taiwan, South Korea
and numerous other coun-
tries on big league rosters.
No country has contributed
more to this globalization
than the Dominican Republic.
If you want to understand the
history of Dominican players
in the big leagues, Felipe Alou
is a good place to start.

© S. F. Giants

Alou was the second Dominican player to play in the National
League, but he was the first big leaguer to have grown up in the
Dominican Republic. Ozzie Virgil Sr., who got to the Giants two
years before Alou debuted in 1958, was born in the Dominican
Republic but grew up in the Bronx. Alou was a very good player, the patriarch of an extensive baseball family, an advocate for
Latino ballplayers and the first Dominican manager. Alou was a
fixture in MLB for more than half a century. You simply cannot
tell the story of the impact of the Dominican Republic on baseball
without Felipe Alou.

Felipe Alou was the best of a trio of brothers who all were
outfielders and all began their careers with the San Francisco

Giants—the first team to tap the rich vein of great Dominican ballplayers. In addition to being the Giants' conduit to Matty and Jesus Alou, Felipe Alou helped the Giants land the great Dominican pitcher Juan Marichal. Felipe Alou also had two sons, Moises Alou and Luis Rojas, as well as two more distant relatives who also played in the big leagues.

Felipe Alou was an outfielder, a career .286 hitter during his 17-year career with a career OPS+ of 113 despite drawing relatively few walks. He fielded his position well and in a good year could hit between 15 and 30 home runs.

Alou also played a key role in one of the most famous games, and indeed innings, in baseball history.

In 1962, Alou had a great year hitting .316/.356/.513 playing left and right field for the pennant winning Giants. He made the All-Star team and finished 13th in the MVP voting. Despite his 25 home runs, Alou frequently batted leadoff because the Giants middle of the order included Hall of Famers Willie Mays, Willie McCovey, and Orlando Cepeda. In the World Series that year, the Giants trailed the Yankees 1-0 going into the bottom of the ninth inning of game seven. Felipe's brother Matty pinch hit for the pitcher and singled to lead off the inning, bringing up Felipe Alou. Alou was asked to bunt his brother over to second but could not get a good bunt down and struck out. Chuck Hiller then struck out for the second out of the inning. The tying run was now on first base for Willie Mays. Mays hit a double to right, but Matty Alou was held at third base. Had Felipe been able to bunt his brother over to second, Mays would have driven in the tying run. Willie McCovey then lined out to end the game and the World Series. For decades after that, Alou would say that his inability to get that bunt down was a memory that still dogged him.

During those years with the Giants, the Alou brothers, Marichal and the Puerto Rican Cepeda were among the Latino players that made the Giants the most diverse team in baseball. They were changing the game, but not everybody understood or welcomed that. The Giants were a team loaded with stars, but they never put it together and after 1962, did not make it back to the postseason until 1971. Many racists blamed that on the attitude of the Latino players. Alvin Dark, who managed the Giants from 1961-1964 was chief among these racists claiming in 1964 that African American and Latino players were "just not able to perform up to the white ballplayers when it comes to mental alertness." Dark also tried to ban the Spanish language in the clubhouse, thus barring Felipe, Jesus and Matty Alou from communicating with their own brothers in their shared native language.

In 1963, Alou, along with the progressive sportswriter Arnold Hano wrote an essay for *Sport Magazine* titled "Latin-American Ballplayers Need a Bill of Rights." This essay drew attention to a number of issues of which many fans and baseball people had been, or chosen to be, unaware and remains a valuable document for understanding the challenges the first generation of Latino players faced. The Giants responded to that article by swapping Alou to the Milwaukee Braves in one of several bad trades the Giants made from the early 1960s through the mid-1970s.

After retiring from play, Alou made it back to the big leagues in 1992 as manager of the Montreal Expos. He stayed there for ten years and later managed the Giants for four years. Today there are numerous great Dominican stars who have had a massive influence on the game. Alou's career, more than that of any other player, is intertwined with that. Alou did not have a Hall of Fame career as a player, but came close. Similarly, as a manager he was a cut or two below most Hall of Fame managers, but few people have been good players, good managers and had such an impact on the game. If I could add one player to the Hall of Fame, it might just be Felipe Alou

Four
Dusty Baker

Dusty Baker is one of those baseball lifers who has been part of an enormous amount of baseball history. Baker was on deck when Henry Aaron hit his 715th home run to break Babe Ruth's record. He was a teammate of Tommy John when he came back from the surgery that bears his name and changed baseball. He was playing left field when Reggie Jackson hit three home runs in the final game of the 1977 World Series. He had a great year as a player during the 1981 strike season. He played alongside Mark McGwire and Jose Canseco before their PED abuse so badly damaged the game. He

Creative Commons - Jerry Reuss https://www.flickr.com/photos/43289453@N03/4802745996

was a coach when the earthquake struck before game three of the 1989 World Series and was a manager during the 2020 Covid season. He was managing the Cubs during the Steve Bartman game and was the manager the Astros hired in 2020 to salvage their image after the cheating scandal was revealed.

Baker was more than just some Zelig like figure who was around baseball for a long time. He was a very good player on three pennant winning Dodgers teams and one World Series champion. A two-time all-star who twice finished in the top ten in MVP voting, Baker was a good fielding outfielder with good, but not top tier, power. His best year was probably 1972 when he slashed .321/.383/.504 for the Braves. Baker was often overlooked, first on a Braves team led by the incomparable Henry Aaron, and later on some very good Dodgers teams that included stars like Don Sutton, Steve Garvey, Ron Cey and Reggie Smith, but he was a very solid player.

Although he played nineteen years in the Major Leagues, ending up with 37 WAR and a career OPS+ of 116, most fans know Baker better as a manger. Since 1993, Baker has managed the Giants, Cubs, Reds, Nationals, and Astros for a total of 26 years. He has taken two of those teams, the Giants and Astros, to the World Series, finally winning a championship as a manager in 2022. Only eight men have managed more big league games than Baker. As a manager, Baker has been more of a player's manager, able to build good relationships with players and the media, while not always distinguishing himself as an in-game tactician.

Baker has also always been one of the most decent people in the game. He was one of the few baseball people that maintained a relationship with his former teammate Glenn Burke as he was dying, and during his long managerial tenure earned a reputation for supporting and helping many young ballplayers. As a manager, Baker was particularly sensitive to the needs and stress of young ballplayers and has mentored many of them, particularly those who are African American. He has long been one of the good guys in the game.

Baker is partly important simply because of his longevity. He had been involved in big league baseball as a player, coach, or manager with very few breaks since 1968. He played with Henry Aaron, managed Bryce Harper, and was a teammate or opponent of pretty much everybody in between. Baseball's appeal rests not only on the excitement of the game, but also on the people. Fans can relate to the game better when there are familiar faces on the field and in the dugout. Over more than a half century Baker has been one of the most familiar and friendly.

All of that is true, but what might be the single most important thing about Dusty Baker occurred on the last game of the 1977 season. Baker came up to bat in the bottom of the sixth against Houston fireballer JR Richard. Baker connected for a solo home run, his 30th of the year, giving the Dodgers a then record four players with thirty or more home runs. After Baker scored, backup outfielder Glenn Burke who had entered the game in the fifth inning was due up. Burke was a young African American outfielder who felt close to Baker because Baker had taken him under his wing, just as Henry Aaron had done for Baker a decade earlier. Burke was so excited for his teammate that instead of holding his hand below his waist for Baker to slap, Burke held his hand up above his shoulders and Baker and Burke slapped hands there. That was the first ever recorded high five. More on Burke later, but it is sometimes forgotten that following Baker, Burke also connected for a home run, the first of the two he would hit in the Major Leagues. Today the high five is ubiquitous. We see it after home runs, touchdowns and three-point shots. It also occurs on the playgrounds, boardrooms and other settings, but it began with a young fringe player and his veteran mentor hitting back-to-back home runs.

Baker is a baseball connector who most famously links Henry Aaron to Glenn Burke in a chain of African outfielders who confronted prejudice. He also links the era when only two teams made the post-season to today's game when the post-season is a month-long tournament featuring twelve teams. Baker has made a positive influence on the lives and careers of hundreds of ballplayers and is, as my grandparents would have said, a real mensch.

Five
Ernie Banks

There are a handful of players in the history of baseball who have been deeply identified with a team and its city: Tony Gwynn and the San Diego Padres, Cal Ripken Jr. and the Baltimore Orioles, Stan Musial and the St. Louis Cardinals are among them. These players are all-time greats who spent their entire career, with that one team. They also had a style, a relationship with fans or some other unquantifiable quality that strengthened that bond between player, team, and city. Not all great players, even if they played only for one

Photo 112145772 / Baseball © Sports Images | Dreamstime.com

team achieved this. For example, Ted Williams, Charlie Gehringer and Jeff Bagwell never really had that kind of tie to the Boston Red Sox, Detroit Tigers, or Houston Astros.

There is no player in the history of the game who is more identified with their team than Ernie Banks. There is no Mr. Yankee, Mr. Giant, Mr. Cardinal, etc., but all baseball fans know that Ernie Banks was Mr. Cub. Banks spent his entire nineteen-year career with the Cubs and played more games, 2,528, for that franchise than anybody else in history.

There is something bittersweet about Banks's career. He was

famous for his love of the game. His catchphrase was "let's play two," something that you can still sometimes hear on baseball fields today. However, Mr. Cub spent his entire career playing for a team that was either not very good or never quite good enough. In the history of the game only four people, Rafael Palmeiro, Ken Griffey Jr., Ichiro Suzuki, and Andre Dawson, played in more regular season games without appearing in the World Series. However, all of them at least played in the post-season, but Banks who spent most of his career before leagues were broken into divisions, never even made the post-season. Perhaps that is why he is so identified with the Cubs, a hard-luck player who is still the face of what was, for decades, a hard-luck franchise.

Banks was an intriguing player. For the first part of his career he was a fine fielding shortstop and fantastic hitter with more power than any shortstop before him. At the time he joined the Cubs in 1953, after playing parts of two seasons with the Kansas City Monarchs of the Negro Leagues, only twice in the history of the American or National League had a shortstop hit 30 or more home runs in a season and none had ever 40. Banks hit 40 or more home runs while playing shortstop five times between 1955 and 1960. Only three other players have done that, Rico Petrocelli and Fernando Tatis Jr. once each and Alex Rodriguez six times.

From 1955-1961, Banks was an extraordinary player averaging 7.4 WAR, 40 home runs and a 145 OPS+ over those seven seasons while generally playing Gold Glove caliber defense at shortstop. He made seven all-star teams, finished in the top five in MVP voting four times and won the award twice, but during those years, the prime of his Hall of Fame career, the Cubs never finished above fifth place.

Banks played 10 more seasons in the big leagues, but was never as good. From 1962-1971, his OPS+ was only 106. That would have been fine if he were still a solid defensive shortstop, but he only played 104 games at shortstop in 1961 and then never played that position again. By the time he retired, Banks had played more games at first base than at shortstop and a 106 OPS+ is simply not very good for a first baseman. Despite this, he remained a hugely important part of the Cub franchise during those years.

Over the course of his career Banks accumulated 67.7 WAR, but 55 of that was through 1961, meaning that after his extraordinary beginning, Banks was just a very slightly above average player for most of his career. Advanced metrics reveal what was not evident at the time. Throughout most of the 1960s, due in part to his early career success and in part to his home run numbers, which were bolstered by playing in Wrigley Field, Banks was still viewed as a star. He made the All-Star team four times between 1962 and 1969 and hit 20 or more home runs six times after moving to first base.

Banks retired with over 500 home runs and was easily, and deservedly, elected to the Hall of Fame in 1977, his first year of eligibility. He is still generally considered as one of the greatest shortstops ever despite playing more games at first base. Banks was, on balance, a great player, but his importance to the game is because players like him, and perhaps nobody more than him, are central to the fan experience. A Chicago area baby boomer first discovering baseball when Banks was starting his career with the Cubs would have immediately been drawn to Banks's great play and personal style. By the time that boy or girl was a man or woman perhaps several years into the workforce, serving in Vietnam or attending grad school somewhere, maybe starting a family of their own, Ernie Banks was still hitting home runs at Wrigley Field. Baseball at its best, as represented by Banks, can provide continuity and stability in the lives of people who may not be able to find it elsewhere.

Six
Moe Berg

Moe Berg might have had the least impressive big league career of any plater in this book. Berg was a backup catcher who rarely played, spending 15 years in the big leagues between 1923 and 1939, and appearing in only 663 games. In 14 of those seasons, he started fewer than 70 games. The primary reason for that was that he could never hit. His lifetime slash line of .243/.278/.299 reflects his anemic bat. His best year was probably 1929 when he was the White Sox regular catcher for much of the season. In the middle of a hitter's era, Berg slashed a paltry .287/.323/.307 for an OPS+ of 64. As bad as that was, it was still significantly better than his career OPS+ of 49.

Photo courtesy of the National Baseball Hall of Fame and Museum (Berg_Moe_B-1963-0177-0019_NBL)

Anybody who makes it to the big leagues even for one day is one of the best ballplayers in the world, so calling any big leaguer a bad ballplayer is not entirely fair. However, when compared to his peers, Berg was not good at all. His career WAR of -4.6 meant that over the course of his career he was significantly worse than the kind of replacement player that could be acquired for almost nothing. That is among the thirty lowest WARs of any non-pitcher in the twentieth century. However, to accumulate that much negative WAR you have to play for a while. Berg was able to do that. Nothing Berg did on the ballfield was particularly significant or even memorable, but few baseball players have had as much of an impact on global history as Moe Berg.

Berg was a fish out of water in the baseball of his, or any, era. Berg was one of the rare players with a college degree and even fewer had an Ivy League degree as Berg did, and he was Jewish at a time when there were very few Jews in baseball. Berg graduated from Princeton University where he had been a baseball star. He was something of a lumpen-intellectual who read incessantly, was knowledgeable on many topics and freakishly good at learning languages, but he was never an academic nor did he publish anything significant. He read newspapers incessantly, spoke many languages and liked to visit museums when on the road. This was a far cry from the hot dogs and beer culture, best exemplified by Babe Ruth, that most ballplayers experienced.

Berg was born in 1902 so, unlike a number of other players, his career was not disrupted by military service during World War II, but he nonetheless played an extraordinary role in that conflict. In 1934, Berg was part of a barnstorming trip to Japan. Among the players on that trip were Babe Ruth, Lou Gehrig, Jimmie Foxx, and Lefty Gomez. The manager of the team was Connie Mack. The US and Japan were not at war then as the bombing of Pearl Harbor was still seven years in the future, but tensions between the two countries were growing and Japan was only a few years away from its aggression in Asia that became part of the second World War.

While in Japan, Berg found time to go on the roof of a Tokyo hospital and take numerous photos of the city and its surroundings from that high place. Upon his return to the US, he then delivered those photos to the US military. Those photos were later used to help identify bombing targets during the war. That bit of spycraft required foresight and deception on an impressive scale, but it was only the beginning for Berg.

Once the war started, Berg did other projects with the Office of Strategic Services (OSS), the predecessor of the CIA. The most extraordinary episode of Berg's war time activities occurred a decade after that initial trip to Japan. In 1944, the allies and the Germans were in a race to develop the atomic bomb and it was likely that whoever got there first would win the war.

The German effort was led by the physicist Werner Heisenberg, who may be best known for the Heisenberg Uncertainty Principle which states that we cannot know both the position and speed of a particle at the same time. In late 1944, Berg, in disguise as a Swiss businessman, was sent to attend a meeting in Switzerland where Heisenberg was giving a talk. Berg's task, based on his strong knowledge of physics and the German language, was to determine if the Germans would develop an atomic bomb and whether they would get one before the US did. If Berg found that to be the case, he was to shoot Heisenberg and then take a cyanide pill. Berg determined the Germans were not going to get the bomb first, so did not follow through with the plan. Berg was entrusted with an extremely critical and dangerous mission at the highest levels of spycraft during World War II and executed it perfectly. The backup catcher was not just a spy, but a war hero as well.

There is nonetheless something strange, even tragic, about Berg's life. He never found consistent or meaningful work after the war inside or outside of baseball, but loved the game till the end. His last words when he was dying, according to legend, was to ask how the Mets were doing. One of the mysteries of Berg's life is why this extremely talented and good looking man, spent the prime of his life in a tough profession, particularly one that, at the time, did not pay well, was not particularly hospitable to Jews and at which he was not very good. There are many possible answers to that. He didn't have to do much, got to travel and had a lot of time to himself, but those answers are not sufficient.

Berg was obsessed with baseball and loved the game so stayed in it as long as he could. Berg was never a great player, but like many of us would have, put the rest of his life on hold as long as he could somehow hang on as a big leaguer.

Seven
Yogi Berra

On Yogi Berra's 90th birthday, I tweeted a photo of Yogi and wished him well. A British colleague responded and said that he was not aware that Berra was a real person, but had just heard Americans attribute all kinds of goofily wise quotations to him. Yogi Berra was indeed a real person, and one of those very rare players who was not just a famous celebrity, but a folk hero.

There is much about Berra that makes him

important, but it should not be overlooked that he was an extraordinary baseball player. Berra was at the heart of the most dominant team in baseball history. During his career he played for 14 pennant winning Yankees teams and ten World Series winners. Between 1950 and 1956, when the Yankees won the AL pennant every year but 1954, Berra won the MVP award three times and finished in the top five in MVP voting every year. During those years, Berra and Dodgers backstop Roy Campanella changed the catcher position by marrying great defense to power hitting.

Berra slugged twenty or more home runs every year from 1949-1958. He was a durable player and despite a reputation as a bad ball hitter, drew a lot of walks, so his career on base percentage of .348 contributed to his 125+ career OPS. No player was a part of more World Series winning teams than Berra who is still the leader in World Series games, at bats, plate appearances, hits, singles and doubles.

As great as Berra was, that alone is not what makes him important. Johnny Bench, for example, was a better all-around catcher but is not among the players in this book. Yogi made his way into the larger American culture through a way of speaking that synergized real wisdom with a dubious command of the English language. Yogi Berra's aphorisms are repeated probably thousands of times a day in the US in almost every imaginable context. I have heard Berra's words repeated at academic conferences, corporate settings, diplomatic events, political campaigns, ballfields and social situations more times than I can possibly count and am pretty certain millions of Americans have had similar experiences.

"It ain't over till it's over." "It gets late early out there." "Pair up in threes." "Nobody goes there anymore. It's too crowded." "Déjà vu all over again." "You can observe a lot just by watching." "It's tough to make predictions, especially about the future." Statements like those made Berra one of the most famous and most recognized names in American culture. These comments are all pretty funny, and we may still chuckle when we hear them for the thousandth time, but there is also some wisdom that applies to both baseball and life. "It ain't over till it's over" is syntactically awkward, but it is also a light-hearted way of saying "never give up." "You can observe a lot just by watching" is similarly mangled syntax but is also a reminder of the importance of noting as much as possible about the world and that sometimes watching quietly is a better strategy than speaking.

Although it is possible to see Berra as a humorous, even clownish, figure, the kind of person after whom a goofy cartoon bear was named, there was much more to Berra than that. Berra's life story is uniquely American. Although the idea of the American Dream has become at times a cliché and for many a cruel joke, Berra's generation still believed the idea. Many lived it, but few Americans ever realized the American Dream as fully as Yogi Berra.

Born Lawrence Peter Berra to Italian American immigrant parents in St. Louis, Berra was raised in an Italian neighborhood of his hometown called The Hill. Like many children of those immigrants, Berra fell in love with baseball, but few were ever as good as he was.

Before joining the Yankees, Berra served in the Navy in World War II. He rarely spoke about his military experience, but was a genuine war hero, and among the first wave of Americans to land at Normandy during that pivotal battle. Berra always had a toughness and pride about him that was often overlooked due to his public persona. He became a Yankee because he refused to sign with the St. Louis Cardinals unless he got as much money as his friend and fellow catcher Joe Garagiola. Berra knew he was the better player and wanted to be treated fairly.

Many years later, after being fired as manager of the Yankees by team owner George Steinbrenner 16 games into the 1985 season, after Steinbrenner had promised Yogi he would manage the entire year, Berra cut all ties with the Yankees. He only resumed those ties when Steinbrenner personally apologized in 1999. Berra insisted Steinbrenner come to him for the public event around the apology—and that is what the Yankee owner did. Berra was a tough man who was not going to be bullied by anybody including the St. Louis Cardinals in the 1940s or George Steinbrenner in the 1980s and 1990s.

Yogi Berra changed the way the game is played on the field by turning the catcher position into one that was not simply about defense and handling pitchers. He was the central player on the most dominant team in baseball history while playing in New York when that city was at the height of its baseball hegemony. This made him one of the most famous and recognizable athletes in the country during the 1950s. Well over fifty years after he played his last game and almost 40 since he last managed, Berra remains one of the most recognized and most quoted athletes in American history—even if he didn't really say all those things he said.

Eight
Vida Blue

In the mid-1970s, the city of San Francisco was not in great shape. Jobs, particularly in the shipping and manufacturing sector, had been leaving for over a decade. Crime was out of control and the city had perpetual budget problems. Political divisions were tearing the city apart as progressive social movements were demanding rights and access to power for racial minorities and gays and lesbians, while a right-wing backlash was mobilizing conservative San Franciscans. And then, in November of 1978, things

© S. F. Giants

went from bad to worse. On November 17th, word made it to the rest of the world that in the Guyana jungle Jim Jones, a demented cult leader, had massacred over 800 members of his Peoples Temple. Jones had based his organization in San Francisco and many of the low-income African Americans and others who had joined the cult had been from the city or other parts of the Bay Area. Ten days later a former supervisor, the city's equivalent of a city councilmember, bitter about not getting his old job back and angry at the city's liberal ascendancy, walked into City Hall and assassinated the progressive mayor George Moscone and Supervisor Harvey Milk.

This was the context in which Vida Blue saved San Francisco. That is an extraordinary claim, but the evidence is strong. The city was reeling after the double blow of Jonestown followed by the Moscone-Milk assassinations. Many newer residents left town while others wondered how our city would survive. If the new mayor, Dianne Feinstein, had to announce a month or so after the horrors in Jonestown and City Hall that the Giants, who had only been there since 1958, were leaving town, San Francisco would have been devastated. More people would have left, there would have been no civic confidence and the city's history would have been very different. That is how Vida Blue saved San Francisco.

In the mid-1970s, the Giants were a terrible team. Willie Mays, Willie McCovey, Gaylord Perry and Juan Marichal were gone, although McCovey would eventually come back. The team was usually last in the National League in attendance and Candlestick Park was a cold, windy and unwelcoming ballpark that was a dreadful place to play night baseball. In January of 1976, longtime owner Horace Stoneham solved that problem by selling the team to the Labatt Brewing Company. The new owners were going to move the team to Toronto. By that time, the consensus in baseball was that the Bay Area was not big enough for two teams and either the Giants or A's—who played across the bay in Oakland—had to go.

New San Francisco Mayor George Moscone, who had been a Giants fan since the team moved west, spent his first weeks in office scrambling to keep the team in the city. Eventually, a local real estate tycoon named Bob Lurie and a partner named Bud Herseth bought the team and saved them from going to Toronto. Part of the arrangement that allowed that to happen was that when the National League agreed to postpone the sale so that Moscone could try to find a new local owner the Mayor agreed that if the team did not average one million fans from 1976-1978, he would not sue or otherwise block them from leaving. In other words, if Lurie could not make a go of it in San Francisco in three years, the team was likely gone. In 1976 and 1977, the Giants drew a combined 1.3 million fans and things did not look good for 1978.

Meanwhile, across the bay, Vida Blue and Bill North were the last members of the great A's teams from earlier in the decade still playing for Oakland. By that time Blue was already one of the most famous, colorful, and cool baseball characters around. His Cy Young and MVP winning 1971 season captured the attention of the country in a way that baseball still could back then. He appeared on the cover of *Time* magazine in August of that year when he was only 22-years-old, shortly after starting the All-Star Game for the American League. Blue also did not like playing for A's owner Charlie O. Finley and wanted out of Oakland. Finley tried to oblige, but the commissioner had vetoed efforts in previous years to sell Blue's contract to the Yankees or the Reds.

In March of 1978, Blue finally got his wish and was swapped to the Giants for seven journeymen players. His new surroundings seemed to agree with the fireballing lefty who responded by going 18-10 with a 123 ERA+ and 5.8 WAR while finishing third in the Cy Young Award balloting and 12th in the MVP voting. Blue's excellent season helped the Giants stay in first place for most of the year and along with players like Jack Clark, Bill Madlock, and an aging Willie McCovey brought excitement back to the Giants. When the season ended, the Giants finished a strong third in a tough NL West, but they had the second highest attendance in franchise history. They drew 1.7 million, meaning the team would not leave. The Giants stayed.

Vida Blue retired with more than 200 wins and a career that fell just a little bit short of the Hall of Fame, but he remained beloved on both sides of the San Francisco Bay for the rest of his life.

Nine
Bert Blyleven

For most of the post-war period, indeed most of the twentieth century, big league baseball was played and managed more or less the same way. Starting pitchers were initially expected to throw complete games, but by 1980 it was increasingly normal to see good starters pitch only seven or eight innings even on a good day. The batting order followed a similar pattern. The leadoff hitter was supposed to be fast and able to steal bases, the number

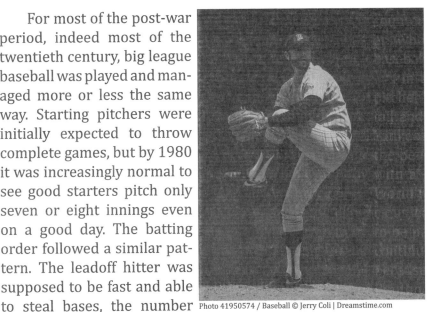

Photo 41950574 / Baseball © Jerry Coli | Dreamstime.com

two hitter needed to be a good bat handler who could get the sacrifice bunt down, and the best hitter on the team batted third.

For almost all of that period evaluations of player value were based on a relatively small number of indicators. For pitchers, wins, strikeouts and ERA were the most important numbers.

Today the way the game is played and managed is completely different. Complete games by pitchers are very rare. In 2021, Gerrit Cole and Sean Manaea had two complete games each, the most in the big leagues. By comparison, fifty years earlier, in 1971, Ferguson Jenkins led all of baseball with thirty complete games while eight pitchers had twenty or more complete games. In 2021 there were only 50 complete games over the course of the entire season, fewer than Jenkins and American League leader Mickey Lolich combined for in 1971. Many games today are started by openers who rarely throw more than two innings. The batting order has changed completely as well. Frequently, the best hitter bats second and the sacrifice bunt has become a very minor part of the game.

Few players have seen their fortunes change as much because of the way baseball is understood as Bert Blyleven. Blyleven pitched from 1970 to 1992 for the Twins, Indians, Pirates, Rangers, and Angels. During those years he was viewed by most of the baseball world as a good and reliable, but certainly not great, pitcher. For most baseball people back then, the idea that Blyleven was a Hall of Famer was laughable. He was known to have a great curve ball, made two all-star teams, finished in the top ten in Cy Young Award voting four times, but never won the award or came particularly close. Blyleven never led his league in wins or ERA, and led in strikeouts only once. He managed to win twenty games only once, in 1973. When he retired, Blyleven was the answer to a great trivia question because the Dutch born righty had more wins, 283, than any foreign-born pitcher in history, but that was the most significant part of his legacy at the time.

Within a few years of his retirement, the analytics revolution began and it became evident that what most people thought about Blyleven was completely wrong. Blyleven became one of analytics first cause celebres because the new approaches showed that Blyleven was, in fact, one of the greatest pitchers in modern times and perhaps the most underrated pitcher in baseball history. Blyleven spent most of his career pitching for mediocre teams out of the media spotlight at a time when wins were still the primary criteria by which pitchers were judged. He racked up 283 career wins, but never reached the magic 300 mark. Blyleven's twelve seasons among the top ten in his league in ERA+ and fourteen in the top ten for Fielding Independent Pitching (FIP) demonstrate that he was an excellent pitcher for a long time, but those measures did not even exist when Blyleven was playing. The three seasons Blyleven led the league in strikeout to walk ratio, and sixteen times he finished in the top ten in that simple, but newish metric, also indicate his greatness.

As WAR became a more popular measure of evaluating pitchers, it was increasingly evident that Blyleven, who was a top pitcher for a very long time, belonged among the game's all-time greats. When he retired, Blyleven's 94.5 WAR was tenth among all pitchers. Blyleven, through nothing he did, became the subject of both an intense Hall of Fame campaign from the new analytical crowd and derision from more traditionally minded fans and writers who believed that any measure that said Blyleven was better than Nolan Ryan or Bob Gibson—and much better than Jim Palmer or Don Drysdale—was axiomatically flawed.

Ultimately the new approach won out and Blyleven's election to the Hall of Fame in 2011 was one of the first major triumphs of the new metrics. Today, the new analytics define the game in everything from pitcher usage, to batting order to in game strategy to player transactions. This change has remade baseball and no player was a bigger part of that discourse than Bert Blyleven.

Ten
Barry Bonds

One of my regrets from my decades as a baseball fan is that I was just a little too young to have seen Willie Mays play. I moved to San Francisco from New York a few months before Willie Mays made the reverse journey and did not go to my first game until after Mays retired. However, since the mid-1970s I have seen many great players including Joe Morgan, Mike Schmidt, Reggie Jackson, Ricky Henderson, Roger Clemens, Greg Maddux, Pedro Martinez, Alex Rodriguez and Mike Trout, but the best player I ever saw play was Barry Bonds.

© S. F. Giants

Barry Bonds is the only player other than Ozzie Smith to steal at least 500 bases and win at least eight Gold Gloves. He is the only player ever to hit 500 home runs and steal five hundred bases. He is one of two players to have five seasons with thirty home runs and thirty stolen bases. The other player in that group is his father Bobby Bonds. Barry Bonds had 162.8 career WAR, behind only Babe Ruth, Walter Johnson and Cy Young. Most famously, and most controversially, Bonds is the all-time leader in single season and career home runs.

Unfortunately, Bonds is also one of the most hated players

in the history of the game. He became the face of the PED era, in large part because of his surly personality, but also because when Bonds started using PEDs, he became so good that he made a mockery of the game. Over the years, MLB and the baseball writers have sent a message that steroids are largely okay if the player is nice to the media, but Bonds was not nice to the media. Many players, including some great ones, used PEDs in the 1990s and first decade of the new century, but only a handful have been singled out for using PEDs. Roger Clemens, Alex Rodriguez, Sammy Sosa and Mark McGwire are in that group, but none of them have been targeted as much as Bonds.

Anybody who has ever watched a big league game closely or played the game at a level above Little League knows how difficult baseball is. Making solid contact against a pitcher who is trying to strike you out, throwing a strike in the first place, even catching a high fly ball, all require excellent hand-eye coordination and physical strength. The only way to learn to do any of these things is practice. The only way to excel is to practice a lot and be fortunate enough to have substantial natural talent. Even big leaguers struggle to do these things consistently, but Bonds on steroids made it look too easy and baseball has never quite forgiven him for that.

The thing about Bonds is that he was a sure Hall of Famer before he ever dabbled in PEDs. We know that he did not use steroids until at least after the 1998 season when he was 33-years-old. Through that season, Bonds had 99.9 WAR. Only 11 other players, Rogers Hornsby, Babe Ruth, Ty Cobb, Willie Mays, Rodriguez, Henry Aaron, Lou Gehrig, Mickey Mantle, Walter Johnson, Christy Mathewson, and Kid Nichols had more WAR at that age. If he had simply retired then, Bonds still would have been 32nd in career WAR. During those first 13 years of his career, Bonds had an OPS+ of 164 and averaged more than thirty home runs and thirty stolen bases with over 100 walks per season. He had already won three MVP awards and finished in the top ten in MVP voting eight times, and seven times in the top five. The pre-PED Barry Bonds was a fantastic and well-rounded player. He was Willie Mays, with a better batting eye and not quite as good on defense. But even then, Bonds was unpopular with the media and had a reputation for being disagreeable and a tough teammate.

And then, at a time when the PED infused home run race between McGwire and Sosa was being celebrated, Bonds decided that he too wanted in on the action. At a key moment, he looked a moral decision in the face and made the wrong choice. To be clear, he didn't kill anybody, rip off old pensioners or seek to overturn a democratic election. Instead, he saw a league that was all but officially embracing PED use and decided he too wanted to be just a little bit better.

PEDs made Bonds more than just a little bit better; they made him cartoonishly good. He led the league in walks and OBP from 2001-2004 and again in 2006 and 2007. He was intentionally walked 120 times in 2004 and slugged 73 home runs in 2001. Bonds added four more MVP awards to his trophy case, winning that award every year from 2001-2004. The PED bolstered Bonds was not the graceful athlete who played gold glove defense and was an elite base stealer as the young Bonds had been. Rather, he was a bloated caricature of a baseball slugger who seemed to hit home runs almost at will. More than 35% of his plate appearances from 2000 through the end of his career in 2007 ended in either a walk or a home run. When Bonds finally broke Henry Aaron's home run record in 2007 it seemed the culmination of a joyless slog. Few outside of the Bay Area seemed happy about it; many including Commissioner Bud Selig barely recognized the event or the new record at all.

Bonds was hated because he used PEDs and was unrepentant about it. He denied it, managed to avoid being found conclusively guilty of using PEDs and ultimately was blacklisted out of baseball after hitting .276/.480/.565 as a 42-year-old in 2007. Bonds often seemed a little angry at baseball, but he was driven to be the best. To understand some of the reason for this, it should be remembered that Barry was the son of Bobby Bonds, an extremely talented ballplayer who had a borderline Hall of Fame career himself. Bobby Bonds was traded a lot, constantly described as not meeting his potential and generally viewed as a malcontent. The racial politics of that in the 1970s are hard to miss. It is very likely Barry saw this and went into baseball with no illusions or expectations. Based on his father's experience, Barry Bonds probably knew what an unforgiving world baseball was and carried some of his father's resentment with him.

Barry Bonds is a complicated man who has led a complicated baseball life, but you cannot tell the story of PEDs, or have a serious conversation about who the best player ever was, without including Barry Bonds.

Eleven
Ila Borders

The longest and most enduring prejudice in baseball is against women. No woman has ever played in the Major Leagues or even for an affiliated minor league team. There is no women's baseball at the college level. It is still unusual to see girls play in high school or other youth baseball programs. The only reasonably high-level women's baseball league, the All American Girls Professional Baseball League lasted only about a decade during and after World War II.

There is a vibrant girls and women's softball culture in the US, particularly at the high school and college level. Softball, when played by men or women at the elite level is a great sport. It is a riff on baseball with some differences and some similarities, but it is not the same sport. There has never been a sustained women's softball league in the US, so the top college softball players do not go on to lucrative careers as professional ballplayers

Photos courtesy of Ila Borders and used with permission.

like many top college and high school male baseball players do. However, there are college scholarships for female softball players. This means that the best young female ballplayers choose, or are pushed, to softball, not least because of the possibility of a college scholarship and are therefore pushed out of baseball at a relatively young age.

This, as well as the deeply ingrained sexism at every level of baseball, too frequently beginning when children are very young, has contributed to the absence of any enduring women's baseball league. There is a national women's baseball team, that is usually very good, but they compete in international tournaments, rather than as part of a league in the US. Thus, it is more likely that as prejudices against women and girls in baseball breakdown that there will be a woman playing for a Major League team before there is another successful women's professional baseball league.

When that woman goes into her windup to throw her first big league pitch, readies herself for a ball to be hit or thrown her way or steps into the batters' box for the first time on a big league field, she will be standing on the shoulders of many women who came before her. One of the most important of those women is Ila Borders.

Borders was a left-handed pitcher and a trailblazer for women in baseball. She grew up in Southern California and attended Southern California College on a baseball scholarship. While in college she played on the baseball team and became the first women to play in a college baseball game when, in February of 1994, she pitched a five hitter against Claremont-Mudd-Scripps. Borders continued to pitch in college through 1996. Southern California College and Claremont-Mudd-Scripps are Division Three (D3) schools, not exactly baseball powerhouses. Southern California College is a small Christian school and Claremont-Mudd-Scripps is a group of three of the five Claremont Colleges, all of which are better known for academics than sports. Nonetheless, even D3 programs, many of which are at historically very liberal schools like Oberlin or Bard, had not had a woman player and still have not had one till this day. That speaks to the extent of the exclusion of women from baseball.

A few pretty good seasons of college baseball is significant, but not enough to make the 100 most important players in the game, but Borders did not stop there. After college, Borders became the first woman to play in a men's professional baseball league. In 1997 she began her career with the St. Paul Saints, a minor league team that was not affiliated with any big league team. Borders spent four years playing in the independent minor leagues, mostly in the Northern League where she played for St. Paul and Duluth-Superior in Minnesota and then briefly in Madison, Wisconsin before ending her career playing the Western League. Some of her teammates included future big leaguers such as JD Drew and former big leaguers including Randy Tomlin and Greg Briley.

Borders was never a great pitcher. She ended up in an independent league because D3 pitchers are very rarely drafted by big league teams, and those that are were dominant pitchers in college. Over the course of four seasons, Borders pitched just over 100 innings with a record of 3-4 and a 6.75 ERA. Her career ended not because of explicit bigotry against her because she was a woman, but because independent league baseball is low-paying and arduous. It is frequently the last stop for players still chasing an unrealistic dream of making it to the big leagues. That is not quite what Borders was doing. She was continuing to play the game, trying to contribute on the field, but also showing that the longstanding prejudice against women in baseball needed to end. While she was not a star, she was effective at times, particularly in 1997 when she had a 3.63 ERA in 34.2 innings and with Madison in 1999 when she posted a 1.67 ERA in 32.1 innings.

One of the things that makes Borders so compelling is that she was not a big star at any point. She was a girl and then a woman who loved baseball and pitched at a higher level, and more effectively, than most boys who ever play on a Little League field, and in doing that helped make it possible for women to continue to break down one of baseball's last remaining bigotries.

Twelve
Jim Bouton

Few players have changed how baseball fans understand and enjoy the game as much as Jim Bouton. Through his 1970 book *Ball Four*, a seminal baseball work that is part of the educated baseball fan's cannon, Jim Bouton became one of the people who most helped shape modern sports culture. Before *Ball Four* most baseball memoirs and biographies were hagiographies and most baseball writers sought to cover up the excesses of star players, but after *Ball Four* that changed quickly and the current media climate around sports began to take shape.

Public Domain Photo

Ball Four was Bouton's journal from the 1969 season, which he spent as a struggling knuckleballer trying to stick in the big leagues, first with the expansion Seattle Pilots and then the Houston Astros. *Ball Four* is a funny, irreverent and highly readable book filled with great baseball stories and more than a few nuggets of wisdom. *Ball Four* was the first baseball book to tell the truth about life in the big leagues and show ballplayers not just in their greatness, but also revealed their pettiness, immaturity, substance abuse problems and humor while giving readers a sense of the stress, boredom, fun and worry of the long baseball season. *Ball Four* chronicled disputes over money between players and ownership at a time when many players were not well compensated. It revealed how managers and coaches often had little of value to say to help players other than inanities like "pound that Budweiser" or surreally obvious platitudes such as "the key to pitching is to throw strikes."

In his hugely influential book, Bouton also explored the deeply conservative culture of baseball in 1969, a time when the national culture was undergoing dramatic change. Bouton was a short-haired jock who was curious about and sympathetic to the counterculture. This made Bouton one of the few baseball players who became a hero to many who live in the overlap between baseball obsession and the counterculture.

In addition to being a writer, Bouton was a right-handed pitcher who began his career with the New York Yankees at the tail end of their mid-century dynasty. He won 21 games for the Yankees in 1963 and 18 more in 1964. Both those teams won the pennant. Bouton was a World Series star as well, going 2-1 with a 1.48 ERA as the Yankees lost both the 1963 and 1964 World Series. In those years, Bouton threw hard and was tenacious, earning him the nickname the Bulldog. He was understood to be part of the young Yankees stars that would help the team continue its dominance through the 1960s. That did not happen because just as the Yankees began to fall apart beginning in 1965, Bouton struggled with arm injuries beginning that year. From 1965-1968, he only was able to pitch 360 innings with an ERA+ of 83, down from 129 in 1963-1964.

Bouton joined the expansion Seattle Pilots in 1969. By then Bouton was no longer the hard thrower he had been early in his career, but was trying to make it as a knuckleballer. He was a below average relief pitcher during 1969-1970 and was then more or less blacklisted from baseball after *Ball Four* was published. Bouton spent the next few years writing, acting and dabbling in politics, even becoming a delegate for Democratic presidential candidate George McGovern in 1972, but could not stay away from baseball. He pitched for the independent Portland Mavericks in 1975, where along with another pitcher and batboy he came up with the idea for Big League Chew, a bubble gum product for children that is shredded and sold in a bag that looks like a pouch to resemble chewing tobacco.

The Atlanta Braves signed Bouton to a minor league contract in 1977. Remarkably, Bouton made it back to the big leagues briefly in 1978 and pitched in five games. Overall, he was not very effective, but on September 14th, Bouton, then 38-years-old, managed to hold the Giants to three hits and one unearned run in six innings.

In addition to several editions of *Ball Four*, Bouton wrote or co-wrote several other baseball books, mostly about his experiences in and around the game. He was also the subject of a 1983 book that was written by his ex-wife Bobbie Bouton and fellow pitcher Mike Marshall's ex-wife Nancy Marshall called *Home Games* about the difficulties of being married to a big league ballplayer.

Bouton was an odd kind of baseball lifer who while never fully welcomed back into the game due to both the book he wrote in 1970 and his irreverent and brash personality, but was still involved in baseball, in one way or another, for most of his adult life, pitching in various semi-professional leagues into his 50s. The final line of Bouton's seminal book "you spend a good piece of your life gripping a baseball, and in the end, it turns out that it was the other way around all the time," is succinctly powerful reflection of the role that baseball plays in our lives and how difficult it is for many of us, including Bouton himself, to get out of its grip.

I am an academic and have spent much of my life reading and writing books. *Ball Four* is on the very short list of books that have influenced me the most. Maybe I shouldn't say this, but if you haven't read *Ball Four*, before you get to number thirteen in this book, you should check it out.

Thirteen
George Brett

Like Ernie Banks, George Brett is deeply identified with the one team for whom he played his entire career. Brett is by far the best player in Kansas City Royals history. Brett's 88.6 career WAR, all with the Royals, is at least twice that of every other Royal in team history other than Kevin Appier (47) and Amos Otis (44.8). However, unlike Banks, Brett did not spend his career with a bad team that never made the post-season. Brett took over as the Royals

starting third baseman in 1974. Two years later, in 1976, the Royals won their division. In the ten years from 1976-1985, when Brett was by far their biggest star, the Royals won the AL West six times, the AL pennant twice and the World Series once.

When the Royals finally won their first World Series in 1985, it was because Brett carried the team with an otherwise mediocre offense to the championship. That year he hit .335/.436/.585 for a 179 OPS+ and led the team in plate appearances, runs, hits, doubles, RBIs, walks, batting average, on base percentage and slugging percentage. In the post season he continued to hit, slashing .360/.475/.600.

Five years earlier, in 1980, Brett hit .390, the closest any player had come to hitting .400 over a full season since Ted

Williams in 1941. Over his 21-year career from 1973-1993, Brett hit .303/.369/.487 and is one of two third baseman with more than 3,000 hits and 300 home runs. For good measure, Brett stole over 200 bases. He was never a great defender, but Brett even managed to win a Gold Glove in 1985.

Brett's relationship with the Royals and being one of the very best third basemen in American League history might be enough to make him among the 100 most important players in baseball history, but one other event—a home run that may or may not deserve to be called that—sealed his place on this list.

On July 24th, 1983 the Royals were playing the Yankees at Yankee Stadium. At that time, the Yankees and Royals had a fierce rivalry. The two teams had met in the ALCS four times between 1976 and 1980. The Yankees won the first three times, but the Royals had swept them out of the playoffs in 1980. The key blow in that series had been a huge three run home run by Brett off of Yankees reliever Goose Gossage in the seventh inning of the third game. When play began that day in 1983, both teams were two games out of first place in their division so another ALCS meeting that October was a very real possibility.

The Yankees led 4-3 in the top of the ninth with two outs and one runner on base when Brett came to the plate. The Yankees manager Billy Martin brought in his best reliever, Goose Gossage, who like Brett was on his way to the Hall of Fame, to get the final out. This was a marquee matchup, one of the best hitters in baseball against one of the game's top relievers with the game on the line. Most fans also remembered how Brett had got the better of the Goose three years earlier in the playoffs. Brett then did it again and smashed a long home run to right field.

Martin, a deeply disturbed and bigoted man who was also an absolute baseball genius, noticed that Brett had too much pine tar, a sticky substance that enhances a batter's grip, on the bat and asked the umpire to examine the bat. Martin's complaint was legitimate and Brett's home run was ruled an out. And then all hell broke loose. Brett was livid and had to be physically restrained from attacking the umpire by his teammates. That video has been watched millions of times on YouTube and is one of the most famous on field arguments in baseball history. The Pine Tar Game, as it came to be known, is still one of the most remembered regular season games in history and Brett was at the center of it.

The Pine Tar Game did not end there. The Royals protested and American League President Lee MacPhail, because of some combination of his belief that Brett had not intended to break the rule, as well as perhaps a disdain for Billy Martin or the Yankees, sided with the Royals. The home run counted, and the final four outs of the game were played the following month and the Royals held on to win by the 5-4 score.

The Pine Tar Game is also significant because it shows how baseball is a game that has long been obsessed with rules and finding small advantages in the rules. Billy Martin had known that Brett had too much pine tar on his bat but waited for the right moment to call the umpire's attention to that fact. Many of the scandals that have always been around baseball such as PEDs, enhanced bats, efforts to either alter the ball or use substances to get a better grip on the ball, and sign stealing all involve pushing the rules to their limits and trying to get away with just a little bit more than the rules allowed. Whether he meant to or not, Brett was at the center of what may have been the highest profile in-game incident of that in baseball history.

One of the strange and forgotten things about the Pine Tar Game was that Billy Martin was right and it was outrageous that the call was overturned. The rules were very clear, but the league sided with Brett. The only reason for that decision that makes any sense is that Brett was a huge star and basically everybody hated Billy Martin.

Watching the video of that game now, another thing strikes me. Brett's anger is so extreme. It would be shocking and lead to police or security intervention in almost any other workplace in America today, but at the time it was seen as funny or part of the game. One of the ways that baseball takes us away from reality is that it indulges what are essentially temper tantrums, and not only from George Brett, that the rest of the adult world does not.

Fourteen
Jim Bunning

There has long been overlap between electoral politics and big league baseball. Lou Gehrig and Babe Ruth campaigned for Al Smith, a Democrat who sought to become the first Catholic President in 1928, decades before John F. Kennedy was elected. George H.W. Bush played college baseball at Yale. Ronald Reagan did reenactments of ballgames on the radio long before entering politics and played pithing great Grover Cleveland Alexander in the 1952 film *The Winning Team*.

Public Domain Photo

Several ballplayers have explored running for office. Before he was engulfed by scandal, Steve Garvey, the Dodgers and Padres first baseman in the 1970s and 1980s, was sometimes said to be a possible candidate for the US Senate from California. As of early summer 2023, Garvey was again toying with a senate campaign in California. Frank White, the slick fielding Royals second baseman and longtime teammate of George Brett, was a legislator in Jackson County, Missouri for several years.

Through all the years, no former big league ballplayer was as successful a politician as Jim Bunning and no politician was ever as good a ballplayer as Bunning. Bunning was a Hall of Fame pitcher who went on to serve twenty-four years in the US Congress, twelve in the House of Representatives and twelve in the US Senate.

Bunning, a hard throwing righty, spent most of his 17-year

career with the Tigers and the Phillies. He was only the second pitcher, after Cy Young, to throw a no-hitter in each league-including a perfect game on Father's Day in 1964. Bunning was also the second pitcher ever, after only Cy Young, to win 100 games in each league. During his 17-year career, Bunning won 224 games and had an ERA+ 115 over the course of 3,760.1 innings. During the second half of his career, primarily with the Phillies, he was a very good pitcher, but never quite as good as other National League aces such as Sandy Koufax, Bob Gibson, and Juan Marichal. Bunning never won the Cy Young Award, but made the All-Star team in seven different years. He was a marginal Hall of Fame candidate who got elected to Cooperstown in 1996, the only sitting member of Congress to ever receive that honor.

Bunning was a native of Kentucky, born in Covington, just across the river from Cincinnati. Being from a relatively small state that could not claim many big league baseball stars, Bunning always enjoyed fame in Kentucky. That fame was essential to his post-baseball life.

Bunning began his political career getting elected to the Kentucky State Senate as a Republican in 1979, eight years after his playing career had come to an end. In 1986 Bunning moved on to the US House of Representatives where he was a solidly conservative, if otherwise undistinguished, member of that body. Today we think of Kentucky as a Republican stronghold that consistently elects Republicans to the senate and delivers its votes to the GOP presidential candidate, but that was not true when Bunning decided to run for the senate in 1998. Kentucky was an increasingly conservative state, but one where conservative Democrats still frequently won elections. Bill Clinton, for example, had carried the state in the 1992 and 1996 elections, and the senator Bunning was running to replace, Wendell Ford, was a Democrat.

That 1998 race was extremely close, as Bunning won by fewer than 7,000 votes. Bunning's baseball fame probably made the difference. Bunning was reelected in 2004 and retired at the end of that term. During his 12 years in the senate, Bunning was very much part of the right-wing movement that took over the

Republican Party. Senator Bunning was better known for his erratic behavior, particularly in his second term, and for his far right views than for any major legislative accomplishments during his time in congress.

Bunning's major contribution to the senate was his ability to win a difficult 1998 election, one that most Republicans who had not been baseball stars, would not have been able to win. In the years that followed, partisan control of the senate was frequently extremely close. If that seat had gone Democratic in 1998, the Democrats would have had just enough seats to be in the clear majority, instead of having control go back and forth between the parties in 2001-2002. The Democrats would have been in a stronger position in the following two years as well.

As his second term wound down, Bunning was preparing to run for a third term, but concerns about his conduct continued to grow. He missed key votes, took some positions that were outliers even in the GOP and gratuitously insulted Supreme Court Justice Ruth Bader Ginsburg, back when that kind of thing was not considered normal political discourse. Ultimately, in part due to his rumors that Mitch McConnell, the powerful GOP senate leader who was the senior senator from Kentucky, had lost confidence in him, Bunning decided not to run. That decision opened the door for Rand Paul who has had a significant, if poisonous, impact on American political life, to get elected to the senate.

It is tempting to see Bunning as a genial old man who parlayed baseball fame into a political career, but his impact goes beyond that. If you are a conservative, you may admire him as a foot soldier in a march to the far right, but if you are a progressive, the full extent of Bunning's impact must be recognized. Bunning voted to confirm John Roberts and Sam Alito to the Supreme Court, but not for Elena Kagan or Sonia Sotomayor. Bunning voted for both Gulf Wars and the Bush tax cuts, but not the Affordable Care Act. The right-hander was also a right-winger.

Fifteen
Glenn Burke

Glenn Burke, as many fans know, was the first big league player who was broadly known to be gay. While he was not exactly out when he was playing, his sexual orientation was an open secret. Burke was an outfielder with the Dodgers and A's who made it to the big leagues in 1976 and played his last game in 1979. He was African American and grew up in Oakland, California, which was a hotbed of baseball and athletic talent in general during the three decades or so after the end of World War II. Among the

Photo courtesy of the National Baseball Hall of Fame and Museum (Burke Glenn 2472.77_NBL)

ballplayers who were Burke's peers in Oakland when they were growing up were Dave Stewart, Lloyd Moseby, Rickey Henderson, Shooty Babbit, Claudell Washington and Rupert Jones.

An extraordinary athlete, Burke was also an excellent basketball player. Burke demonstrated this athleticism through his play in the outfield, where he earned a reputation as an excellent defender, and on the basepaths where he stole 35 bases in 51 tries over the course of his brief big league career. The speedy outfielder tore up the bases in the minor leagues, peaking with 63 stolen bases while only being caught stealing 13 times in about two thirds of a season with the Dodgers AAA affiliate Albuquerque Dukes in 1976.

There is another aspect of Burke's game that is often over-looked, but gives his story some nuance. Like a lot of other talent-ed prospects, Burke always struggled with the bat. In the minors, Burke hit around .300 most years with great speed and decent power, but never put up the kind of numbers that top hitting prospects are expected to produce. While he played under extraordinary stress and pressure at the big league level, Burke simply never hit. His career OPS+ of 57 and slash line of .237/.270/.291 was the stuff of backup catchers not starting outfielders.

Despite that, there is no question that Burke's big league career was shortened because he was gay. However, the widely reported notion that he would have been the next Willie Mays, based on a comment by longtime Dodger player and official Jim Gilliam, is wrong and should be seen in some context. First, virtually all outfielders from about 1965-1980 who hit for power and could run, especially if, like Burke, they were African American, were at one time or another called the next Willie Mays. None were, although the son of Bobby Bonds, the first next Willie Mays, came close. Without belaboring the point, one way to see this is that at 23-year-old, Burke had a solid season at AAA hitting, .300 with seven home runs and then did not hit well after being called up to the big league team at the end of the year. That is a respect-able, but not standout, prospect season. However, when Mays was 23, he hit .345 with 41 home runs, won the NL MVP and led the New York Giants to victory in a World Series where he made the greatest catch in baseball history.

Burke had the misfortune not just to play at a time when big-otry towards LGBTQ people was still very strong in baseball, but also to play for two managers, Tommy Lasorda and Billy Martin, who shared the widespread homophobia of the time. Lasorda was not just prejudiced against Burke because he was gay, but was very upset that his young gay outfielder was friends with his son, Tom Jr. who was also gay. Tom Jr. was a teenager when Burke was a Dodger and Lasorda did not approve of the friendship.

After his career with the A's ended, Burke moved across the bay and was a mainstay of San Francisco life for years where he was also a star in that city's very competitive gay softball league.

Burke died in 1995 from AIDS. By then, he was largely forgotten by the baseball world and many of his former teammates. One of the exceptions was the man who was part of Burke's most famous moment in baseball, Dusty Baker. Burke and Baker were part of the first recorded high five and Baker remained in contact with his onetime teammate until he succumbed to AIDS.

There is one more thing about Burke that needs to be said. Part of the narrative around the first gay player is that the Dodgers dumped him because he was gay. Burke was undoubtedly the victim of prejudice, not least from his manager, but his trade to the A's is more complicated than that. On the morning of May 17th, 1978, the Dodgers were tied with the Reds for second place in the NL West, one and a half games behind the Giants. That day, they traded Burke, who still had some potential, for a proven veteran who could help that team named Bill North. North was an excellent leadoff hitter who could get on base, play the outfield well, but not as well as Burke, and was an elite base stealer. After coming over to the Dodgers, North posted a .371 on base percentage and stole 27 bases in 35 tries, usually batting first or second in the lineup. The Dodgers ended up winning the division by two and a half games and probably would not have won if they had not made that trade.

The idea the Dodgers got nothing in return for Burke, or that the next Willie Mays missed out a career because he was gay, dramatizes the bigotry Burke faced, but it also makes it one dimensional. If Burke had been as talented as Mays, he might have been a ground-breaking player, a kind of gay Jackie Robinson if you will. Instead, the career he missed out on was that of a backup outfielder, who in a good year plays almost every day. Burke's glove and speed were enough to help any team, but his difficulty hitting would always have prevented him from being a real star. In order to have long careers, those kind of fourth players need to be well liked and not be seen as troublemakers. Homophobia is what prevented Burke from having that type of career due to the bigotry of the time. Nonetheless, as society and baseball grow more tolerant, Burke's role in baseball history is increasingly recognized.

Sixteen
Miguel Cabrera

As baseball has become more globalized in the 21st century, Venezuela has become one of the top international exporters of talent to MLB, behind only the Dominican Republic. Pitcher Alex Carrasquel became the first Venezuelan to play in the big leagues in 1939. Luis Aparicio, a shortstop who played excellent defense and stole over 500 bases during his career, was the first, and thus far only, Venezuelan elected to the Baseball Hall of

Creative Commons - Keith Allison KeithAllisonPhoto.com

Fame. Since the days of Carrasquel and Aparicio there have been hundreds of Venezuelan big leaguers including standouts like Dave Concecpion, Bobby Abreu and Felix Hernandez.

Five years after he retires, Miguel Cabrera will join Aparicio in Cooperstown. Cabrera, a right-handed slugger who has spent his career with the Marlins and Tigers, is the greatest Venezuelan player ever. He is a twelve time All-Star and is one of only seven players with more than 3,000 hits and 500 or more home runs. His career OPS+ through 2022 was an excellent 142, tying him with several good players like Kevin Mitchell and Frank Howard, but is considerably less than all-time greats like Mays, Aaron, Ruth, Bonds or Frank Robinson. Similarly, his 67.7 career WAR through 2022 is tied with Ernie Banks at 126th on the all-time list, just behind Graig Nettles and Ryne Sandberg, but just ahead of Roberto Alomar and Dwight Evans.

The gap between Cabrera's raw numbers and his advanced metrics is due to his having played most of his career during a high offense era, the long decline phase of his career that began in 2017 and his inability to contribute anything with the glove. Cabrera was never a strong defender, but his poor defense was too often exposed by managers who insisted on playing Cabrera at third base rather than even his natural position of first base or his even more natural position of designated hitter.

Cabrera's best season was 2013 when he slashed .348/.442/.636, leading the league in all three categories. His OPS+ that year was 190. Even then, he was limited to 7.5 WAR that year because had -1.3 defensive WAR due to his poor play at third base. Cabrera won his second consecutive MVP award in 2013. However, it was the previous year's MVP voting that is remembered more and is one of the reasons why Cabrera is, in the context of the evolution of how baseball is understood, a very important player.

For decades the supreme accomplishment for a hitter was to win the triple crown by leading the league in home runs, RBIs and batting average. In the twentieth century there were only ten triple crown winners including Mickey Mantle, Frank Robinson and Carl Yastrzemski. Ted Williams and Rogers Hornsby won it twice each. Since Yastrzemski in 1967 nobody had won a triple crown until Miguel Cabrera in 2012 when he led the league with a .330 batting average, 44 home runs and 139 RBIs.

Batting average, home runs and RBIs are not exactly cutting age quantitative indicators and are no longer seen by many fans, or teams, as the most valuable way to measure a player's ability. RBIs, in particular, are a questionable measure because they are so dependent on team play. Nonetheless, Cabrera also slashed .330/.393/.606 and had an unquestionably excellent season in 2012. There were also some less than excellent numbers for Cabrera. He hit into a league leading 28 double plays and played generally sub-par defense at third base. When it came time for award voting, most fans assumed Cabrera would win the MVP.

There was another player that year, Mike Trout, a rookie centerfielder with the Angels who also had an excellent year slashing

.326/.399/.564 while playing an excellent centerfield, stealing a league leading 49 bases in 54 tries while only grounding into seven double plays. Trout's 10.5 WAR was substantially more than Cabrera's 7.1. The MVP vote between Trout and Cabrera was one of the most contentious in baseball history. It was not just a vote between two players, but a referendum on the new quantitative approaches that was beginning to take over baseball. To those committed to the new methods, it was clear that Trout's comparable slash lines, slightly higher OPS+ due to ballpark effects, superior baserunning and defense made him a significantly more valuable player than Cabrera. To Cabrera's backers, it was axiomatic that a triple crown winner should be the MVP, particularly as nobody had accomplished that feat in 45 years. Many of the people supporting Cabrera also seemed to believe that those supporting Trout were somehow destroying the game with their data obsessions.

In the end, the vote wasn't close as Cabrera won 22 of 28 first place votes and beat Trout 362 to 281 in the points system used for MVP voting. It was a victory for the traditionalists, but given how the game has changed, it may have been their last one. Today there are few fans, and increasingly few sportswriters, who think indicators like RBIs are important. The quantitative revolution has remade baseball and Cabrera is one of the players who most symbolizes the contentiousness around that.

Seventeen
Jose Canseco

Jose Canseco was the Ur steroid abuser and a kind of prime mover among players in what became the PED era. By the end of his career, in the early 2000s, Canseco was almost a caricature of a bloated, PED using slugger. Unlike some other great players of the PED era, we do not know when Canseco started using PEDs with some speculating that he was juicing as early as the late 1980s.

Photo 44437521 / Baseball © Jerry Coli | Dreamstime.com

Canseco never threatened to break long cherished records the way Barry Bonds, Mark McGwire, Sammy Sosa, Alex Rodriguez, and Roger Clemens did. Similarly, there is not much of a Hall of Fame debate around Canseco. He wasn't good enough, and by age 28 was no longer a consistently standout player. However, Canseco differs from all of the other big name players accused of using PEDs because he was unapologetic about it. Canseco was frank about his own use of the banned substances and about how widespread the problem was throughout baseball. In other words, Canseco, uniquely among baseball players, told simple truths about PED abuse and, for his efforts, was ridiculed, criticized and all but blacklisted from the game.

Canseco played for seven American League teams during his career including the Rangers, Red Sox, Blue Jays, Rays, Yankees, and White Sox but will always be remembered most for his time with the Oakland A's. He had his biggest on-the-field success with Oakland as well as his first exposure to PEDs. Canseco was drafted out of high school by the A's and made it to the big league team in 1985 for the last few weeks of the season. By then a highly touted prospect, Canseco performed well posting a 130 OPS+ in 100 plate appearances. The next year, he was the Rookie of the Year, which he followed up by a solid if unspectacular second year in 1987.

In those early years, Canseco was the rare power hitter who looked like a big slugger, but who could run extremely well. He was never a great outfielder, but he fielded his position well enough. In 1988 Canseco broke out and established himself as one of the best players in the game. He became the first player ever to hit 40 home runs and steal 40 bases in a season while slashing .307/.391/.569 for an OPS+ of 170. Canseco's A's won their division handily by thirteen games and Canseco received all 28 votes in the MVP balloting. Unfortunately for Canseco, the A's lost that World Series to the Dodgers despite being heavy favorites. In 1987, another young slugger, Mark McGwire, joined Canseco on the A's. McGwire had even more power than Canseco, but Canseco was by far the better all-around player. McGwire and Canseco became known as the Bash Brothers and led Oakland to three straight pennants, and one World Series Championship between 1988 and 1990.

During the late 1980s and into the early 1990s, Canseco was one of the best and most famous players in the game. His off-the-field fame included a high-profile speeding ticket for driving 125 miles per hour and rumors of a liaison with Madonna when she was one of the biggest pop stars in the world. During these years there was no talk of Canseco and PEDs because few people in the game were even aware of steroids. However, Canseco later claimed to have used PEDs with McGwire as early as 1988, meaning that all of three of those pennant A's teams could well have been led by PED users at a time when few other players were using.

Canseco's last great year was 1991 when he again led the

league in home runs, but by then the A's felt they'd seen enough of Canseco and sent him to the Rangers midway through the next season. The slugger spent the next ten years bouncing from team to team, always hitting reasonably well, every now and then at an elite level, but rarely staying healthy. By the mid-1990s, the PED era was in full swing, and Canseco continued to use PEDs to bolster his numbers.

In recent years Canseco has become something of a joke for many baseball people. His sometimes unusual behavior including having a goat wearing a diaper in the back of his car that was discovered when he was pulled over and his odd use of social media were sources of ridicule. He also accidentally shot off part of finger while cleaning a gun. His post-baseball personality has been strange, but also at times funny.

Canseco's importance is that underneath the distractions he was a truth teller. Unlike so many players and executives who denied or tried to minimize the impact of steroids. Canseco was very honest. He did it flamboyantly and was not the best messenger, but telling simple truths in simple language is always valuable. There were many villains of baseball's PED era, but in some odd, but real way, Canseco may have been one of the heroes.

Eighteen
Hal Chase

Hal Chase is one of the more obscure players in this book, but he was well known during his playing days. Chase may have been the most famous, although not the best, Yankees player, until Babe Ruth came along. Prince Hal, as he was known, even was briefly the Yankees player-manager at the end of the 1910 season through the following year. Chase was a first baseman who, in addition to the Yankees—then known as the Highlanders—played for

Sporty News Archive - Public Domain - Photographer: Charles M. Conlon

the Reds, White Sox, and Giants. Because he played during the deadball era, Chase had little power hitting only 57 home runs in his entire career, but he hit some doubles and triples, stole a lot of bases and was generally viewed as the best defensive first baseman of his era.

The deadball era refers to baseball before 1920. During those years bats and balls were heavier and remained in play longer. This meant that balls got scuffed, damp, and dirty and thus harder for batters to see, making it very difficult to hit for power. Baseball in those years had many fewer home runs, but many more bunts and stolen bases than during the last 100 years.

Chase played from 1905-1919 during a time when big league baseball was just taking shape. The America League and National League had more or less arrived at their present form with each league stabilizing at eight teams. Those sixteen teams would play in their same cities for almost half a century. However, the hegemony of those two leagues over professional baseball was not yet complete. In addition to the Negro Leagues that were formed during this time, a rival major league emerged seeking to poach players from the American and National League. Several big stars went over to the new Federal League including Chase, who played for the Buffalo Blues in 1914 and 1915. That last year of Chase's career should stand out to most fans as the year that the Chicago White Sox threw the World Series to the Cincinnati Reds.

The World Series of 1919 is usually understood to be an aberration that led to Kenesaw Mountain Landis, the game's first commissioner, to ban the players who threw the World Series and rid baseball of gambling. There is some truth to that, but it overlooks the extent to which gambling had been compromising the game in the years before 1919-and no player symbolized that more than Hal Chase.

It is tempting to look at baseball in the first two decades of the twentieth century and see it as leading to the MLB of today. Rules evolved, franchises moved, racial barriers were lifted, but none of that was inevitable. During Hal Chase's time, there was no precedent for baseball or organized professional sports in general. If history had played out slightly differently, baseball might have been a passing fad and disappeared by mid-century or been relegated to schools, colleges and amateur clubs. Chase going to the Federal League, briefly and earlier in his career, and threatening to leave the Highlanders to play for a new league in his home state of California, are reminders that the dominance of the American and National Leagues was not a given until much later. Chase's gambling is a similar reminder that baseball during those years was not at all the American institution it later became.

The stories of Chase's gambling, throwing games and consorting with criminals are widespread in the early history of baseball. Several of his managers, including Hall of Famers Frank Chance and Christy Mathewson accused him of throwing games. Chance succeeded Chase as manager of the Highlanders, raising the very real possibility that Chase not only was involved in gambling as a player, but as a manager as well.

Mathewson, one of the game's first and most widely respected stars, managed Chase for the Reds from 1916-1918. Chase had his best years playing for Mathewson, leading the league in batting average in 1916. Not even two full seasons later in 1918, Mathewson suspended Chase for trying to bribe a teammate.

By 1919 Chase was playing with the Giants and was no longer with the Reds, the team that benefited from the White Sox throwing the World Series, but Chase was also at the center of that scandal. In 1920, when Chase was playing in the Pacific Coast League, the news of the World Series scandal broke and Chase was quickly identified as being one of the people who helped broker the arrangement between the gamblers and the White Sox players involved.

Too frequently baseball history is dominated by stories of the great players and heroic figures, but there were many people around the game whose impact was negative and either jeopardized the future of baseball, as Chase did with his gambling, or denied people the right to play based on the color of their skin, as numerous players and executives did. Unfortunately, they too are important people in the story of baseball.

Writing in 2023, it is also impossible to look at Chase outside of the context of today's game. From 1920 until very recently baseball had a very strong zero tolerance policy towards gambling, but in the last few years that has changed dramatically and quickly. Today, gambling is advertised throughout baseball and fans are encouraged to gamble not just on who will win, but also on things like how many hits or strikeouts there will be in the game. Promoting gambling to fans not only seeks to addict people to a potentially very destructive habit, it also will eventually raise ethical specters about the game itself. Turns out maybe Hal Chase was just ahead of his time.

Nineteen
Roger Clemens

Roger Clemens is the Barry Bonds of pitchers, kind of. Other than Clemens pitching in about 35 games in 1984 and 1985, their careers overlapped exactly, from 1986-2007. They both won the major award for their type of player, the Cy Young for Clemens and the MVP for Bonds, seven times. There is a good argument that they were the best pitcher and the best hitter respectively of the last half century, and possibly ever. They were also both linked to

Photo 74060047 / Baseball © Jerry Coli | Dreamstime.com

PED abuse which has led to them being kept out of the Hall of Fame and never fully welcomed back into big league baseball after their retirement.

Like Bonds, Clemens established himself as an all-time great before he was thought to have started using PEDs following the 1997 season. Through that year, and through age 34, Clemens had already won four Cy Young Awards and had accumulated 92.7 WAR. The only pitchers to exceed that through their age 34 season were Cy Young, Kid Nichols, Christy Mathewson, and Walter Johnson. Young and Nichols did that mostly in the 19th century and Johnson and Mathewson at a time when pitchers threw more innings and thus generally accumulated more WAR.

The PED era is a blemish on big league baseball, but one where the responsibility is spread around. Players like Clemens,

Bonds, and many who were not as talented, used PEDs. Before we claim that Clemens' or Bonds' records and accomplishments are less legitimate, we need to recognize that many of the players they batted or pitched against were also PED users. MLB, for its part, took an attitude during most of the 1990s that could charitably be described as turning a blind eye to PED use, and at times seemed to almost tacitly encourage it. Even after MLB tried to change this approach, they never fully confronted the problem and its impact. One of the issues that was never addressed was Hall of Fame eligibility. That was left to the writers to navigate on their own—and those writers have excluded both Bonds and Clemens.

Because Clemens pitched in such an offense rich era, some of his raw career numbers can be deceptive. His 3.12 lifetime ERA puts him just behind John Tudor and just ahead of Dave Dravecky. Those were both very good pitchers, but Cooperstown is never going to be calling for them. On the other hand, Clemens career ERA+ of 143 is tied for 16th on the all-time list behind mostly relievers and deadball era pitchers. He is also one of only three pitchers since World War II to have at least 350 wins.

Clemens was a great pitcher who pitched at the height of the PED era and got caught up in that scandal, but he was also part of several big moments that reflect the complexity of the game as well as its ugliest and most poignant sides. One of those occurred in the 1986 World Series. At age 23 Clemens had his first great year for the Red Sox in 1986 going 24-5 with a 2.48 ERA. He led the league with a 169 ERA+ and accumulated 8.8 WAR. Clemens won the MVP and Cy Young award that year.

The Red Sox took a 3-2 lead over the Mets in that World Series and gave the ball to Roger Clemens to close it out in game six. Their young ace did not disappoint, striking out eight and giving up one earned run in seven innings. He left with his team leading 3-2 and only six outs away from their first World Series win since 1918. An hour or so later, Mookie Wilson hit a slow roller through the legs of Bill Buckner. The Mets had come back to tie the series. They won it the next day. This was one of the most famous, dramatic, heart-breaking or exhilarating, depending on who you were rooting for, moments in baseball history. It was baseball at its best and Clemens was part of it.

Fourteen years later, Clemens was again in the World Series, this time pitching for the Yankees. He'd helped the Yankees win the World Series the previous year, after a stopover in Toronto where he stayed just long enough to win the Cy Young Award twice. Clemens' World Series opponent again was the Mets, but this time the series was not as close.

The 2000 World Series occurred at the height of the steroid era. Clemens was the Yankees starting pitcher in game two. That was when he became one of those rare great players whose most famous on the field moment demonstrates not his greatness, but his strangeness. In the first inning of that game, Mets star Mike Piazza, with whom Clemens had already clashed earlier in the season, hit a broken bat grounder back to Clemens. The Yankees pitcher instead of picking up the ball, inexplicably grabbed a shard of the bat and seemed to throw it at Piazza. The fury in Clemens' actions was clear and a little frightening. Many attributed it to either steroid rage or the intensity of the moment. That is still the image that comes first to the minds of many fans when they think of Clemens, but many forget that Clemens went on to throw eight shutout innings in that game, striking out nine and only allowing two base runners. That was also Roger Clemens.

Twenty
Roberto Clemente

Roberto Clemente was one of those very rare players whose extraordinary abilities were matched by a grace and beauty on the field. Clemente was an excellent hitter whose career batting average of .317 is particularly impressive because much of his career was played in the low offense era of the late 1960s. He also had enough power to hit 240 home runs, but Clemente is equally remembered for his defense, specifically his throwing arm.

Public Domain Photo

His 255 career assists are second to Harry Hooper among right fielders and 76 more than any right fielder from the post-World War II era. Clemente and Willie Mays are the only outfielders ever to win twelve Gold Gloves. People who saw Clemente play still speak of how he carried himself, how fluidly he played the game and how smooth he looked in the outfield.

Clemente's place in baseball history is grounded not just in his superior play and statistics. Clemente was the first great Puerto Rican player in MLB and the first Puerto Rican elected to the Hall of Fame. Clemente, who began his career with the Pirates in 1955, encountered prejudice as a player due to both the color of his skin and for being Puerto Rican. Those struggles were shared, and continue to be shared, by many Latino ballplayers today, but Clemente and others of his cohort, like Orestes Minoso, faced indignities that many of today's players have been spared.

Clemente spent his entire big league career with the Pirates, one of the teams during the 1950s-1970s that was most active in bringing in African American and Latino players. He was a respected leader on that team and mentor for many younger Latino Pirates. On September 1, 1971, Clemente took his usual spot in right field for the Pirates and was part of the first lineup ever fielded by a National or American League that consisted entirely of Black players.

On September 30th, 1972, Clemente doubled off of Mets lefty Jon Matlack in the fourth inning and left the game a few innings later. That hit was his 3,000th and would turn out to be his last time at bat. He only played in one more game that year, as a defensive replacement in the 9th inning of the season's final game.

Clemente spoke English with an accent, as many non-native speakers of any language do. The Pirates, like all teams then, did not provide Spanish translators, so the press would interview Clemente and other Latino players of his generation and then render their words onto paper with exaggerated accents and poor syntax. For example, the word "big" often became "beeg". "I don't want" would be "me no want." Many readers and writers thought this was authentic, or even funny, but it was really just bigoted and hurtful. Also, like many Latino players in the 1960s, Clemente was frequently accused of not playing hard all the time and of exaggerating injuries. Similarly, Clemente's first name was Roberto, but he was frequently described in print as "Bob." This may seem to be a small thing to some, but refusing to call people by their real and preferred names is a power play that is often grounded in prejudice.

Clemente remains one of the absolute giants of Latino baseball history. One small way to see this is that his number, 21, is frequently worn by Latino ballplayers, particularly Puerto Ricans, from Little League through the big leagues. Clemente hasn't played in fifty years, but in his community his legend may be stronger today than it was back when he was playing. Clemente is still broadly recognized not only as the greatest Puerto Rican player in history, but as an important trailblazer who played the game with a style and pride that raised up all Puerto Rican ballplayers.

A few months after the 1972 season ended a major earthquake rocked the country of Nicaragua, killing and displacing many. Clemente became involved in humanitarian efforts to send supplies to help the victims of the earthquake. Clemente decided to travel from Puerto Rico to Nicaragua on a plane heavily loaded with supplies to make sure that the distribution of those supplies went smoothly. Shortly after takeoff the airplane crashed into the sea. Clemente's body was never recovered.

The death of Roberto Clemente is one of baseball's great tragedies, but it also further demonstrated the integrity and decency of the man. Other great baseball players died during their careers. Lou Gehrig struck down mid-career by disease, Thurman Munson by an airplane crash while he was practicing flying, Ed Delehanty fell, or was pushed, off a train near Niagara Falls, and a handful of other players have died in the middle of their career, but none in the way Clemente did.

The death of a great player just months after achieving a major milestone and only a year removed from the 1971 World Series, where Clemente led the Pirates to an upset victory over the Orioles, shook the baseball world. Clemente was inducted into the Hall of Fame in 1973, becoming the first player since Lou Gehrig for whom the five-year waiting period was waived. The impact Clemente's death had on Latino ballplayers particularly on his teammates, including star catcher Manny Sanguillen, who hailed from Panama, was devastating and enduring. After Clemente's death, Sanguillen came to Puerto Rico and spent weeks diving into the sea where Clemente had died fruitlessly searching for Clemente's body.

Because of his extraordinary play, humanitarian actions, and dignity on and off the field Roberto Clemente's meaning to Puerto Rican baseball is difficult to overstate. One measure of this is that in a game with a long history of excellent players, only Clemente is known as "The Great One."

Twenty-one
Ty Cobb

The reason Ty Cobb is not the most hated player in baseball history is that he played before social media, and to a great extent, even before mass media. Cobb played the game with an aggression that was so extreme that it spilled over into cruelty and anger. He slid into bases hard, was never reluctant to knock over an opposing infielder or spike them so hard that it caused them pain or injury. Once he climbed into the stands and beat up a heckler who had lost his hands in an accident. This is

Public Domain Photo

not the behavior of a mentally healthy, or decent, person. Cobb grew up in the deep south and although obviously he cannot be blamed for the segregation that kept all Black players out of the National and American League for decades, he was also, according to many accounts, a pretty nasty racist as well.

Cobb played in the big leagues from 1905-1928, spending all but the last two years of his career with the Tigers. Although his career outlasted the deadball era, which ended around 1920, Cobb never adjusted his style of play to the newer more home run centered game that emerged in the last years of his career. However, there is probably no other player who, in everything from temperament to how they played the game, better reflects baseball during the first two decades of the twentieth century.

72

Cobb was also the best player of that era and one of the best ever.

Baseball from 1900-1920 was played hard by men who hailed mostly from rural America, in many cases from the south, lacked formal education and were extremely competitive. Fights were common and violence was very much part of the game. In short, it was a mean game and Cobb was a mean man.

There was also nobody who played as well as Ty Cobb during that era. Cobb retired with a .366 batting average, still considerably higher than that of any other player, while his .433 on base percentage is the 11th best ever. His career record of 4,189 hits lasted well over fifty years until it was broken in 1985 by Pete Rose. Cobb's record of 897 stolen bases fell to Lou Brock a few years before that. Cobb was not by today's measures a power hitter, hitting only 117 home runs, but he hit a lot of doubles and triples and led the American League in slugging percentage eight times. Due both to his character as well as his extraordinary ability, if there is a face of baseball in the deadball era, it is Ty Cobb's.

Cobb had 151.5 career WAR, good enough to still be sixth ever and 16 more than the second highest position player from the deadball era, Tris Speaker. The real value of WAR is that it allows us to compare players across time, but still relative to their own context because replacement level also varies over time and ballpark. The three position players ahead of Cobb in this broad category include Barry Bonds, who began his career twenty years after Cobb died, and Willie Mays who finished his career after Cobb's death. Mays is generally viewed as having been better than Cobb and Bonds is rarely compared to him. However, the other player with more WAR than Cobb is Babe Ruth. Today, it is axiomatic to most thoughtful fans of the game that Ruth was better than Cobb and rivaled only by Willie Mays for the title of best player ever.

For much of the twentieth century this was different. The idea that Cobb was better than Ruth was broadly held by many fans and writers well into the 1960s. Cobb died in 1961. Most of the obituaries described him in one way or another as the greatest baseball player ever. Ruth hit all the home runs, but the general argument was that Cobb did the other, more important, things better. To believe Cobb was better was a way to signal you really understood the game and that you were a sophisticated fan.

The problem with the argument was that it is essentially indefensible. Even without more modern measures, Ruth's superior on base percentage and slugging percentage constituted a pretty convincing case as to who was the better player. Somehow, Ruth having 600 or so more home runs than Cobb and 800 more walks almost counted against him and were sometimes seen as proof that he couldn't do the small things. Ruth's impressive pitching record was also not seen as tipping the balance in his favor.

Baseball, like almost everything, is defined, at least in part, by a tension between change and continuity. Ty Cobb represented the latter and the Babe the former. Ruth was baseball's great disruptor who, more than any player, changed how the game was played. In doing that he angered a lot of people including legendary Giants manager John McGraw who never embraced the new style of play. Cobb did not change the game of baseball, but simply played it on the terms he found it better than anybody else.

Traditionalists and purists have a loud voice in baseball. Sometimes this puts them on, in my very subjective view, the right side of an issue like the designated hitter or interleague play, but other times that resistance to change is unhelpful. Resistance to new ways of evaluating talent, or more damningly, criticism of the way non-white players approach the game are examples of this. No player was a better symbol of this resistance to change on and off the field as Ty Cobb.

Twenty-two
Eddie Collins

Baseball history is full of heroes both on and off the field. Yogi Berra and Ted Williams were great players and war heroes. Jackie Robinson was a civil rights hero who was also a fantastic ballplayer. Felipe Alou and Roberto Clemente were trailblazers who cared about their communities and were very good (Alou) and great (Clemente) players. Eddie Collins was different. He was one of the greatest players ever who at a key inflection moment put himself on the wrong side of history and morality.

Like Ty Cobb, Eddie Collins played in the deadball era and excelled at the style of play from that time. Collins played in the American League from 1906-1930 and was a teammate of Cobb's on the Philadelphia Athletics from 1927-1928. Collins career totals include a .333/.424/.429 slash line, more than 3,300 hits and more than 700 stolen bases, but he hit even fewer home runs

Library of Congress, Prints & Photographs Division [Bain News Service - LOC LC-DIG-ggbain-14025]

than Cobb. Over a 25-year career, Collins hit only 47 home runs and never hit more than six in a season. Unlike Cobb, Collins was unusual for that era because he had gone to college and is, along with Lou Gehrig, one of the two best players who are alumni of Columbia University.

Despite his lack of power, Collins remains the greatest second baseman in American League history. From 1911-1914, as a member of the Philadelphia Athletics, along with Stuffy McGinnis, Frank Baker and Jack Barry, Collins was part of the famous "$100,000 infield." That nickname developed because the infield was seen by many as the greatest ever, not because their combined salaries even approached that number.

Four years later, now with the White Sox, Collins was part of one of the first early memorable World Series moments. In the top of the fourth inning of game six of the 1917 with the White Sox leading three games to two, Collins led off by reaching second on a two-base error. The next batter, Shoeless Joe Jackson also reached on an error, putting runners at the corners with no outs. Happy Felsch then hit a ground ball to pitcher Rube Benton who threw to third and caught Collins in a rundown. The Giants executed the rundown poorly and the play ended with Collins sprinting for home and Heinie Zimmerman, the Giants third baseman, trying to chase down the speedy Collins because the catcher was not near the plate. Collins scored the game's first run as his White Sox went on to win the game and clinch the World Series.

That White Sox team was back in the World Series two years later. The 1919 World Series was one of the biggest baseball stories ever. The White Sox threw the World Series to the Reds, leading baseball to crack down on gambling. Collins was one of the White Sox stars who was not in on the fix. He took the ethical route and played his best in the World Series. It turned out he ended up having a bad series anyway hitting .226 with only one extra base hit, but he did it honestly.

Collins was also part of one of my favorite obscure historical games. On May 24, 1928, the Yankees beat Collins's Philadelphia Athletics 9-7. Collins pinch hit and flew out in the bottom of the seventh. An amazing 13 future Hall of Famers appeared in that game including Babe Ruth, Lou Gehrig, Jimmie Foxx, Lefty Grove, Collins, Ty Cobb, and Tris Speaker. Collins, Speaker, and Cobb were playing their last years with the Athletics, while most of the other Hall of Famers were in, or entering, their prime years. For good measure, both team's managers, Miller Huggins of the Yankees and Connie Mack of the Athletics also made it to the Hall of Fame as well.

The reason Collins makes this list is because of what he did after he was no longer an active player. During the 1930s and 1940s, Eddie Collins was an executive with the Boston Red Sox, serving as the team's general manager for most of that time. In 1945 as World War II was winding down, the pressure was growing for the American and National League to integrate and be open to all players. Naturally, this pressure came from the left. One Boston politician, City Councilman Isadore Muchnick, made this a top priority and sought to pressure the Red Sox to hire an African American ballplayer.

Muchnick succeeded in arranging the tryout and the Red Sox gave three African American players an opportunity to show what they could do. Eddie Collins was the Red Sox executive charged with determining whether the players were good enough to play in the American League. By 1945, it was apparent to any sentient baseball person that the top Negro League players were certainly good enough to play in the big leagues. Collins did not see it that way and dismissed the three players as not having the skills to play in the American League. One of those players was Jackie Robinson, who two years later was starring with the Dodgers and four years later was the National League MVP. Collins looked at a young Jackie Robinson and decided that upholding racism was more important than either racial equality or signing a star player for his Red Sox.

The racists and racism, represented by Collins decision, that kept baseball segregated for so long are as much part of baseball history as Jackie Robinson or Roberto Clemente. The Red Sox, for their part, missed out on having Jackie Robinson getting on base ahead of Ted Williams. They did not have an African American player until Pumpsie Green in 1959, making them the last big league team to integrate. Collins had the chance to change that and make the Red Sox the standard of integration. When the chance came to make his biggest play, Collins booted it.

Twenty-three
Joe Cronin

Joe Cronin is probably the second best player named Joe to have grown up in San Francisco. He was one of many great ballplayers to come out of that city in the 1920s and 1930s including Tony Lazzeri, Lefty O'Doul, Harry Heilmann (who attended the same high school as Cronin) and the DiMaggio brothers, but that is not why Joe Cronin is on this list. Nobody has ever had a life in baseball quite like Joe Cronin's. Cronin had a Hall of Fame career as a player, served as a team executive, taking over from Eddie Collins as general manager of the Boston Red Sox, and later became president of the American League during a period of significant transition for the league and for baseball in general.

Until Cal Ripken Jr., Robin Yount and Alan Trammell came along in the 1970s and 1980s, the greatest shortstop in American League history was either Luke Appling or Joe Cronin. Cronin began his big league career with the Pirates in 1926 and 1927, but by the end of the 1928 season was the shortstop for the Senators, where he played until he was sent to the Red Sox following the 1934 season. Cronin always fielded his position well, but was also a very good hitter at a time when shortstops generally did not do much with the bat. His career .301/.390/.468 slash line and his 119 OPS+ would be impressive even in today's game where there are many power hitting shortstops, but during his era, Cronin contributed much more offense than most who played his position. Cronin started for the American League in the first three All-Star Games from 1933-1935, and was the last of the five consecutive batters Carl Hubbell struck out in the 1934 All-Star Game.

Cronin followed Eddie Collins as the Red Sox general manager, serving in that capacity from late 1946 through the 1958 season. During those years, the Red Sox initially contended, coming extremely close to winning the American League pennant in 1948 and 1949, but then began to fall behind in the American League because they were unable to compete with the Bronx Bombers during what was the pinnacle of the Yankees dynasty. The Red Sox, and Cronin, made that more difficult by refusing to sign non-white players. At a time when people such as Larry Doby, Orestes Minoso, Luis Aparicio, and Elston Howard were beginning to make an impact in the American League, the Red Sox clung to their racist ways until 1959. By then Cronin was no longer running the Red Sox and had become President of the American League.

Today Major League Baseball is one entity, usually known as simply MLB, led by a strong commissioner who is empowered to represent and advocate for the owners of all thirty teams, but for most of baseball history, that structure was different. Until late in the twentieth century, each league had a fair amount of independence. That is why, for example, the designated hitter rule was adapted by the American League in 1973 and by the National League in 2022. There were other differences as well. For example, today franchise movements, which rarely occur, and expansion, are issues that are addressed by all of MLB, but for decades each league individually made those decisions. For these reasons, league presidents were very important.

When Cronin took over the American League before the 1959 season, the two leagues felt quite dissimilar from each other. In the American League, the Yankees had won nine of the ten previous pennants, whereas over that ten year period, four teams had won National League pennants. The National League was also way ahead of the American League with regards to integration. By 1958, the best African American and Latino players like Mays, Aaron, Clemente, Frank Robinson, and Orlando Cepeda were almost entirely in the National League.

Cronin would lead the American League through a period of transition that all but remade the league. In 1959, there were eight American League teams, six of which had been playing in the same city for more than half a century. Several of these franchises were struggling under the twin related problems of poor attendance and Yankees dominance. American League baseball was also an inferior product as many of the best players continued to be excluded because they were not white.

By the time Cronin left his position following the 1973 season, all of that had changed. African American and Latino stars like Reggie Jackson, Vida Blue, Frank Robinson, after his trade to the Orioles, Willie Horton, Rod Carew and Luis Aparicio were evidence that the league was now as integrated as the National League. The amateur draft had helped make the league more competitive with fully six teams winning the AL pennant in the final ten years of Cronin's presidency. Moreover, the league itself had expanded to twelve teams with teams as far west as California and as far south as Texas, a major change from the late 1950s when the southern and westernmost American League team was the Kansas City Athletics.

Cronin, who as Red Sox general manager continued that team's ugly history of segregation did not bring that approach to the American League. That reversal helped keep the American League competitive and improved the quality and style of play. Cronin also hired Emmett Ashford, the first African American umpire in the history of the American League. Cronin spent just short of half a century in baseball and is one of the few players in history who combined a Hall of Fame playing career with an impactful league executive role.

Twenty-four
Dizzy Dean

No player better captures the myth of baseball as a magical rural pastime that brought goofy, but well-meaning country boys to the big city than Jay Hanna "Dizzy" Dean. Dean who was born in Arkansas, and as a youth also spent time in Oklahoma and Texas, began his big league career with the Cardinals in 1930. Dean was a hard throwing righty who quickly became one of the best pitchers in baseball. Between 1932 and 1936 he won an average of 24 games a year with an ERA+ of 130.

Public Domain Photo

It is not an accident that Dean was signed by the Cardinals. First, at that time the Cardinals were probably the most popular team in the south, where Dean was growing up. The two St. Louis teams, the Cardinals in the National League and the Browns in the American League, were the southernmost teams in the big leagues. The Cardinals were a winning franchise while the Browns were generally pretty hapless. Dean joined the Cardinals organization just as team executive Branch Rickey was building up a large network of affiliated farm teams. That approach would revolutionize baseball; Dean was one of Rickey's first successes in that project.

In 1934 Dean had a year that has given him a special place in baseball history. He went 30-7 becoming the last pitcher to win thirty games in a season in the National League. That MVP year helped the Cardinals make it to the World Series where Dean won two games and lost one and had a 1.73 ERA as the Cardinals bested the Tigers in seven games. In that game seven Dean gave up six hits, no runs and no walks as the Cardinals coasted to an easy 11-0 victory.

Before the 1934 season, Dean boasted that he and his brother, Cardinals pitcher Paul Dean, would win fifty games that year. That was an absurd idea because fifty wins for two pitchers was an unrealistic goal. The Dean brothers predictably came up short. They only won 49. In the World Series, Paul Dean picked up two wins, so the Dean brothers got all four of the Cardinals' wins. Those champion Cardinals were known as the Gashouse Gang and were one of the most colorful teams of the era. Dizzy Dean was by far their best player and the face of the team. Dean's legend as a player was burnished not just by his great pitching and good-natured boasting, but by his aw shucks image as Ole Diz who was just a country boy. At a time when the US was still a very rural country, Dean quickly became a well-known national star.

A line drive off of his toe in the 1937 All-Star game all but destroyed Dean's career. Through the end of the 1936 season, his age 26 season and last full year before the injury, Dean had accumulated 35.4 WAR. In the twentieth century, only 13 other pitchers exceeded that number by age 26. Up until the 1937 All-Star Game, Dean had won 133 games and pitched 1,689.2 innings. After the injury he would pitch only 277.2 more big league innings and win 17 more games.

Dean was one of many great players whose career was cut short by injury. He was also almost the prototype of the good-natured man-child from a small town who takes the big leagues by storm with his pitching ability, charm and media skills. Dean was, for example, an earlier version, of Mark Fidrych or Tim Lincecum, but Dean's impact on the game did not end when he wrapped up his playing career with the Cubs in 1941, or even when he came back in 1947 and managed to pitch four scoreless innings for the St. Louis Browns.

From the 1940s into the 1960s, Dean enjoyed a second career as a broadcaster, becoming one of the most successful in the business. He called games for the Cardinals, Browns, Yankees, and Braves as well as for the national networks. Dean's colorful personality and rural style and aphorisms helped make him popular with baseball fans around the country. Lacking much formal education, Dean did not exactly have a strong command over grammar and syntax. Dean frequently drew exasperation from grammarians by saying things on the air like "he slud into third" and his liberal use of the word "ain't," but baseball fans liked it. His post-playing fame kept him in the national spotlight enough that in 1952 a mediocre film "The Pride of St. Louis" was made about him. Dan Dailey played the lead role.

Dean, whose broadcast career included both radio and television, was an important figure in the early years of baseball on both those media. Because the technology of the time, even television broadcasting during Dean's time required announcers to speak more, tell more stories and entertain fans beyond what they do today because they could not rely on the pictures on the screen to tell the story. Dean's easy-going and conversational style was perfect for the role.

Through his work as an announcer, Dean helped baseball adapt to new media and new ways of reaching fans. We now live in era where video is a big part of how we experience baseball, but that was relatively new during Dean's time as a broadcaster. Nonetheless, he helped popularize the game and showed new fans new ways of experiencing the game. And if that line drive off the bat of Earl Averill in 1937 had gone somewhere else, Dean might have won 300 games.

Twenty-five
Joe DiMaggio

In the 1960s Paul Simon asked, "where have you gone Joe DiMaggio?" Fifteen years or so before that, Santiago, the fisherman in Ernest Hemingway's *Old Man and the Sea* spoke of "the Great DiMaggio" who was the son of a fisherman. That was only a few years after theater goers seeing the play *South Pacific* heard a song about a woman whose "skin is tender as DiMaggio's glove." Somewhere in there, shortly after he retired from playing, DiMaggio

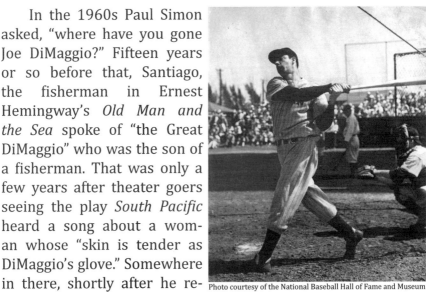

Photo courtesy of the National Baseball Hall of Fame and Museum (DiMaggio Joe 1362-70_Bat_NBL)

married Marilyn Monroe. This should provide a sense of just how famous and significant a part of the culture Joe DiMaggio was.

My father was born in 1934 and lost interest in baseball around the time Stan Musial retired. However, once, when my father was in his 70s sometime in the 2010s, Joe DiMaggio's name was mentioned. My father then told me how he remembered the summer of 1941 when in his little New Jersey town people waited anxiously every day to see if DiMaggio got a hit to keep his hitting streak alive. DiMaggio's fame, role in the culture and grip on the country in 1941 are all reminders of how important baseball was in mid-twentieth century America.

DiMaggio was a national figure who, like his teammate Yogi Berra and a handful of others, had a national profile that went beyond his abilities on the ballfield. He was also enormously important to Italian Americans. There have been many great Italian American ballplayers including Berra, Tony Lazzeri, Mike Piazza, Ron Santo, Frank Viola, and Craig Biggio, but none were as central to the history of Italian Americans as DiMaggio.

To understand DiMaggio's significance as the first Italian American with widespread crossover appeal, it is first necessary to understand that in first decades of the twentieth century there was substantial prejudice against Italian Americans, some of which lingers on today. In the 1920s and 1930s, much of America saw Italians as dirty, greasy, eating strange food and prone to crime, and due to their growing numbers, particularly in big cities, a threat to democracy.

DiMaggio grew up in one city, San Francisco, with a large Italian American population, and played his entire career in another city, New York, with an even larger Italian American population so he was beloved on both sides of the country, but it was DiMaggio's extraordinary success that helped break down prejudices. DiMaggio cultivated an image of cool, grace, and sophistication that was also in part to conceal his shyness and in response to the pressure he faced throughout his career. That image also helped reshape how Italian Americans were viewed and made DiMaggio a hero to that community.

The 56-game hitting streak in 1941was the highlight of DiMaggio's career, but he was one of the greatest players ever, despite battling injuries for much of his career. DiMaggio was one of three brothers who played in the big leagues. Vince, Dom, and Joe were all great defensive centerfielders, known for their grace and range in the field but while Vince and Dom were good hitters, Joe was one of the very best. He had career slash line of .325/.398/.579 and an OPS+ of 155. Because he missed three years because of military service between the age of 28-30, and wrestled with injuries for most of his career, DiMaggio only played 1,736 games. He only played 140 or more games five times in a career that lasted from 1936-1951. Accordingly, some of his counting numbers, such as his 2,214 hits or 361 home runs don't seem impressive at first glance. The home run figure was also not helped by Yankee Stadium's unforgiving dimensions for right-handed hitters. Even more impressive is the fact that DiMaggio struck out only 369 times in his entire career, an extremely low total for a slugger.

DiMaggio lived for 48 more years after his playing career ended in 1951. His post-baseball life had a poignancy to it as he never quite found a place for himself, while his moment, the 1940s and 1950s America, receded. When Paul Simon first sang about him, DiMaggio was only 51-years-old and had not gone anywhere. He was briefly a coach for the Oakland A's, although he looked terribly out of place in the offbeat A's uniforms rather than Yankees pinstripes, appeared at Yankees functions, and was a pitchman for various products such a coffee making machine.

DiMaggio's marriage to Marilyn Monroe solidified his position as a cultural icon, but the marriage was not a happy one and did not last. As the news of the eminent divorce between DiMaggio and Marilyn Monroe spread, the press descended on their home in Southern California. As soon as DiMaggio left in a waiting car driven by a childhood friend, the media asked where he was going. DiMaggio responded "home, to San Francisco." Growing up in the 1970s and 1980s in San Francisco, DiMaggio was part of the fabric of an older San Francisco, that as a newer migrant I could never quite know even though DiMaggio lived only a few blocks from me.

When the Loma Prieta earthquake, also known as the World Series earthquake, hit in 1989, DiMaggio's house in the Marina District was badly damaged and he was seen at a local schoolyard lining up with everybody else, rather than using his celebrity status to cut the line.

Joe DiMaggio was a great player who was a star on nine World Series winning Yankees teams, but he was also more than that. He became an icon for Italian Americans and something of a symbol of a lost American golden age.

Twenty-six
Larry Doby

On July 5th, 1947 in the bottom of the seventh inning with two out and one on, Cleveland Indians manager Lou Boudreau sent Larry Doby up to pinch hit for pitcher Bryan Stephens. Doby struck out, but in doing that he became the first African American to play in the American League. Doby's first game was only about seven weeks after Jackie Robinson's storied first game with the National League's Brooklyn Dodgers. Doby's appearance for Cleveland received much less attention, but demonstrat-

Public Domain Photo

ed that Robinson was not a one off and that African Americans were going to be a permanent part of the American and National Leagues. Over the next years Doby's experience in the American League was, in some respects, more challenging than Robinson's in the National League because there were so many fewer African American players in the American League.

Doby struggled badly while playing for Cleveland in 1947 slashing .156/.182/.188, but after that year it would be over a decade before Doby would again struggle against big league pitching. Between 1948 and 1958, Doby slashed .285/.389/.496 for an OPS+ of 139. Doby was a fine defensive centerfielder and formidable power hitter who also had a very good batting eye. For most of the 1950s he was the best American League center-fielder other than Mickey Mantle and the best centerfielder in the game who was not playing for a New York team.

In 1948, his first full season with the Indians, Doby was one of the best players on a very good and very interesting World Series winning Cleveland squad. Jackie Robinson had helped lead his Dodgers to the World Series in 1947, but Cleveland became the first team with an African American player to win the World Series. That team had not one but two African American stars including an aging Satchel Paige who joined Cleveland in July and provided key support out of the bullpen. The Indians manager, Lou Boudreau, was a 31-year-old who also won the league's MVP award in 1948. That year Boudreau became the first, and thus far only, Jewish manager to win a World Series.

Doby remained one of the best players in the American League for the next several years, making the all-star team every year from 1949 to 1955. In 1954, Doby hit a league leading 32 home runs with an OPS+ of 129 as the Indians won the pennant again, the only time between 1949 and 1958 when a team other than the Yankees would represent the American League in the World Series. Unlike in 1948, this time Cleveland, despite winning 111 games during the regular season were swept out of the World Series by the New York Giants.

The turning point in that series came in the top of the eighth of game one. Doby led off with a walk and slugger Al Rosen singled him to second. Vic Wertz then hit what looked to be a double or triple to deep centerfield, but Giants centerfielder Willie Mays ran it down and made what is generally considered the greatest catch in World Series history. Doby made it to third on the play, but did not score. Momentum is rarely a real thing in baseball, but it was in that moment. The Giants went on to win the game and the series in four games.

Doby and Paige were brought to Cleveland by Indians owner Bill Veeck. Veeck, who owned several teams during his long life in baseball, is viewed today as something of an iconoclastic innovator who was also a good baseball man. He built a winning team in Cleveland, but also had his Chicago White Sox play in short pants in the 1970s. Veeck's role in integrating baseball is sometimes overlooked because it does not fit in with the rest of his image.

A native of New Jersey, Doby was a star for the Negro League

Newark Eagles in 1947 when Veeck bought his contract and put him on Cleveland's roster. This happened without much fanfare or discussion in the media beforehand. However, unlike Branch Rickey who signed Jackie Robinson to play for the Dodgers, Veeck compensated Doby's team when acquiring him, thus treating the Negro League more respectfully than Rickey did.

Veeck and Doby's paths would cross again, almost thirty years to the day after Doby struck out in his first big league at bat. By then Veeck was in his second stint owning the White Sox who were managed by Doby's old teammate the Hall of Fame pitcher Bob Lemon. The team got off to a slow start and on July 1st of 1978, Lemon was fired and replaced by Doby. This made Doby the second African American manager in the big leagues three decades after becoming the second African American to play in the big leagues.

Doby's 56.8 career WAR place him 17th among all center-fielders, below the elite all-time greats and alongside other very good players like Jim Edmonds and Jim Wynn, but if Doby had played a few more years in the American League before 1947, he would be a notch or two higher on that list. Doby was elected to the Hall of Fame by the Veteran's Committee in 1998. It was a well-deserved honor for a trailblazing ballplayer and manager who also was an extremely good ballplayer. Almost a decade after his death, during the Obama administration, the US postal service issued a stamp commemorating Doby's contributions to baseball and the country.

Twenty-seven
Dock Ellis

Dock Ellis was one of the best pitchers on a Pittsburgh Pirates team that won the NL East five times from 1970-1975, but lost the NLCS each of those years except 1971 when they won the World Series. Those Pirates teams were unusual because they were led almost entirely by Black stars. Roberto Clemente, Willie Stargell, Manny Sanguillen, Al Oliver, and Dave Cash were among the highest profile players on that team. White players on the teams including Bob Robertson and Steve Blass were much less visible and well known. Ellis was the best African American pitcher on that team and was the pitcher the day in 1971 when the Pirates became the first team to start nine Black players in one game.

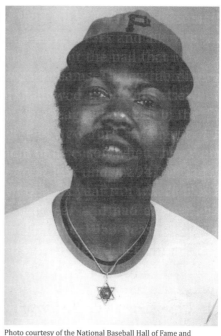

Photo courtesy of the National Baseball Hall of Fame and Museum (Ellis Dock 1745.75_HS_NBL)

In 1971 Ellis was 14-3 with a 2.11 ERA at the All-Star break. Those were excellent numbers, but the biggest story of the 1971 season was over in the American League where Vida Blue was 17-3 with a 1.42 ERA. Because they were having such strong first halves, Ellis and Blue were both chosen to start the All-Star Game. That marked the first, and so far only, time that two Black pitchers started against each other in the All-Star Game. Today that seems like an interesting footnote or answer to a good trivia question, but the early 1970s was a time when baseball was still central to African American sports and culture in a manner that has not been true for decades. Veteran stars including Clemente, Aaron, Mays, and Bob Gibson as well as younger stars such as Reggie Jackson and Dick Allen were among the biggest names in the game. It turned out that neither Blue nor Ellis pitched well. Ellis got through the first two innings smoothly but gave up four runs in his third and final inning including a mammoth two run home run to Reggie Jackson and then a two run home run with two outs to Frank Robinson.

The year before starting the All-Star game, Ellis also had a very solid season going 13-10 with a 3.21 ERA for a Pirates team that won the division with its bats and, in particular, a great year from Roberto Clemente. On June 12th of that year, Ellis pitched one of the strangest, and in its own way most impressive games in baseball history. The Pirates were playing in San Diego, not far from where Ellis, a native of Southern California, had grown up.

Ellis, starting the first game of a doubleheader, pitched a no-hitter, but walked eight batters while hitting one. There have been a handful of no-hitters where so many players reached base, but what made Ellis's game extraordinary is that he did it while tripping on LSD-at least that is the story that has been told and retold and that has become part of baseball lore. Pitching a no-hitter in any conditions is extremely difficult; doing it while under the influence of a powerful hallucinogen seems extremely unlikely. We will probably never know whether Ellis actually pulled off this amazing feat, but we know that Ellis was a heavy drug user, which makes the story slightly more plausible.

On another occasion, in 1974, Ellis starting against a powerful Cincinnati Reds team and trying to avenge some previous slight the Reds, a famously conservative organization, had made against the Pirates, hit the first three batters in the Reds lineup.

By the end of 1975 Ellis was increasingly seen as a problem by the Pirates management, so they traded him to the Yankees in exchange for another pitcher, Doc Medich. Unlike Ellis, whose given name was Dock, Medich came by his nickname because he

studied medicine while playing in the big leagues and later became a doctor.

Ellis went 17-8 with the Yankees in 1976 helping them get
back to the post-season for the first time since 1964, but was out
of baseball within a few years. However, that trade remains one
of the best in Yankees history, and worst for the Pirates, because
the Yankees also acquired Willie Randolph who went on to have
a borderline Hall of Fame career mostly in pinstripes.

This all suggests that Ellis was some kind of hothead or
oddball character, but he was much more than that. Ellis was an
outspoken African American player, like Dick Allen and Reggie
Jackson, at a time when the culture was changing. Ellis spoke his
mind, called out racism when he saw it and chafed at the extremely conservative institution that baseball had always been. Ellis
pitched at a time when the counterculture and social movements
of the 1960s were flourishing and was one of the most visible
players who embraced that world and still managed to succeed
in the big leagues.

Baseball is still very conservative and there is still tension
between those who believe that African American and Latino
players are too flashy or don't obey all the unwritten rules—
whatever that means. Ellis, and those Pirates teams he played on,
were at the forefront of trying to change that baseball culture.

Twenty-eight
Bob Feller

There is an old baseball legend about a country boy from somewhere in the Midwest who throws harder than anybody has seen for years, makes it to the big leagues as a teenager and keeps striking batters out. In the particularly shmaltzy version of this story, that kid than goes on to serve his country heroically in World War II before coming back and helping his team, naturally the only team he ever played for, win the World Series. Sounds like a myth, but that was the true story of Bob Feller. By seventeen, Feller was pitching for Cleveland and striking out more than a batter an inning in the big leagues. By his early twenties Feller had established himself as the best pitcher in the American League. The great fastball pitcher who can throw the ball past everybody is a stock folk hero in baseball. Feller was that kind of pitcher, widely believed to throw faster than any of his peers or predecessors. He pitched years before there were good tools to determine how fast he threw, so we cannot put a number on Feller's fastball.

Library of Congress, Prints & Photographs Division [Harris & Ewing - LOC LC-DIG-hec-23126]

Through Feller's age 22 season, which was 1941, he had pitched 1,448.1 big league innings with an ERA+ of 136. No other pitcher in the 20th century managed even 1,300 innings with an

ERA+ of 130 by that age. Feller then missed all of the next three seasons and most of a fourth because he enlisted in the Navy two days after Pearl Harbor was attacked. Like many big league stars Feller spent some time playing baseball in the military, but he also saw extensive combat as a gun captain. Feller was a genuine war hero whose record included six campaign ribbons and eight battle stars.

In his first full year back from the war, 1946, Feller led the American League in wins, complete games, shutouts, innings pitched and strikeouts. There was no Cy Young award back then, but if there had been one, Feller would have won several including in 1946. When Feller retired after the 1956 season, he had 266 wins, 2,581 strikeouts and 63.5 WAR. Those are excellent and solid Hall of Fame numbers, but had he not lost four years to military service in the prime of his career, Feller would have easily won well over 300 games, struck out a lot more than 3,000 batters and had at least 80-85 WAR.

Feller's early years occurred when the American League was still segregated, but as a member of the Cleveland Indians, he was playing alongside African Americans shortly after he came back from the war. As the biggest Cleveland star at the time, Feller could have led the opposition to Larry Doby joining the team, but never did anything like that. However, Feller was more closely tied to the second African American to join the Cleveland team, the great pitcher Satchel Paige. Feller and Paige had pitched in numerous barnstorming events before Paige came to Cleveland in 1948. The two pitchers, who never had the chance to face off against each other when they were at the height of their respective powers, became teammates and helped Cleveland win that 1948 World Series. They have not won one since.

Feller retired after the 1956 season. He was 37-years-old, but his arm was shot, as he had struggled to an 0-4 record and a 4.97 ERA in his final year. Five years later he was handily elected to the Hall of Fame. His 93.8% of the vote far exceeded the only other player voted in by the reporters that year—Jackie Robinson who received only 77.5% of the vote, barely exceeding the required 75% threshold. Feller lived a very long life and died in 2010 at the age of 92.

After retiring from baseball, Feller did some broadcasting, was involved in youth sports programs and worked in the private sector, but mostly he was Bob Feller former baseball great. During the last decade of his life, Feller emerged as one of the most visible curmudgeons of the game. He was a voice of old school baseball, critical of PED users, Pete Rose, the designated hitter and pitch counts. In general, he believed baseball had gotten soft and pitchers simply needed to throw more. Feller also indicated he was unimpressed with the great catch Willie Mays made against Feller's team in the first game of the 1954 World Series, and suggested that Mays was playing too shallow to begin with on the play.

It seems that for as long as baseball has been around, some player from a previous era is eager to explain what's wrong with the game. Feller was very much a part of that tradition, but because he lived so long, he was also an important part of baseball history for the last years of his life. In the 21st century, he could still talk about barnstorming pitching duels with Satchel Paige or striking out Lou Gehrig 12 times. Feller was baseball mythology come to life. A kid who came from nowhere and threw faster than anybody had seen who went to become the best in the game for almost a decade interrupted only by serving his country heroically. That is a simplified telling of the story, but baseball is sometimes a game of simple stories that become legends.

Twenty-nine
Curt Flood

Curt Flood is one of the hand-ful of players whose courage and vision was most instrumental in changing labor relations in base-ball. He helped make hundreds of players extremely wealthy, but he is one of the only players who paid a price for it. Most of the peo-ple who radically remade baseball economics beginning in the mid-1960s, leading to players making much higher salaries which, in turn, brought much more money into the game, were recognized as heroes.

Public Domain Photo

Marvin Miller, the labor lawyer who led the Major League Baseball Players Association (MLBPA) became a widely respected figure in the labor movement and was posthumously, and against his wishes, elected to the Hall of Fame. Sandy Koufax and Don Drysdale who participated in a groundbreaking joint holdout in 1966 won healthy salary raises. The early free agents in the 1970s who challenged the reserve clause were well compensated by their new teams.

Curt Flood was different. He was one of the first players in the modern era to challenge the economic structures of baseball and for his efforts was essentially blacklisted from the game. Flood was born in Texas, but grew up in Oakland and was one of many great ballplayers to come out of that small city in the decades following World War II. Flood played alongside Vada Pinson in high school. Frank Robinson attended the same school, but was a few years older than Flood.

Flood began his career with the Reds, but at age twenty he became the starting centerfielder for the St. Louis Cardinals, a position he would hold for the next decade. Flood had a skill set that was very valued in baseball for decades and is much less common now. He was a top-notch defender in centerfield, who had limited power, but got on base enough to bat at the top the order, usually leadoff or second. Flood won a Gold Glove award every year from 1963-1969 and had a career on base percentage of .342. His 41.9 career WAR is in solid Hall of Very Good territory.

Following the 1969 season, the Cardinals sent Flood, who at 31 had just completed another very strong season, to the Phillies. It was a multi-player trade that included Flood and catcher Tim McCarver going to Philadelphia in exchange for Dick Allen and Cookie Rojas. It was a very big trade that might have helped both teams, but Flood did not want to go to Philadelphia. He was aware of how poorly many African American players were treated by that franchise and its fans, not least because of the experience Allen had there. The Cardinals, by contrast, had won three pennants in the 1960s with a talent base that included African American future Hall of Famers Lou Brock and Bob Gibson, as well as Flood himself and Puerto Rican slugger Orlando Cepeda.

For decades players had just accepted trades because the reserve clause that tied them eternally to the team for which they were playing, leaving no options other than to accept the trade or go home. Flood courageously sought to challenge that system. Marvin Miller and the MLBPA were happy to support Flood's challenge, but were also aware of the risk Flood himself was taking. Flood sat out the 1970 season as his legal challenges to MLB went all the way to the Supreme Court. Flood lost at every level, but his struggle was a major baseball story.

The late 1960s and early 1970s were still a time when ballplayers were seen as fortunate to be able to play baseball for a living. The public had little sympathy for players asking for more money. Flood had clashed with management over money while with the Cardinals as well. Flood was also African American, so many whites viewed him as another overpaid and ungrateful African American. Flood did not back down at all and referred to himself as a "well-paid slave."

Flood wanted more rights and chafed under a system where wealthy white men has so much control over a substantially non-white workforce. In some sense, Flood was making a general protest against how few rights players had and how easily their lives could be disrupted by a trade or similar action by a team. Flood's case was not aimed specifically at creating free agency as we know it, but more at finding a way to restructure player-management relationships and to ensure more rights for players.

There was no happy ending to Flood's saga. After missing the entire 1970 season, almost no team wanted to employ Flood. He finally landed with the Washington Senators in 1971. He played poorly in 13 games for that team and never played in the big leagues again. Flood's decision to challenge a trade he did not want after playing for the same team for twelve years nonetheless changed baseball. Within a few years the reserve clause was weakened to allow for free agency, players with ten years in the big leagues and five with the same team were given an automatic veto over any trade and many other players negotiated a similar veto over trades into their contracts. Flood's challenge was the first major step in those victories, but he did not enjoy any of the fruits of the advances made by the MLBPA.

Thirty
Rube Foster

Rube Foster was an African American man born in 1879. Because of the color of his skin, he never had the opportunity to pitch in the American or National Leagues. Moreover, because the Negro Leagues were not fully formed at the time Foster was at his pitching prime, the statistical record of his pitching is very hazy. However, Foster played an enormously critical role in creating the Negro Leagues that thrived in the decades between the two World Wars.

Photo courtesy of the National Baseball Hall of Fame and Museum (Foster Rube 274-81_HS_PD)

Foster was a right-handed pitcher who was of the same generation as white pitching greats like Mordecai Brown and Christy Mathewson. Foster briefly worked with a young Mathewson and may have helped him develop his famous fadeaway pitch. Like many Black stars from both the US and the Caribbean in the first half of the twentieth century, Foster pitched in both regions. The US team for which he pitched the most was the Chicago American Giants. The scant records of Foster's career show him having a record of 64-28 with a 2.31 ERA.

There have been many player-managers in baseball history, although the last one in the big leagues was Pete Rose in 1986. However, Foster was one of the very few player-owners, or more accurately, player-owner-manager. In 1910, Foster along with a white partner bought the Chicago American Giants and built that franchise into the best Negro League team of the decade. That team featured stars like pitcher Smokey Joe Williams, infielder John Henry Lloyd as well as Foster himself.

Foster had built an excellent team, one that could almost certainly have competed with the best American and National League teams of the era, but his team was not always able to find regular opponents or play a full schedule, so instead engaged in barnstorming, tournaments, and other forms of competition. This led Foster to his next idea and his greatest contribution to the game.

In 1920, Foster was the driving force in consolidating existing Black baseball teams into cohesive and functioning Negro Leagues. Initially Foster's Negro National League had eight teams and played under the famous, if cryptic, slogan "We are the ship. All else is the sea." The Negro Leagues as they are remembered today, good baseball teams led by fantastic stars like Josh Gibson, Satchel Paige, Cool Papa Bell and so many others, were the structures that Foster created. However, the Negro Leagues, even after 1920, were never an exact African American parallel of the white major leagues. Because of the deep institutionalized racism of that era and the financial hardship in African American communities around the country, teams frequently encountered financial problems leading to, among other things, occasional shortened seasons, players leaving teams mid-season to pursue more lucrative baseball opportunities and teams leaving and new teams entering the leagues.

Despite that, the scope of Foster's accomplishment must be recognized. Through his baseball skills and reputation, business savvy, force of personality and national network, he built a functioning African American business, indeed a whole industry, that employed thousands, and offered top quality entertainment to a people that in much of the country were denied these opportunities. Foster also created an organization that now, deservedly, has an honored place in the African American history and culture. Moreover, he did that in the face of the deep racism of the early 20th century. In 1920 simply finding eight African Americans who loved baseball and had the means to own a team was not easy, but nothing about starting the Negro League was. Once Foster found teams and owners, those owners had to find places to play which sometimes meant renting from big league teams who would always have priority at the ballpark, but often it meant finding other facilities.

In those days, decades before the amateur draft, competitive balance was a problem throughout baseball, but it was a bigger problem in a league where both the players and executives were accustomed to players changing teams quickly, and to promoters assembling what looked like All-Star teams for barnstorming and other related purposes. Foster himself had to move some of his better players off the Chicago American Giants, which he continued to control. Additionally, all owners and players had to navigate a society where young African American men, particularly if they seemed to have money, as some players did, were a constant target of police and other harassment. All of this had to be done while still providing a product that was good enough that low income African Americans with limited resources for entertainment would pay for it. Foster somehow managed to succeed in overcoming most of these challenges.

Tragically, Foster's life was cut short by exposure to toxic fumes from a leaky gas pipe that damaged his mental health and ultimately made it impossible for him to continue to serve as president of the Negro National League. He was institutionalized in 1926 and died in an Illinois facility for the mentally ill in 1930. It was a tragic end to an extremely impactful life in baseball.

Foster was only 51 at the time of his death. Had he not become ill, he probably would have been able to continue to lead the Negro Leagues for at least another decade. The loss of Foster's leadership and the beginning of the Great Depression a few years later were a dual challenge to the Negro Leagues. Although they survived into the 1950s, by the 1930s, the Negro Leagues were not quite the same after Foster's illness and death and evolved into more of a hybrid of a formal league and barnstorming. Rube Foster was the person most responsible for creating the Negro Leagues which, for decades, were a central part of both the baseball universe and of African American economy and culture.

Thirty-one
Frankie Frisch

Frankie Frisch was a Hall of Fame second baseman who hit for average, had limited power, fielded his position well and could steal bases. He played from 1919 to 1937. Frisch began his career with the New York Giants but was sent to St. Louis following the 1926 season in a blockbuster trade for Rogers Hornsby. Frisch was the kind of player who would today be seen as having that intangible quality of being a winner, playing on eight pennant winning teams, four of which won the World Series including as the player-manager on the Cardinals World Series winning Gashouse gang team of 1934. That was the year Dizzy Dean won thirty games for the Cardinals. Frisch managed for a total of 16 years, but that was his only pennant.

A more recent player who would be a good comp for Frisch is Lou Whitaker, but Frisch had slightly less power, more speed,

Frankie Frish at bat. Library of Congress, Prints & Photographs Division [Underwood & Underwood - LOC LC-DIG-ppmsca-18595]

a higher batting average and fewer walks. Both were excellent defenders. Frisch had a 71.8 career WAR and an OPS+ of 110. Whitaker's numbers were just a little bit better, 75.1 WAR and a 117 OPS+. There is one big difference between the two players. Frisch was elected to the Hall of Fame in 1947, his seventh year on the ballot. Whitaker failed to get even five percent of the vote in his first year of eligibility and was therefore removed from the ballot. Whitaker's only chance of getting to the Hall of Fame is through one of the committees charged with reviewing various groups of players from previous era.

Hall of Fame debates can be endless and are not the purpose of this book, but the case of Frisch and Whitaker is particularly illustrative because of the disproportionate role Frisch played in who got into the Hall of Fame.

Frisch being in and Whitaker being out is consistent with a pattern in Hall of Fame voting. Players from the 1970s and 1980s remain very underrepresented in the Hall of Fame while players from the 1930s and 1940s are overrepresented. For example, Whitaker is only one of several American League second baseman of his era, the others are Bobby Grich and Willie Randolph, who have received very little attention from Hall of Fame voters while clearly inferior second basemen from the previous era like Billy Herman or Bobby Doerr are in.

One of the people most responsible for the Hall of Fame tilting so heavily towards players from the 1920s and 1930s was Frankie Frisch. Frisch served on the Veteran's Committee of the Hall of Fame from 1967 until his death in 1973. The committee was charged with reexamining the careers of overlooked players from the past. Frisch was widely respected by his peers and wielded substantial influence on the Veterans Committee. During his years on the committee Frisch shepherded through the candidacy of many players who were very good, but not Hall of Fame caliber. Some of these players were former teammates Chick Hafey (31.2 career WAR), High Pockets Kelly (25.9 career WAR), Jesse Haines (32.6 career WAR) as well as others from Frisch's era like Kiki Cuyler (47.9 career WAR), Earle Combs (44.7 WAR) and Rube Marquard (32.4 career WAR).

These were good players, but they got to Cooperstown through Frisch's cronyism. Some might say this is not important because the Hall of Fame itself is not important, but that is not right. Regardless of whether your favorite player is in the Hall of Fame, it is the physical and virtual space that is the premier place for baseball history and memory. One of the most significant ways we remember the game, its history and its great players, is through the Hall of Fame and players who are fortunate enough to get elected to the Hall of Fame are remembered differently.

The players Frisch ushered into Cooperstown were all very good players and a Hall of Fame case, albeit a weak one, could be made for some of those players. For example, Earle Combs was an excellent leadoff hitter on the Ruth and Gehrig era Yankees who played a solid centerfield and, despite having a truncated career, always produced and retired with a .397 on base percentage and a 125 OPS+. The problem is that putting so many players from that era in the Hall of Fame suggests there was something special about that era-and there was. The 1930s were largely special for being the last period before baseball was integrated. Anybody from later generations played against much tougher competition.

Frisch's Veterans Committee activism leads to an understanding of baseball that suggests that modern players with numbers that are much better than Frisch's friends somehow were not quite as good as they were. Among the players who were superior to the ones Frisch helped get into the Hall of Fame are Keith Hernandez, Will Clark, Jack Clark, Bert Campaneris, Bobby Abreu, Rick Reuschel, and many others.

Frisch was instrumental in creating a big Hall of Fame, which would have been fine if it had stayed that way, but that hasn't happened. When a borderline candidate is up for the Hall of Fame, some baseball wag will inevitably explain why that player is not deserving by saying the Hall of Fame should be for people like Willie Mays or Babe Ruth. But the reality is the Hall of Fame is also for players like Kiki Cuyler and Jesse Haines, all thanks to Frankie Frisch. Like all cultural and folk institutions, baseball is deeply tied to the projects of memory and history, and few players have influenced that project as much as Frisch did.

Thirty-two
Eddie Gaedel

Eddie Gaedel had, if you will pardon the pun, the shortest playing career of anyone in this book. Between 1900 and 2015, 224 players, not counting pitchers, had only one plate appearance in the big leagues. Gaedel was one of a subset of 38 of those players who reached base in that appearance. In his case by drawing a walk. Gaedel's one plate appearance came as a pinch-hitter in the bottom of the first inning of the second game of a double-header on August 19, 1951

Public Domain Photo

in which the St. Louis Browns were hosting the Tigers. Gaedel walked, was removed for a pinch-runner and never played again.

This was a very unusual way to begin a game, but Gaedel was an unusual player because he was only three feet seven inches tall and had been sent to the plate with orders not to swing at any pitch. Tigers pitcher Bob Cain could not throw the diminutive leadoff hitter a strike and walked him. The whole idea was an elaborate stunt thought up by Browns owner Bill Veeck who only a few years earlier had put together a championship team in Cleveland.

Following the game, Gaedel's contract was declared void by the American League. He never again played in the big leagues. Gaedel's one plate appearance is reasonably well known among baseball fans, but it is generally presented as something funny, another offbeat idea by that showman Bill Veeck, whose role in integrating the American League is often overlooked. However, Eddie Gaedel's career was much more significant than that.

In baseball lore, the 1950s are often described as some kind of Golden Age. After all, this was the time of Jackie Robinson and the Boys of Summer Brooklyn Dodgers, Willie, Mickey, and the Duke roaming three centerfields in New York. Bobby Thomson's shot heard 'round the world, Willie Mays's great World Series catch, and Don Larsen's perfect game.

All of those events have something in common. They all occurred in New York and all, with the exception of Cleveland's Vic Wertz who hit the ball that Mays caught in 1954, involved only New York teams. The extraordinary baseball events in New York overshadowed problems elsewhere. The more complex truth about big league baseball in the 1950s was that it was in crisis outside of New York. In August of 1951, the Browns were in the middle of a season when they would win only 52 of 154 games and draw just under 294,000 fans. That season occurred in the midst of a six year run where they averaged fewer than 330,000 fans per year and had an overall winning percentage of .367. Following the 1953 season, they moved to Baltimore and became the Orioles. Other teams such as the Philadelphia Athletics and to a lesser extent teams like the Washington Senators and Cincinnati Reds struggled with attendance as well. By 1951 many teams, such as the Athletics, Senators and Pirates were at least a decade removed from their last World Series appearance. The Athletics were in the midst of a forty-year period without a post-season appearance.

The idea of sending a very short batter up to the plate is more than a joke. It is almost a way to hack baseball. A player whose strike zone was so small that he could walk even sixty percent of the time would be extremely valuable either leading off the game or as a pinch-hitter. The value of that player would be limited if he could not field well, but it is possible that baseball could devolve into a strange and boring game where very short players simply tried to draw walks.

This is obviously a not entirely serious idea, but Veeck was one of baseball's great innovators who was frequently looking for an edge. In 1948 he built a World Series winner by signing top African American players Larry Doby and Satchel Paige. About thirty years later he almost won a division title in 1977 with a Chicago White Sox team that was the first of the free agent era to build a team around players on the cusp of free agency like Richie Zisk and Oscar Gamble.

The other reason Gaedel occupies a significant role in baseball history is that it is a legacy from a time when baseball did not take itself quite as seriously as it does now. Even when a team is bad, and those Browns of the early 1950s were very bad, they are still in the entertainment business. Sending Eddie Gaedel to the plate was a funny idea, but it is one that fans undoubtedly enjoyed.

I am a believer in modern metrics for evaluating players and building teams, but am acutely aware of how this leads to a style of play, with batters trying to run up counts, few pitchers going deep into games and many plate appearances ending with a walk, strikeout or home run that is not very interesting to fans. The answer is not to send more Eddie Gaedels to the plate, but the spirit of both Veeck and Gaedel should be cultivated more. Owners who spend more time entertaining, and less time trying to separate fans from their money at every turn, would be good for the game and Gaedel reminds us of that.

Thirty-three
Lou Gehrig

Before discussing Lou Gehrig's importance to baseball and to America, let's take a moment and talk about Lou Gehrig the hitter. He had a career OPS+ of 179 and eleven seasons of seven or more WAR-among position players only Babe Ruth, Willie Mays, Henry Aaron and Barry Bonds had more. Gehrig was also in the top five in OPS in the American League every year from 1926-1937. He had an eleven-year run from 1927-1937 when he averaged 39 home runs and 154 RBIs and

Public Domain Photo

slashed .350/.459/.659 with an OPS+ of 189. At the time he retired, Gehrig had the second highest on base percentage and slugging percentage in the history of the American or National League since 1900, behind only Babe Ruth. In the first 40 years of the twentieth century only Ruth and Cobb had scored more runs in the twentieth century and only Ruth had more home runs and RBIs.

Those numbers help secure Gehrig's status as baseball's greatest first baseman ever, but it was the 2,130 consecutive games played and his tragic death from Amyotrophic Lateral Sclerosis (ALS), that define Gehrig's place in the culture. For decades, Gehrig's consecutive game streak was, along with Joe DiMaggio's 56 game hitting streak, viewed as one of the most unassailable records in the game. Gehrig's record lasted 56 years, much longer than Ruth's career or single season home run records.

Gehrig also played every day when there were frequent doubleheaders and much less adequate healthcare than players enjoy today. He also did it at a time when the game was much rougher. Pitchers threw at batters more and batters did not wear helmets at the plate. The thing that is often overlooked about a consecutive game streak is that not only does the player have to stay healthy, but he has to remain good enough to be in the lineup every day. It requires a consistency that only the best players can demonstrate.

Sadly, it is the tragedy of Lou Gehrig that elevated him from the status of great ballplayer to American icon. After a 1938 season when the 35-year-old Gehrig hit only 29 home runs and slashed .295/.410/.523, it was clear when Gehrig arrived at spring training in 1939 that something was wrong. He was not moving the way he had in the past. The once strapping athlete was losing his strength and bat speed. Nonetheless, Gehrig was in the Opening Day lineup, but he only played in eight games managing four singles and five walks in 33 trips to the plate. By May, Gehrig was out of the lineup and never played again.

It was soon learned that Gehrig was suffering from amyotrophic lateral sclerosis, a devastating disease that gradually destroys the muscles. The disease is now generally known as ALS or Lou Gehrig's disease. People who do not know who Lou Gehrig was, or even anything about baseball, now know of Lou Gehrig's disease. Today people live can live with ALS for years, but Gehrig died in 1941 shortly before his 38th birthday.

Gehrig was the ultimate supporting actor in baseball. He spent the first part of his career in the shadow of his better and more flamboyant teammate Babe Ruth. After one year, 1935, of being the biggest star on the Yankees, Joe DiMaggio joined the team in 1936 and the two were teammates until the end of Gehrig's career, but DiMaggio was placed in the spotlight by the media. Gehrig was perpetually Spock to Ruth's, and later DiMaggio's Captain Kirk. And like Spock, he was enormously strong, extremely dependable, and very even tempered.

There are different kinds of stock heroes in American culture and sports. One of them is the strong, handsome type who quietly goes about his or her business, but is always there when you need them. Gehrig was the baseball archetype of that as demonstrated not just by his consecutive game streak, but of the awesome numbers he put up every year for over a decade.

New York City is at the center of baseball history and some of the best teams and players ever have called New York home. Babe Ruth, Joe DiMaggio, Tom Seaver, Christy Mathewson, Derek Jeter, and many others spent most or all of their career there. Willie Mays began and ended his career playing for New York teams. Jackie Robinson made baseball history playing for the Brooklyn Dodgers. Many great players like Whitey Ford, Hank Greenberg, Alex Rodriguez, and Edgar Martinez were born there.

Today New York is still very much a baseball town. However, in the long history of baseball in New York, no player had a stronger connection to the city than Gehrig. Lou Gehrig was born in the Bronx, attended college at Columbia University and spent his entire career with the Yankees. He is buried a few miles north of the city in Valhalla, New York. You could do a tour of Lou Gehrig's life on a bicycle in New York City and not even tire yourself out, although you might decide to take the train to visit his grave.

Thirty-four
Josh Gibson

Josh Gibson was one of the greatest hitters in baseball history. Because he played in the Negro Leagues, the data on Gibson is sparse, but it shows that during roughly 600 official games he hit .373/.458/.718, for an OPS+ of a Ruthian 214. Those 600 games are only a small part of Gibson's career, because in those days African American players barnstormed, played in tournaments and in other competitive settings including in Mexico and the Caribbean.

Photo courtesy of the National Baseball Hall of Fame and Museum (Gibson_Josh_BL-2397-71_NBL)

Gibson was born in 1911 so was of the same generation of white big league players as Mel Ott, Jimmie Foxx, and Hank Greenberg. As with the Babe himself, Gibson was a slugger whose accomplishments can only be partially captured by numbers. Like Ruth, Gibson evolved into the realm of legend with stories abounding about him being the only player ever to hit a fair ball out of Yankee Stadium and the home runs he hit in some obscure ballpark somewhere in the south, at some tournament or in the Caribbean.

There is a strong argument to be made that Gibson was both the greatest catcher and the greatest hitter that ever lived. Monte Irvin who played against Gibson in the Negro Leagues and with Willie Mays and against Henry Aaron in the National League considered Gibson the best player of the three. White players such as

Walter Johnson thought Gibson was easily good enough to star in the American or National League.

Gibson is one of a small handful of great Negro League players for whom there is enough of statistical footprint to have a sense of how good they were, but by the time of integration was too old to play in what was then considered the Major Leagues. Therefore, for the entire time Gibson was playing, Americans of all backgrounds were denied the chance to see perhaps the greatest hitter of the day compete against all the great pitchers of that era.

The peripatetic career path Gibson pursued, moving back and forth from US based Negro League teams to Mexico and the Caribbean, reflects how African Americans played professional baseball in the pre-1947 era and of how in the US institutionalized racism was much stronger than in many neighboring countries.

Gibson hit wherever he played, but is probably most remembered for playing on the Pittsburgh Crawfords in the 1930s. Those Pittsburgh Crawfords may have had the best collection of front-line talent of any team ever. Among the stars playing with the young Josh Gibson were Satchel Paige, Cool Papa Bell, Judy Johnson, and Oscar Charleston. Charleston and Johnson were already in their late 30s. Charleston was also the manager of the team, but he could still hit. Johnson, who may have been the greatest third baseman in Negro League history, was already slowing down. That team may have been the best team anywhere in the US, but they did not have the opportunity to compete in a true series against the Yankees, Tigers, Cardinals, New York Giants, or any of the other great white teams of that era.

Gibson was never considered as a candidate to be the first African American player in the twentieth century to integrate what were then considered the Major Leagues. This was due largely to his age and his reputation as heavy drinker. However, in 1945 and 1946 Gibson led the Negro National League in home runs and slugging percentage, and was undoubtedly still the best African American hitter in the US. He could have helped many big league teams, but at that moment there were other criteria besides simply baseball skill for making the jump from the Negro

Leagues to the American or National League. That was another way that racism denied fans the best baseball product in those years.

Not only did Gibson never have a chance to play alongside, and against, the best white players, but by the time Jackie Robinson played his first game for the Brooklyn Dodgers, Gibson had been dead for about four months, succumbing to a brain tumor a few days after his 35th birthday. By 1948, Satchel Paige, Gibson's one time teammate who was a few years older, was pitching for the Indians, so it is possible that if Gibson had been healthy, he too would have had his chance, but we will never know.

Gibson played a total of 14 full seasons in the Negro Leagues. During those years, he led his league in home runs 11 times, on base percentage seven times, slugging percentage nine times, and OPS eight times. Gibson also never played more than 70 official regular season games in one season and had countless other hitting accomplishments in tournaments, while barnstorming or playing outside the US. This means that the evidence remains scant. We don't have Gibson's full oeuvre or a good enough sense of the competition against which he played. Thus, in a sport obsessed with numbers it is more than ironic that we cannot determine who the greatest hitter of the twentieth century was because racism in baseball, and in America, precluded Gibson from playing against the best competition or even in leagues that had a consistent structure and schedule from year to year. The racism that defined the National and American Leagues before 1947 means that baseball history can never be completely understood and that we will never have enough data to know who truly were the greatest players ever, but Josh Gibson should be part of that discussion.

Thirty-five
Hank Greenberg

On a Sunday in Detroit in the middle to late 1930s some people might have listened to the ranting of Detroit based Father Charles Coughlin, the fascist Nazi sympathizer whose radio show was extremely popular. Others might have gone to the ballpark to take in a Tigers game. If they chose the latter, they would have seen a pretty consistently good team whose biggest star was a Jewish slugger named Hank Greenberg. Greenberg was one of the greatest sluggers in baseball history, but his story and importance cannot be separated from his background.

Public Domain Photo

In 1938, when Coughlin was still ranting and blaming the Jews, and Hitler was beginning the genocide against the Jewish people, Greenberg was one of the most important and famous Jews in the US. That was the year he almost broke Babe Ruth's record of sixty home runs in a season, a record that was already seen as unassailable. Greenberg ended that year with 58. No right-handed hitter slugged more in a single season until Sammy Sosa and Mark McGwire in 1998. Greenberg's slugging accomplishments made him one of baseball's biggest stars as well as a symbol of strength and hope for many American Jews.

Greenberg was about eight years younger than Lou Gehrig, but they were both slugging first baseman who grew up in New York. Greenberg had been born in Manhattan but moved north

115

to the Bronx as young boy. Both went to college in New York, but Greenberg went to New York University, not Columbia. Greenberg might have been a great fit for the Yankees, but with Gehrig firmly set at first base and Greenberg's generally limited defensive skills, the fit would not have been perfect. Greenberg, as a right-handed hitter, would not have been able to take advantage of Yankee Stadium either. Rather than go to his hometown team, Greenberg spent most of his career with the Tigers.

Like so many players of his generation, Greenberg lost time to World War II, in his case beginning with military service in 1941 before Pearl Harbor and ending midway through the 1945 season. Had he not missed those almost four and a half seasons in his early thirties, Greenberg would have had well over 400 home runs, instead of a career total of 331. He retired with 55.4 WAR about the same as Will Clark and David Ortiz. The war probably cost Greenberg twenty WAR. A total 75 WAR would have put him easily in the top ten ever for first baseman. Greenberg's career OPS+ of 159 is tied with Stan Musial for the 19th best ever.

After returning from his military service, Greenberg rejoined the Tigers on July 1, 1945. In only 78 games he hit 13 home runs and slashed .311/.404/.544. The Tigers won the pennant by 1.5 games and went on to win the World Series. They clinched the pennant on the last day of the season when Greenberg hit a grand slam in the ninth inning to give the Tigers a 6-3 win over the Browns. Greenberg's contributions were recognized as the difference in that pennant race. Despite playing only half a season, he finished 14th in the MVP voting. The 1945 World Series was the fourth and final one in which Greenberg played. Across those four World Series, Greenberg slashed a remarkable .318/.420/.624 with five home runs in 23 games.

After the 1946 season, Greenberg was sold to the Pittsburgh Pirates. Early in the 1947 season the Dodgers came to town to play the Pirates. Greenberg, the game's best and most famous Jewish player, became one of the few non-Dodgers to go out of his way to offer support and encouragement to Jackie Robinson. This occurred when many other opposing players were regularly taunting Robinson with racial epithets. Those supportive words also came from one of the few players who could relate to what Robinson was experiencing almost every day.

Although Greenberg never seemed to like playing in Pittsburgh, he had a very impressive season, although by the counting stats of the day it was less appreciated. Greenberg only hit .249, but because of his 25 home runs and 104 walks in not quite full-time play, he had a very respectable OPS+ of 132, good enough for ninth in the league. Greenberg clearly still had enough left to help many teams, but he retired after that 1947 season. After his playing days, Greenberg was a baseball executive who served as general manager of the Cleveland Indians, where he won a pennant in 1954, and then part owner, along with Bill Veeck, of the White Sox.

Greenberg was a big tough Jew who stood up against anti-Semitism wherever he encountered it. By doing that, he became an important symbol for American Jews at the darkest time in our long history. He also joined the fight against fascism, signing up for the military after Pearl Harbor even though he had already completed his military service. Combined with his time before Pearl Harbor, Greenberg spent more time in the military during the war than any other big league ballplayer.

Today there are many Jewish players in the big leagues including stars like Alex Bregman, Max Fried and Joc Pederson, but that was not the case when Greenberg began his career. The stereotype of Jews as being weak and unathletic, which persists today, was much stronger when Greenberg was playing. Anti-Semitism in general was also more widespread. On Sundays in Detroit in the 1930s, Greenberg gave people who were not interested in hearing Father Coughlin's lies about the Jewish people the much better option of spending a day in the sun seeing what a real live Jew could do with a baseball bat.

Thirty-six
Ken Griffey Jr.

Ken Griffey, Jr. had a strange career. From 1989-2000 he was one of the best players in the game. He then stuck around for another decade, but during those years he was usually injured or not playing well, and occasionally both. During the 1990s, Griffey was the clean face of baseball during the steroid era. He was a good-looking man with a great smile, who made it to the big leagues at age 19 and was one of those players who seemed

Photo 68944243 / Baseball © Jerry Coli | Dreamstime.com

to drip with enthusiasm for playing the game. He wore his cap backwards and pulled it off with panache while excelling at every aspect of the game for a decade or so. In some respects, Griffey was the last real face of baseball. He endorsed well-known brands like Nike and Frosted Flakes, made a cameo on the Simpsons and The Fresh Prince of Bel Air and even had a candy bar named after him. It is hard to imagine Bryce Harper, Juan Soto or Mike Trout doing that today or being as widely recognizable as Griffey was.

In 1987, Griffey was taken in the baseball draft with the first overall pick by the Seattle Mariners. Two years later he was in the Mariners lineup; and a year later found himself frequently joined the lineup by his father, Ken Griffey Sr. who was winding down his own excellent big league career. In one of the great father and son baseball moments of all-time, on September 14, 1990, the two hit back-to-back home runs.

During the 1990s Griffey was the consensus best player in the game, but a closer look at the data reveals the consensus was wrong. That may sound nitpicky given just how good Griffey was, but he was also the last great player who, while active, was evaluated almost entirely on conventional statistics. In the 1990s Griffey and Barry Bonds were the two biggest stars in the games. The two players, who seemed able to anything on the ballfield, had a lot in common. They were both second generation stars, sons of fathers who had been very good ballplayers, but who they surpassed. Griffey's grandfather had also played high school basketball with Stan Musial and in one of baseball's coincidences, both Ken Griffey Jr. and Stan Musial were born on the same date, November 21st, and in the same small town, Donora, Pennsylvania.

Bonds was the better player, but Griffey was the more marketable of the two due to his more upbeat personality and stronger media skills. Griffey had a remarkable peak from 1990-2000 slashing .299/.384/.579 for an OPS+ of 151, averaging 38 home runs and 14 stolen bases in 19 tries. During that period, he won nine Gold Gloves in centerfield. His total WAR for those 11 years was an extraordinary 73. That was an amazing peak, but by any measure Bonds' 11 year pre-PED peak was considerably better. From 1986 through 1996, Bonds slashed .288/.404/.548 for an OPS+ of 161 and an average of 30 home runs and 35 stolen bases in 45 tries. Bonds also won six Gold Gloves during that period. His WAR during this 11-year stretch was 83.6. His higher WAR reflected Bonds being a better base stealer, playing in a tougher hitters' park and, according to advanced metrics, being a slightly better defender.

After 1996, Bonds went on to have two more pre-PED excellent years, while Griffey was never a great player after 2000. From 2001-2010, Griffey had an OPS+ of 114 while devolving into a poor defender. This due largely injuries, but few players have had as long a decline phase Griffey. During the last ten years of his career Griffey only was worth 7.6 WAR, meaning he was essentially a replacement level player for a decade, getting by on his fame and past accomplishments.

On balance, I am not sure the story is quite that simple. While Bonds' play in the 21st century was, in part due to PED use, far better than Griffey's, the overall impact of the PED era on both players is hard to measure. Griffey's long decline period is yet another example of how the PED era, and the failure of MLB to address it in real time, had an impact on the game and its best players.

In the 1990s, Griffey was talented enough to excel without PEDs against pitchers, and relative to other batters who were using. Bonds was similarly dominant during those years. Their numbers in the 1990s, given that, are even more impressive. However, for much of the first decade of the 21st century Griffey, who was getting older, was unable to continue to excel. Additionally, his numbers looked even less impressive because of all the other sluggers, not just Bonds, who were using PEDs.

The tradeoff for Griffey was absolutely worth it. He still ended up with 630 career home runs, behind only Aaron, Ruth, Albert Pujols, and Mays among players who did not use PEDs. There was also no great debate over whether Griffey should be in the Hall of Fame as in his first year of eligibility over 99% of the Hall of Fame voters deemed Griffey worthy of the honor.

Griffey is what baseball might have become in the early 21st century, but somewhere in there it made a wrong turn. PED use was encouraged and tolerated for several years before it wasn't, and Griffey's star faded in the wake of barrages of home runs by bloated sluggers.

Thirty-seven
Bryce Harper

Bryce Harper is one of the best players in the game today. Beyond that, his career demonstrates, more than any other big league star, how youth baseball and the pipeline to the big leagues for American players have changed since the days when hard throwing high school kids and slugging farm boys were discovered in the backroads, fields and inner city high schools of what feels like a different country. Harper is illustrative of several changes in what might be best

Photo 64340785 / Baseball © | Dreamstime.com

described as the gestalt of big league baseball as it consolidates its transformation from a hybrid of pastime, folk tradition and business into a much more unambiguously corporate creation. There is a soullessness around much of baseball today and while it would be unfair and inaccurate to somehow blame that on Bryce Harper, who is in no way responsible for those changes, he is the best player through which to show that.

By the time Harper was taken with the first overall pick in the 2010 draft, he had been preparing for, and been tracked into, a professional baseball career for years. Harper played on US national teams for players 16-years-old and younger and then 18-years-old or younger, after playing in competitive travel baseball programs for much of his youth. From the time he entered high school, Harper's life was structured around not just making it to the big leagues, but around becoming a big league star. He left high school early, took his GRE, and began playing at community college so he could be eligible for the big league draft a year sooner than if he had stayed in high school through graduation.

The first time most fans encountered Harper was when he was 16-years-old and featured on the cover of *Sports Illustrated* described as the "Chosen One," and then as "Baseball's Lebron." Harper was starting for the Washington Nationals when he was nineteen-years-old in 2012 and was the National League Rookie of the Year. Harper's career path is unusual only because of his success in the big leagues, but most American players today are tracked, from a very young age, into travel programs, various tournaments and national teams if they are good enough. Many are also following Harper's path through junior college.

This is a perfectly rational ways to identify, cultivate, and draft the best young American baseball players, just as offenses built around home runs and walks and using six pitchers to strike out fifteen batters over the course of one game are good strategies. However, all of this leads to a baseball product that feels very different and is less appealing to many older fans. There is something less poetic about the game today. The players, particularly the American ones, are products of a similar approach to the game and are evaluated by things like exit velocity, spin rates and even body type from a young age leading to a homogeneity that takes some of the magic out of the game.

Harper is part of a group of superstars of his generation including players such as Mike Trout and Gerrit Cole who have been consistently excellent on the ballfield and consistently unable to break through to the larger culture in any way. That is also evidence of the changing nature of the game. The social critic Greg Proops has said the problem with baseball is that too many players are named Dustin. That was not a literal comment, but suggested too many of players, particularly the American ones, have interchangeable backstories and skill sets.

Willie Mays, Babe Ruth, Stan Musial, Rickey Henderson, Sandy Koufax and Barry Bonds are some of the greatest American players ever, but they also have personal stories that are compellingly interesting. Baseball was a more fascinating and fun game for many because Ruth learned to play the game in Catholic orphanage or that Sandy Koufax was a Jew from Brooklyn who went to college intending to play basketball and was enrolled in classes at Columbia during his first year with the Dodgers, or that Willie Mays learned the game from his father who loved baseball and taught his son to play every position. Those were stories that made the players more relatable, interesting and accessible to fans. Today's process is more logical and makes more economic sense, but something is lost in that transition.

For his part, Harper has been a great player, winning two MVP awards and making six All-Star teams. Through the 2022 season, when he was only 29-years-old, Harper had slashed .280/.390/.523 for an OPS+ of 143 with 285 home runs and 42.5 WAR. Although Harper has been an excellent player and is on a path that will very possibly lead him to being enshrined in the Hall of Fame, there has frequently been a sense of disappointment around him. This is less of a reflection of anything he has done on the ballfield than it is of the absurdly high expectations of a player who was described as a can't miss prospect in the national media before he was old enough to vote.

The story of the corporatization of big league baseball is more than just new stadiums, rising ticket prices, labor disputes and teams moving into the real estate sector. It is also about youth baseball and how young players are developed. The players today are more physically talented than any in history, but big league baseball is in the entertainment business and it is no longer clear that the product is as entertaining as it could be. Harper is the face of that paradox.

Thirty-eight
Rickey Henderson

I was just a bit too young to see Willie Mays, Henry Aaron, Roberto Clemente, or Frank Robinson in person, but I have seen pretty much every great player since then. I've seen Barry Bonds, both pre- and post-PED use hit home runs and steal bases, Mariano Rivera save numerous games, Greg Maddux pitch a World Series masterpiece, Derek Jeter play many times. I saw Mike Trout during his rookie year and Joe Morgan in his prime and on his way out. I've sat in the stands and watched Seaver, Carlton, Clemens, Alex Rodriguez, Buster Posey, and many others.

None of those players were as exciting or fun to watch as Rickey Henderson, particularly in his early years with the A's. I wasn't even an A's fan, but in my grammar school, where most of the kids were Giants fans, I became friends with a boy who had roots in the East Bay and was a big A's fan, so beginning in 1980

Photo 139017905 / Baseball © Sports Images | Dreamstime.com

124

we would take BART over to Oakland and see the A's from time to time. In that season Rickey Henderson was the most disruptive, dynamic and athletic player in the game-and he stayed that way for a decade.

In the early years of his career, whenever he got to first base, which was often, the whole ballpark would watch Henderson take his lead, draw a few pickoff throws and then steal second, and frequently third as well. He also played great defense, and along with Tony Armas in right and particularly Dwayne Murphy in center, was part of an outstanding defensive outfield. Henderson had not yet developed his real power, but he still had some pop in those days.

Any discussion of Rickey Henderson begins with base stealing. There are players who change the game because of how they play. Babe Ruth was instrumental in bringing power hitting into the big league game. Willie Mays combined power and speed in a way that had not been seen before. Cal Ripken Jr. became the archetype of the power hitting shortstop that is relatively common now. It is tempting to say that Henderson changed baseball by reintroducing the stolen base as a big weapon, but that is not true. Henderson began his career while the base stealing renaissance led by people like Ron LeFlore and Omar Moreno was already underway. Within a few years that had faded away. Henderson did not change the game in a lasting way because nobody had his skills both in stealing bases and reaching first base, so he could not be imitated well.

Few players have dominated in one area of the game the way Henderson did with regards to stolen bases. The gap between Henderson's record 1,406 stolen bases and Lou Brock, who is second all-time with 938, is the same as the gap between Brock and Jimmy Rollins who is 46th all-time. Henderson led his league in stolen bases 12 times, also the most ever. Willie Wilson and Kenny Lofton are considered among the best base stealers ever. They are 12th and 15th on the all-time list and led their league in steals a combined six times. Together they have fewer stolen bases than Henderson.

Those extraordinary stolen base totals obscure just how good

Henderson was. He scored more runs than anybody in baseball history and only Barry Bonds drew more walks. His 111.2 career WAR is the 19th highest ever and 14th among position players. Henderson had a very solid OPS+ of 127 over a 25 year career, but as a leadoff hitter, his .401 career on base percentage was more significant. Henderson also accumulated more than 3,000 hits, and slugged just shy of 300 home runs, while scoring more runs than anybody in baseball history.

Stolen bases come and go as an offensive weapon. They have recently been in a lull just as they were in the 1940s and much of the 1950s, but are experiencing a revival beginning in 2023 due to MLB's rule changes. Nonetheless, Henderson's complete domination of the leaderboards in this category is striking. There is more to Henderson than stolen bases. He was, in some sense, ahead of his time as a ballplayer, because he was extremely athletic, trained rigorously and blended power and patience in a way that was much less common when he was at his peak from about 1980 to 1991. Henderson also managed to excel as an older player in the PED era while never being associated with steroids. In the parts of four seasons he played after he turned 40, Henderson had a .381 on base percentage while averaging 22 stolen bases in 29 tries playing part time.

There is a question that is increasingly raised about Rickey Henderson that goes something like: in today's game with the stolen base deemphasized and home runs so much a bigger part of the game, what kind of player would Henderson have been? The hypothesis is that along the way a coach or team would have told Henderson to stop damaging his body by stealing bases and to focus more on home runs. This would have turned him into a very good player with a high on base percentage 35 or so home runs a year and 15-30 stolen bases. In some years that might have been more valuable, but again the conflict between the best strategy for winning games and providing the best product is apparent. For a quarter century Henderson was both one of the very best players in the game and a compellingly exciting player for fans to watch. That seems like the kind of combination baseball should try to cultivate.

Thirty-nine
Catfish Hunter

The Oakland A's, looking to win their second consecutive World Series in 1973, fell behind the New York Mets three games to two. The Mets had their ace, Tom Seaver, ready to go in game six. Seaver, the best pitcher of that era, pitched a great game giving up two runs in seven innings against a very loaded A's lineup. Unfortunately for the Mets, the A's countered with their ace Catfish Hunter who pitched just a little better, allowing only one run in 7.1 innings. The A's won that game and the next to win the World Series. In 1974 they won again for their third championship in a row.

Photo 105402766 / Catfish Hunter Baseball © Jerry Coli | Dreamstime.com

From 1972-1974, when the A's were winning those three consecutive World Series, Catfish Hunter was their ace and one of the best pitchers in the game. Over that period, he averaged 22 wins, an ERA+ of 125 and fully 290 innings a year. In the postseasons during those three years he went 7-1 with an ERA of 2.45. In that same span, he won one Cy Young award and finished in the top five in the other two years. In the early 1970s and into the middle of the decade, Hunter was one of the most famous names in baseball. His real name was Jim, but the owner of the

A's, Charlie O. Finley, made up the name Catfish, for the North Carolina born and raised Hunter, as well as an absurd back-story involving running away from home as a young child and catching some catfish in a nearby stream.

As a nineteen-year-old in 1965, Hunter started twenty games for the Athletics, who were then in Kansas City, and by 1967 was a very solid big league pitcher. In 1968, he pitched a perfect game against the Minnesota Twins. On the back end of his career in 1978 as a sore armed pitcher for the Yankees, Hunter turned his season around and had one last period of greatness, going 9-2 with a 2.23 ERA after August 1st as the Yankees won the most exciting division race of the four division era and went on to win the World Series. That was Hunter's fifth championship, three with the A's and two with the Yankees.

Hunter is one of those players to whom advanced metrics are not friendly. His career WAR of 40.9 and ERA+ of 104 are not Hall of Fame caliber, but it did not seem that way in the 1970s, when he was one of the top pitchers in the game and, along with Seaver, probably the most famous. Catfish was, in part due to Finley's clever marketing, one of those players who was known through-out baseball by his first name, or in his case, his nickname. Seaver, was the better pitcher, but Bob Dylan never wrote a song about Seaver. Dylan wrote one about Hunter called, what else, "Catfish."

In addition to his pitching accomplishments, Hunter was one of the key figures in the early years of free agency. Unlike Curt Flood, Hunter did not make any sacrifices, financial or otherwise, in his journey to free agency. Instead, Hunter became the first player to sign a major multi-year free agent contract. Following the 1974 season, Hunter demanded his free agency because Finley, who still owned the A's, had not fully honored Hunter's contract. Specifically, he had failed to pay a life insurance premium as specified in the contract. The case went to arbitration and Peter Seitz, the arbiter who heard the case, ruled in favor of Hunter and made him a free agent.

This was not a direct challenge to the reserve clause, but it was nonetheless a major step in the name of player's rights. Because Hunter was the only major free agent between the 1974 and 1975 seasons, there was a lot of competition for his services. Hunter finally agreed to a five year deal with the Yankees worth $3 million. That was by far the biggest contract in history at that time. Hunter's contract was the first sign of how much money would be available for players if free agency continued.

In his first year with the Yankees, Hunter went 23-14 with a 144 ERA+ and finished second in the Cy Young Award voting. The following year, his record slipped to 17-15, but he pitched almost 300 innings and helped the Yankees win their first pennant since 1964. Over the next three years, the more than 3,000 innings he had pitched over the previous 12 years caught up with him as Hunter succumbed to arm injuries. Other than the second half of 1978, when the Yankees needed absolutely every win they could get, Hunter was never again a good pitcher and was out of baseball after 1979.

Hunter's contract with the Yankees was groundbreaking for several reasons. In addition to being a harbinger of how free agency would change baseball's economy, it also signaled the return of the Yankees as a contending team. The Yankees had been building a good team in the early 1970s, but the signing of Catfish Hunter sent a message to the rest of the league that team's owner, George Steinbrenner, was going to pay whatever price was necessary to build his team into a winner.

Forty
Monte Irvin

Monte Irvin was a Negro League star who moved to the National League in 1949 when he was 30-years-old. Irvin and Sam Thompson became the first African American players on the New York Giants. Irvin had spent his entire Negro League career with the Newark Eagles where he was a four time All-Star and one of the top hitters in the league. Irvin and Larry Doby played together in the Eagles outfield in 1943 and 1946. In 1942, Irvin only played four games with the Eagles and spent the rest of the season with Veracruz in the Mexican League where he slashed .397/.502/.772.

Photo courtesy of the National Baseball Hall of Fame and Museum (Irvin Monte 2887.70 NBL)

During his time in the Negro Leagues, Irvin seemed like the kind of person, both on and off the field, who was poised to be the first African American to play in the National or American League in the twentieth century. Dodgers president Branch Rickey made an overture to Irvin to fill this role, but Irvin declined believing he was not quite ready yet.

In his first four full years with the Giants, Irvin continued to be a top hitter and slashed .314/.503/.511. Irvin was probably the best player on the Giants when they won the pennant in 1951. In 1954 when the Giants won their final World Series in New York, Irvin slugged .262/.363/.438. In 1951 Irvin was joined in the Giants outfield by another, much younger, African American player, Willie Mays. Irvin was about 12 years older than Mays and was a valuable resource and mentor for the young rookie who, like Irving, was from Alabama. In the World Series of Mays's rookie year, Irvin, Mays, and Sam Thompson became the first all African American outfield to start together in the World Series.

Irvin was a power hitting outfielder who typically hit 15-25 home runs in a season with the Giants and had a career OPS+ of 125 during his years in the National League. However, by the time he got to the Giants' Irvin's best years were behind him. He only played 120 or more games three times and retired after the 1956 season, which he spent with the Cubs. At that time, he was nearing 40 and had starred in the Negro Leagues, the National League and in the Mexican League, but his impact on the game was, in some respects, just beginning.

After working briefly as a scout for the Mets, Irvin became the first African American to work in the front office for Major League Baseball when he was hired in the Commissioner's Office. His portfolio there was primarily in public relations. Six years into his time working for the Commissioner, Irvin found himself at the center of an historic moment because then Commissioner Kuhn, the same genius who a few years later would ban Willie Mays and Mickey Mantle from baseball for life, decided that being physically present when Henry Aaron broke Babe Ruth's career home run record wasn't all that important. Kuhn sent Irvin to represent the Commissioner's Office. This was a slight to Aaron, particularly in the face of the ugly racism that Aaron confronted as he closed in on the Babe's record. The white Commissioner was sending a clear message that he was not going to stand beside, literally, the new home run champion, who was African American, at that key moment. The racial politics of sending Irvin instead were complicated. It was a snub on the part of Kuhn, but Irvin was widely respected, particularly among older African American ballplayers.

Monte Irvin's life in baseball lasted six decades. He was a good enough player to be the only person ever elected to the Mexican League, Negro Leagues and Major League Halls of Fame and was part of many historic moments. Irvin made the first out of the inning minutes before Bobby Thomson's shot heard 'round the world in 1951 and three years later was in left field when Willie Mays made the greatest catch in World Series history. Irvin integrated one team and had the opportunity to integrate all of white organized baseball, was a star in the Mexican League when it was at its strongest and for over a decade was the highest ranking person of color in Major League Baseball.

Over the course of those six decades MLB, as it came to be known, grew to dominate professional baseball in the Americas in a way that was not true when Irvin was playing. Irvin's journey shows how MLB grew into the baseball hegemon it is today and how a big reason for that was because people like Irvin were included; and the racism that kept them out slowly, and not yet completely, began to be weakened.

Forty-one
Bo Jackson

Nobody ever played big league baseball quite like Bo Jackson who was probably the best athlete ever to play the game at its highest level. Jackie Robinson starred in track and field and football in addition to baseball. Jim Thorpe won gold medals in the pentathlon and decathlon at the 1912 Olympics. Deion Sanders also played in the Major Leagues as well as the NFL, but Jackson stands out even among players like that.

Photo courtesy of the National Baseball Hall of Fame and Museum (Jackson_Bo_BL-7172-89_NBL)

In college at Auburn, Jackson played both baseball and football, but was better at the latter. He won the Heisman Trophy in 1985 and was widely considered to be on the path to stardom in the NFL. Jackson was drafted by the Tampa Bay Buccaneers with the top overall pick in the 1986 NFL draft, but instead chose to play baseball, despite having played only one season at Auburn. He was a fourth round pick by the Kansas City Royals in the 1986 baseball draft and was in the Royals lineup by the end of the 1986 season. They Royals were not having a great year in 1986, but they had been a very good team over the previous decade and had won the World Series in 1985, so playing Jackson was not just a stunt aimed at getting attention and drawing fans.

By 1987 Jackson was starting for the Royals. That year, he showed signs of what he could be, hitting 22 home runs and stealing ten bases in only 116 games, but he also struck out in 36% of his plate appearances. Back in the 1980s, that was an extremely high percentage. By the end of the season, it was clear that although Jackson had power, speed and great athleticism there were still flaws in his game that were preventing him from becoming a big league star.

The Raiders had taken a seventh round draft pick flyer on Jackson in 1987 thinking he might come back to football. Over the next three seasons, from football in the fall of 1987 through baseball in 1990, Jackson did not just play two sports, he starred in both. On the football side he emerged as one of the better running backs in the game. On the baseball side, the strikeouts never went away, but everything else came together. He had an OPS+ of 124 from 1988-1990, hitting 25 or more home runs in all three of those seasons.

Jackson made highlight reels with acrobatic catches and fantastic throws in the outfield and extremely long runs in the NFL. In 1989, until then his best season, Jackson hit 32 home runs, stole 25 bases and slashed .256/.310/.495. He finished tenth in the MVP balloting, but the highlight of that season, and of Jackson's career in baseball, was the All-Star Game. Jackson, the starting left fielder for the American League, led off the bottom of the 1st inning off of Giants ace Rick Reuschel with a mammoth home run to centerfield, stole a base a few innings later and was named the MVP of the game.

Jackson had an even better year in 1990, slashing .272/.342/.523 in 111 games, but the following January he badly injured his hip while playing for the Raiders. He was never the same player in either sport again.

For a few years in the late 1980s and early 1990s Jackson was probably the most recognizable athlete in America. He was a star in two sports whose feats on both fields were impressive even to the very casual fan. Jackson was also charismatic and telegenic so was sought after for product endorsements and other forms of advertising. The "Bo Knows" campaign by Nike which featured

Jackson in a range of situations with lines like "Bo knows tennis" or "Bo knows basketball," was ubiquitous in those years. The other people in these commercials talking about Bo Jackson were the likes of John McEnroe, Michael Jordan and Bo Diddly. That is how big Bo Jackson was at the height of his fame. The biggest stars in other sports and other parts of American society appeared in commercials in which Jackson starred.

The height of Jackson's fame was just before the PED era, but by the time Mark McGwire, Sammy Sosa and others were breaking home run records, Jackson, due to his damaged hip, was out of the game. In some respects, Bo Jackson represents a path not taken by baseball. He was the face of a fun, athletic game that did not always take itself all that seriously. Even in 1989, Jackson was not one of the best players in the game. He struck out too much, very rarely walked and, despite the highlight reels, was not consistent enough to be a great fielder, but fans loved him and voted him onto the All-Star team.

Bo knew baseball and football and, for a brief time, everyone seemed to know Bo as well.

Forty-two
Joe Jackson

The saga of Joe Jackson is a tragic one that has long captured the American imagination. There was something almost mythic, even poetic, about Jackson's baseball demise, from his deeply rural and impoverished origins, complete with the colorful nickname Shoeless Joe, probably apocryphal plea "say it ain't so, Joe" from a young boy saddened by the final chapter in Jackson's baseball career, to the remaining thirty years of his life lived in the shadow of his actions.

Library of Congress, Prints & Photographs Division [LOC LC-USZ62-78070]

Jackson is widely known as one of the eight players on the Chicago White Sox who threw the 1919 World Series. Of those eight, he was both the best player and one of the least connected to the gamblers. However, Jackson went along with a very bad idea, and because of that was banned from baseball for life following the 1920 season. That is the bare bones story of Jackson and the scandal, but his career was much fuller and more important than that.

First, Jackson was an extremely good hitter. During the height of the deadball era, the only hitter who was clearly better was Ty Cobb. Cobb began his career in 1905, Jackson in 1908. Through 1920, Cobb slashed .369/.433/.512 for an OPS+ of 181. Jackson's numbers through 1920 were a notch behind at .356/.423/.517

for an OPS+ of 170. Nobody else had an OPS+ that high over the first two decades of the twentieth century. If you were to make an all deadball era team, Jackson would be in the outfield along with Cobb.

Jackson played all three outfield positions, but was more noted for his batting than for his glove. He was not a base stealer like Cobb was, but over the course of his career, Jackson stole just over 200 bases. Like many of the best hitters of his era, Jackson hit few home runs but his power came through by hitting lots of doubles and triples. Jackson had begun his career with the Philadelphia Athletics and then went to Cleveland, but is still most famous for his play with the White Sox.

In 1917, Jackson had, by his standards, a bad year as he only slashed .301/.375/.429, but he helped lead a very good White Sox team to a World Series championship. Two years later, the White Sox were back in the World Series. Jackson hit .351 with an OPS+ of 159 that year so he was once again among the best hitters in the league. Jackson and star pitcher Eddie Cicotte were the two best players on the team. Their opponents in that World Series were the Cincinnati Reds. The story that has been handed down through the ages is that the White Sox were heavily favored, but the Reds had won eight more regular season games, and the two teams were relatively evenly matched.

A group of gangsters persuaded eight White Sox players including Jackson and Cicotte to throw the World Series in exchange for what turned out to be a relatively modest sum of money. The Reds went on to win the series five games to three. The scandal was not uncovered until the following year and all eight White Sox players were banned from the game for life by baseball's first Commissioner Kenesaw Mountain Landis. Landis had been hired earlier that year and charged with rooting gambling out of the game.

The 1919 World Series, and its aftermath, have become symbols of how baseball was threatened by gambling in its early years and then cleaned itself up just as Babe Ruth was taking the game to new levels of popularity. Jackson became the face of the scandal. Naturally, in addition to being banned from the game he was never enshrined in the Hall of Fame.

There is some truth to that symbol, but banning the eight players who threw the World Series, particularly those who played a relatively minor role, also is an example of the self-righteousness that sometimes is a bit much in baseball. A league that had quietly tolerated gambling, banned non-white players, and was often very violent, harshly punished all, not just the leaders, of the players, who were involved in the scandal. Jackson, for example, had hit .375 with three doubles and a home run in the World Series, leading all regulars on both teams in batting average. If he was not trying his best, it is not very obvious from the numbers. Perhaps he deliberately struck out at key moments, but even that is unlikely has he only struck out twice in the whole series. There are lots of ways for one player to change the outcome of a game, but it is not clear how Jackson tried to do that. Jackson's crime was his association with the gamblers and taking money from them, but he may not have actively done anything else to throw the World Series. A milder punishment, perhaps a suspension of a year or two, might have been a better solution. Today, MLB has embraced gambling so it may be time to revisit Joe Jackson's Hall of Fame candidacy.

Baseball is, like life, a game of what might have been, and Joe Jackson is one of the best examples. Unlike others who were denied opportunity because of racism or injury, Jackson's own foibles cost him the rest of what should have been one of the greatest careers in baseball history.

Forty-three
Reggie Jackson

There has never been a player quite like Reggie Jackson. During the 1970s, Reggie was the biggest name in baseball. He was the best player on the A's teams that won five consecutive division titles and three straight World Series during that decade. Then, after a year with the Orioles, he spent five years with the Yankees and helped them win two consecutive World Series.

Reggie was much more than just one of the best players of the decade. He was a phenomenon who captured so much of the vibe of the time. During the 1970s, which Tom Wolfe called the "Me Decade," no player embraced the egoism of the era more than Reggie. He was visible in the media, referred to himself as "the straw that stirs the drink" during his first spring training with the Yankees, became the face of free agency and the new

Photo 104961096 / Baseball © Jerry Coli | Dreamstime.com

money in baseball when he signed with the Yankees, used phrases like "the magnitude of me" unironically and even outrageously claimed that if they played in New York, they would name a candy bar after him-and they did. The Reggie Bar was released by the Curtiss Candy Company in 1978. Catfish Hunter, who won three World Series with Reggie in Oakland and two more with him in New York, quipped that "When you unwrap a Reggie Bar, it tells you how good it is."

Two of the best, most controversial and newsworthy teams in baseball history were the A's in the early 1970s and the Yankees in the second half of the decade. Both were led by owners, Charlie O. Finley and George Steinbrenner, who were impatient and mercurial with their players, and cycled through managers. Players on both teams frequently, and publicly, fought with each other. Both were also very good, combining to win five World Series between 1972-1978. Reggie, along with Catfish was on all five of those World Series winning teams.

Reggie was selected by the A's with the second overall pick in the second ever amateur draft. The Mets had the first pick on the draft but opted for a high school catcher named Steve Chilcott. It has been widely reported that the Mets soured on Jackson, who is African American, because his girlfriend was white. (For what it's worth, she was Mexican-American.) By 1968, Reggie was in the A's starting lineup and he stayed there through 1975. During those eight years he slashed .268/.362/.509 for an OPS+ of 152 with 253 home runs.

The young Jackson could do almost everything on a ballfield. He had a great arm. As a former college running back, he was fast enough to play right field well and even play center field with some frequency. Jackson drew a lot of walks and averaged 18 stolen bases a year with the A's, but the biggest part of Jackson's game was the home run.

In 1969, Reggie had 37 homers at the All-Star break and was briefly threatening Roger Maris's single season record. Over the course of his career, Reggie hit 25 or more home runs in a season fifteen times. When he retired his 563 home runs were the seventh most in big league history. His 2,597 strikeouts are still the most ever. Reggie hit massive home runs, but watching Reggie strikeout and twist himself into a pretzel in the process was always entertaining too.

Reggie's three most famous home runs came in the final game of the 1977 World Series. That was Jackson's first year with the Yankees. The team had squabbled all year. Yankees manager Billy Martin, Steinbrenner and Jackson had been in a three-way feud that had generated nonstop media attention, but in the final game of the season, Reggie hit three long home runs on three successive swings of the bat bringing the Yankees their first championship since 1962. That was the night he earned one of baseball's great nicknames, Mr. October.

The following year, the controversy and fighting on the Yankees got even worse and the team seemed to fall out of contention, but they battled from a 14 game deficit and forced the Red Sox into a one game playoff for the AL East crown back before there were wild cards. That game was one of the most famous in baseball history. The highlight was a three-run home run by a light hitting Yankees shortstop named Bucky Dent. The final score of that game was 5-4 with the last Yankees run coming on a home run by Reggie in the top of the 8th.

Reggie was not the first free agent, but after the 1976 season, when free agency had arrived in earnest, he was the biggest name in that first free agent class. He signed a five-year deal with the Yankees for over three million dollars, and when that contract expired Reggie signed an even more lucrative five-year contract with the Angels. The 1970s was when the narrative of ungrateful athletes who only thought about money began to take hold. Reggie was the player to whom the media pointed most when seeking to make this point. The racial politics of that were evident, as Jackson was a smart and outspoken African American man who was not inclined to sit quietly in the face of criticism.

During and after his playing career, Jackson wrote three memoirs all of which were called either *Reggie* or *Reggie Jackson* followed by a subtitle. The stories of Jackson's ego were not fabricated, but he was also a wonderful player who knew how to work with the media and was baseball's biggest star for a decade.

Forty-four
Derek Jeter

Derek Jeter was the most famous player on the most famous team in baseball for about twenty years. During that time, he led the Yankees to five World Series championships and eventually fell one vote short of unanimous election to the Hall of Fame. Because he played in New York, Jeter was an extremely visible player and a face of the game type for much of his career. He was seen as a bit of a throwback to another era. He did not use PEDs, referred to his manager as Mr. Torre and was way too media savvy to ever say much to the media other than platitudes about winning.

Photo 109746695 / Baseball © Sports Images | Dreamstime.com

Jeter was also a fascinatingly polarizing player. The New York media, and a big segment of the national media loved him. He was portrayed as baseball's golden boy-respectful, hard-working, a team player and an elite talent. Jeter was the kind of player older fans and older reporters loved. Off the field, the worst thing that people said about Jeter was that he canoodled with too many models, starlets and other women. On the field, he did the kinds of things that old school baseball people like. He got a lot of hits—the sixth most ever—eight seasons with 200 or more, regularly hit over .300 and played every day. Jeter also had a way of coming up with big plays at big moments. For example, the 2001 flip play in the ALDS remains one of the most famous defensive plays of the century.

The other side of Jeter's image was that for some fans the worshipful media coverage of Jeter engendered resentment and the view that Jeter was overrated. His defense was the focal point of this as his four Gold Gloves told a very different story than advanced metrics. According to the latter, Jeter was, beyond not being a Gold Glover, an historically bad defender, costing his team 185 more runs than the average defensive shortstop over the course of his career.

By the time Jeter's star was rising, around the turn of the century, and he was supplanting Ken Griffey Jr. as the face of the game, it seemed as if it was no longer popular for baseball fans, let alone the culture more broadly, to feel so positively about one player. Dodgers fans never loved Willie Mays, for example, but other than that he was broadly beloved and respected in baseball and, outside of the most racist corners, the US generally. That was never the case with Jeter. The merchandise branded with his number 2 and the word "respect" seemed, and was, over the top and a bit forced by MLB. The comedian Will Farrell satirized this in a video clip that went somewhat viral during Jeter's last season. By the time Jeter was in his last season he was being called, by a small minority of fans, writers and teammates, the greatest Yankees player ever, the greatest shortstop ever and even the greatest player ever. None of those assertions were true; and all reflected the cloyingly positive media that followed Jeter, and annoyed so many fans. Although the attention Jeter got from fans and the media was never simple or all positive, he was a larger-than-life figure in a way that is increasingly unusual in 21st century baseball.

Ironically, although many who believed in advanced metrics were generally among Jeter's critics, his numbers are also the kind that should resonate with people who have a sophisticated understanding of baseball data. Jeter was never, other than in the minds of the most loyal Yankees fans, a slick fielding defensive whiz. Nor was he ever a true power hitter, but Jeter had a skill set that was unusual and very valuable. He played a demanding position at an average or slightly below average defensive level for many years while getting on base all the time.

The two greatest shortstops ever were Honus Wagner and Cal Ripken Jr., but after that it is complicated because so few shortstops have long careers at that position. Alex Rodriguez, Robin Yount, and Ernie Banks were, at their best, better all-around shortstops than Jeter, but they all moved off the position in mid-career. Jeter played more games at the position, 2,674, than all but one other shortstop. Among the 19 players with 2,000 or more games at shortstop, only Barry Larkin, by one point, had a higher OPS+ and only Luke Appling had a higher on base percentage. Jeter was never truly a power hitter, but of those 19 shortstops only Larkin and Ripken had a higher slugging percentage. There is value in longevity and consistency and Jeter provided that to the Yankees for almost two decades.

Jeter spent his entire career with the Yankees, baseball's most successful, visible, storied and controversial franchise. He was not the greatest Yankee ever-Babe Ruth was, but nobody ever played more games for the Yankees. No team pays more attention to its history than the Yankees. Jeter became an important part of that history joining Lou Gehrig, Joe DiMaggio, Mickey Mantle, Whitey Ford and followed by his teammate Mariano Rivera as Yankees Hall of Famers who spent their entire career with just that one franchise. Jeter was alternately, one of the greatest players ever, beloved by some, hated and resented by many, the divisive face of an increasingly divisive sport and the best and most famous Yankee since Mickey Mantle.

Forty-five
Tommy John

Tommy John has not thrown a pitch in a big league game in well over thirty years, does not coach or manage and has almost no public profile, but his name might appear in print, and in other media more than any other retired pitcher. The reason for that is because when John was 31 years old, having an excellent year for the Dodgers and already in his 12th big league season, he badly injured his arm, tearing his ulnar collateral ligament (UCL). It was not clear if he would ever be able to pitch again.

Photo courtesy of the National Baseball Hall of Fame and Museum (John Tommy AL76-798_HS_NBLMcWilliams)

John agreed to undergo an experimental surgical procedure that would essentially use a tendon from another part of his body to replace the torn ligament. This was a very unusual experimental surgery that had never been done before, but Dr. Frank Jobe, the surgeon and inventor of this groundbreaking procedure, believed that while the surgery was risky, it was the only way John would have a chance to pitch again. John missed the second half of the 1974 season and spent 1975 rehabilitating his arm, but by 1976 was back in the Dodgers' rotation, starting 31 games and going 10-10 with a 3.09 ERA. Over the next two years, he was one of the top starting pitchers on pennant winning Dodgers teams.

Since John's comeback, UCL surgery, known throughout

baseball as Tommy John surgery, has changed the game. An injury that had ended numerous careers even before many pitchers made it to the big leagues could now be treated through a reliable, although arduous, surgery and recovery. However, this also meant that young pitchers were no longer as afraid of arm injuries. By the 21st century it was not at all unheard of for college and even high school pitchers to have Tommy John surgery. In some respects, it almost feels like a rite of passage for young pitchers, or a rite of spring, when we learn which pitchers will be out for 18 months or so, sometimes for the second time, because they need Tommy John surgery.

The prevalence and relatively easy availability of Tommy John surgery has contributed to the larger trend in baseball of pitchers pushing themselves, and being pushed by coaches and managers, to throw as hard as possible knowing that UCL injuries can now be repaired. This, in turn, has helped bring about today's game with high strikeout totals and frequent pitcher injuries. It has also contributed to a sense, among fans and teams, that pitchers are somewhat interchangeable. Some might have several good years and then fall into a cycle of arm injury, surgery and rehab that does not always land them back in the big leagues. Over the last sixty years, first complete games virtually disappeared and now starters going even seven innings, which pitchers managed to do on average 22.7 times on every team in 2022, compared to 74.7 times per team in 1982, is rare. There are many causes of this, but one of them is the throw as hard as you can until you drop approach that was, in part, facilitated by the possibility of Tommy John surgery.

I have encountered younger fans and players who were surprised to learn that Tommy John had been a real pitcher, but he was, and a very good one at that. John was very comparable to, but according to every conventional and advanced metric, better than recently elected Hall of Famer Jim Kaat. Both were lefties whose careers largely overlapped and who pitched for a very long time. John won 288 games and pitched 4,710.1 innings with an ERA+ of 111 and a career total of 62.1 WAR. Kaat's numbers were slightly less than John's in all those categories except for

WAR where he trailed John by 17. John was a sinkerball specialist who got a lot of ground ball outs and was never a big strikeout pitcher, but because he rarely walked batters or gave up home runs, he was very effective. John was also a good big game pitcher going 6-3 with a 2.65 ERA in the post-season.

John had an extremely long career, lasting 26 years in the big leagues. Tommy John started pitching a few years before I was born and threw his last big league pitch a few weeks before I graduated from college. He pitched his first game for Cleveland when John F. Kennedy was in the White House. The Cuban Missile Crisis had occurred only six months earlier. John's last game, when he was 46-years-old, occurred when George H.W. Bush was the president and only about six months before the fall of the Berlin wall.

The length of John's career helped highlight the success of Tommy John surgery generally, suggesting that the process not only repaired arms, but made them stronger. John pitched 2,544.2 innings and won 164 games after the surgery. Similarly, his best seasons, with the Dodgers from 1976-1978 and with the Yankees in 1979 and 1980 all occurred after Dr. Jobe replaced his UCL.

At 31-years-old, Tommy John was not looking to forever change baseball and sports medicine, nor did many people think he would still be pitching in the big leagues almost fifteen years later, but through the surgery that now, informally at least, bears his name, that is what happened. His omission from the Hall of Fame seems increasingly strange, particularly as clearly inferior pitchers of his era, like Kaat and Jack Morris, have been favored by the Veterans Committee in recent years. Maybe they also forgot Tommy John was real pitcher.

Forty-six
Walter Johnson

There is something magical about a great fastball pitcher who reduces the game to its most primal battle between pitcher and batter. The names of the truly great fastball pitchers, those who were successful for years relying on heat, are a special group of pitchers. People such as Lefty Grove, Bob Feller, Bob Gibson, Nolan Ryan, and Randy Johnson constitute an honor roll among pitchers. Walter Johnson was the first of this American archetype to be widely recognized and successful at the highest levels in the modern game.

Throwing sidearm and in a manner that appeared almost effortless, Johnson was the hardest throwing pitcher of his generation. He spent his entire career, from 1907-1927 with the Washington Senators and was by far the best and most famous player that franchise ever had.

Johnson may be the greatest pitcher in the history of the

American or National League, particularly since the beginning of the 20th century. His 417 wins, 110 shutouts, 5,914.1 innings pitched, 531 complete games and 165.1 WAR are much more than any other pitcher since 1900. He is currently ninth on the career strikeout list, but when he retired, he was first. Johnson kept that record for well over fifty years. Johnson led the America League in strikeouts 12 times and was elected to the Hall of Fame as part of its inaugural class in 1936.

Because he played so long ago, there is not a lot of film of Johnson pitching. The film that is available shows his odd side-arm motion and suggests that he threw hard for his era, but not by today's standards. Older players, as well as fans and writers of a certain age, have always held the view that ballplayers from twenty or more years go were better than today. However, all the evidence suggests the opposite is true—and if you don't believe that, go online and look up some video not just of Walter Johnson pitching, but of any player from more than 60, or even 40, years ago.

Walter Johnson is a baseball legend of the highest order. He was a fastball pitcher who threw so hard that nobody could hit him and, according to the mythos around him was such a nice man that he never threw at opposing hitter. Decades later, the same thing would be said about Sandy Koufax. As the years passed, Johnson's legend faded, but only somewhat. His wins and complete game totals seemed from another era altogether while his strikeout totals were eclipsed by modern players. However, he was never entirely forgotten. Bob Dylan may have written a song about Catfish Hunter when he was at the height of his fame, but in one of the stranger links between popular culture and baseball, the quirky proto-punk, singer Jonathan Richman wrote a song about Johnson almost forty years after he died.

Johnson's career provides a fascinating perspective and raises several questions about the historiography of baseball and the challenge of comparing players across eras. The numbers substantiate that no pitcher ever dominated the game quite like Johnson, who led his league-not just among pitchers-in WAR seven times and is second only to Babe Ruth in that career category.

The substantial increase in athleticism, particularly in the last 25 years or so, has changed baseball. It is essential to recognize that when we are tempted to become kvetchy about modern players. Players don't bunt well anymore because the average fastball is much faster than a generation or more ago. Similarly, hitting against the shift, and place hitting in general, is much more difficult against faster pitching. From the pitching perspective, it is more difficult to throw a complete game when lineups have hitters from top to bottom, batters are much stronger, bats lighter and video equipment allows hitters to study pitchers much more effectively.

None of this is to suggest that Walter Johnson was not a great pitcher. One indication of this is that Johnson played well into the live ball era, finally retiring at age 39 after the 1927 season. During the 1920s, Johnson was 120-88 with a 119 ERA+ and led the American League in strikeouts three times, including in 1924 when was the league MVP. Understanding baseball history requires wrestling with the complexity of a pitching career like Johnson's which was both absolutely dominant and the product of a different baseball world.

Forty-seven
Dorothy Kamanshek

A few years ago, I took a trip to San Diego to visit an old friend. Before I left, my friend told me he and his middle school aged daughter were beginning to play baseball together and I should bring my glove, so I did. At one point during my visit, the three of us went out to play ball at a nearby park. My friend's daughter was having trouble catching the ball. I could see that the problem was that her glove was not broken in, but my friend could not switch gloves with her because he was a righty and she, like Dorothy Kamanshek, was a lefty. Fortunately, I am left-handed too, so I lent her my well used glove. Immediately, she was able to catch the ball. After a few throws back and forth with her father, the girl yelled out "baseball is fun." My friend and I laughed and agreed.

Public Domain Photo

Baseball is indeed fun. It is also a sport and a pastime where sexism is very deep and very institutionalized. There are no professional or college baseball leagues and girls are usually pushed out of youth baseball at a very young age. However, this was not always true. In the middle of the last century, World War II changed pretty much everything in America, including baseball. With many big league players serving in the military and many men who should not have been playing at that level filling up big league rosters, the quality of play in the American and National Leagues waned. At the same time, the large number of men in the military meant that women were being asked, and had the opportunity, to do things they had never done before.

One of those things was to participate in an women's professional baseball league. The All American Girls Professional Baseball League (AAGPBL) lasted from 1943-1954. Over the course of the AAGPBL's history, Dorothy Kamanshek was one of the best players. Kamanshek joined the league in its inaugural season and played until 1953, spending her entire career with the Rockford Peaches. Kamanshek, and the Rockford Peaches are probably best known today from the 1992 film *A League of Their Own* in which Geena Davis played Kamanshek.

Kamanshek played first base where she was said to be an excellent defender. It is difficult to interpret AAGPBL statistics because the league was generally low scoring and not a lot of home runs were hit. For example, Eleanor Callow was the all-time league leader in home runs with only 55. Kamanshek was not a power hitter, slugging only thirteen home runs in 4,251 plate appearances. However, her .292 career batting average was the fourth highest ever in the AAGPBL and her .378 on base percentage was also very high for that league. Kamanshek was the all-time AAGPBL hit leader with 1,090 and made the All-Star team six times. That number might have been higher, but the AAGPBL did not have an All-Star team until the 1946 season.

Like the Negro Leagues, the AAGPBL was not a parallel league that was just like the men's leagues but with women players. There was an element of entertainment to the AAGPBL that focused on the novelty, to many, of women playing baseball and was also a product of its time. The teams not only had managers and coaches, but chaperones as well. The women were expected to abide by a code of conduct and had to attend the league's charm school course. The dimensions of the diamond changed over the course of the league's history but was never quite as big as men's baseball diamonds. Additionally, overhand pitching was not allowed in the AAGPBL until 1948.

Some might say that means that the AAGPBL was not really baseball, but it is more accurate to describe it as a different kind of baseball. Baseball evolved over many years and continues to evolve today. To Cap Anson, Charlie Radbourne or Willie Keeler baseball today might not seem like baseball, just as many fans today would not consider the 19th century game at which those men starred to be real baseball. Baseball can take many forms and can benefit from innovation and experimentation. The AAGPBL was part of that. When it ended, something was lost in the baseball universe both because women lost an opportunity to play professionally and because fans no longer could watch a different kind of baseball, one less dependent on home runs and where the smaller diamond made for a differently paced game.

Kamanshek did not play professionally after the league folded in 1954. Instead, she worked for the County of Los Angeles for many years. The question of whether Kamanshek, perhaps the best player in the AAGPBL, could have played in the big leagues, is a good one, but my sense is that the answer is no. This is not to say that no woman could have then or now, but Kamanshek's skill set would not translate into the American or National League. As a first baseperson with no power, she would not have found much opportunity in men's baseball of the time. Because she was left-handed, she would not have been able to move to another position other than to the outfield. But that question misses the bigger point because the AAGPBL demonstrated seventy years ago that there was a market for women's baseball. Kamanshek was the best player in a competitive and successful, for a while, league.

Forty-eight
Sandy Koufax

On October 6, 1965, Sandy Koufax made life easier for every Jewish American who has ever had to explain to a teacher, boss, or colleague why they were not coming in to work or school on a High Holiday. That year Koufax's Dodgers were scheduled to open the World Series in Minnesota against the Twins on Yom Kippur. They wanted to give the ball to their ace, but Koufax declined to pitch that day, and by doing that showed what Jewish religious observance meant to a country that still, for the most part, knew little about it. Koufax's decision took on even larger significance because he was not a religious Jew. The media spent that day visiting synagogues in the Twin Cities trying to catch a glimpse of the great pitcher, but they never did. Koufax spent the day in his hotel room, but he made his point.

Public Domain. University of Southern California Libraries and California Historical Society

154

In 1965, Koufax wasn't just the Dodgers' ace. He was the best pitcher on the planet coming off a season where he had gone 26-8 with a 2.04 ERA and leading the league in wins, winning percentage, ERA, complete games, and innings pitched, while setting a single season record with 382 strikeouts. Koufax received all twenty first place votes in the Cy Young balloting and finished second to Willie Mays in the MVP voting.

Because Koufax could not start game one of that World Series, Dodgers manager Walter Alston gave the ball to Don Drysdale, the Dodgers' other ace who was also one of the best pitchers in the game. However, the big righty did not have it that day. Drysdale gave up seven runs and did not make it out of the third inning. After he was taken out of the game , Drysdale told Alston, "bet you wish I was Jewish today too."

Koufax was, along with Hank Greenberg, one of the two greatest Jewish players ever. Unlike Greenberg, who also never played on Yom Kippur, Koufax played his entire career in cities with huge Jewish populations—New York and Los Angeles— and he did it in a different media era, so his position in Jewish American history is even greater than Greenberg's. Koufax is not just a Jewish sports star, but a Jewish American hero.

In 1965, Koufax was at the top of his game, but he did not have a very long peak. Although he had an enormous amount of talent, it took him several years to find his groove as a pitcher and he retired due to arm troubles at age 30. However, from 1961-1966 he averaged 22 wins and 286 strikeouts with an ERA+ of 156. For those six years, he was the best pitcher in baseball and, other than Mickey Mantle and Willie Mays, the most famous player in America.

Koufax was born and raised in Brooklyn and after briefly attending the University of Cincinnati, where basketball was his main sport, he signed with the Dodgers. Because of baseball's rules around players who signed large bonuses, known as bonus babies, Koufax went directly to the big league club in 1955, the year the Dodgers won their only World Series in Brooklyn. During that championship, Koufax pitched remarkably well for a 19-year-old going 2-2 with a 136 ERA+ with two shutouts.

Koufax stayed on the big league team for the rest of the decade pitching well, but never entirely consistently. In the early 1960s something clicked for the lefty and he became a different, and much better, pitcher.

If you watch old videos of Koufax pitching now, it is not hard to see why he was such a great pitcher. Koufax's delivery was extremely graceful with a long stride. His arm came fully over the top of his body. However, averaging 22 complete games and almost three hundred innings per season from 1963-1966 ultimately destroyed his arm.

Koufax and Drysdale were teammates from 1956 until Koufax retired, due to his arm injuries, following the 1966 season. Together, they led the Dodgers to three pennants and two World Series championships between 1963 and 1966. It was not unusual for them to start about half of the Dodgers regular season and World Series games. They were the two best, and most famous, players on one of the best teams in baseball. And in spring training of 1966, together they did something that helped change and modernize big league baseball.

We generally think of Koufax as a great player and important figure in Jewish American history, but in 1966 he was also a pioneer for what was then baseball's embryonic labor movement. That spring Koufax and Drysdale held a joint holdout demanding a total of one million dollars over three years to be split evenly between the two pitchers. That was a lot of money in those years, but the two pitchers realized that they had more power negotiating together. The Dodgers might attack one in the media, but not both. Similarly, the Dodgers could not have been a competitive team if both players held out into the regular season. Ultimately, Koufax and Drysdale did not succeed in getting all they wanted, but both got big contracts and demonstrated the value of players working together to increase their salaries. That was the first successful case of players bargaining collectively for better wages and was an important first step towards the economic changes over the following decade that would remake the game.

Oh, and if you're wondering what happened in that 1965 World Series, Koufax still managed to start three games and pitch

24 innings. The Twins scored a total of one earned run off of him, but Koufax threw a complete game shutout in game seven and the Dodgers won the series.

Forty-nine
Tommy Lasorda

Tommy Lasorda had one of the least impressive playing careers of anybody in this book. His entire big league career consisted of only 58.1 innings pitched between 1954-1956. He lost four games without winning any and had a career ERA of 6.48. He also walked more batters than he struck out. A left-handed pitcher, Lasorda spent his career with the Brooklyn Dodgers and Kansas City Athletics. Lasorda's stint pitching for the Dodgers ended when he was sent down to the

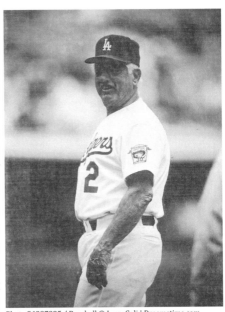

Photo 26387325 / Baseball © Jerry Coli | Dreamstime.com

minors in 1955 to make room for Sandy Koufax. After appearing in 18 games with Kansas City in 1956, Lasorda was back in the Dodgers system by 1960.

Lasorda is one of many players who had very limited success in their own playing careers, but went on to become very successful managers. Lasorda took over the helm of the Dodgers at the very end of the 1976 season and managed them through 1996. During those years they won their division seven times, the pennant four times and the World Series twice. Lasorda was Kirk Gibson's manager when he hit the home run off Dennis Eckersley in 1988 and was on the other side 11 years earlier when Reggie Jackson hit three home runs in the final game of the 1977 World

Series. Lasorda's success as a manager is apparent, but during the twenty years he managed the Dodgers he was never seen as a great strategist or innovator. Instead, Lasorda was a different kind of manager who understood the importance of media relations, keeping his players productive over the course of a long season and in building their confidence.

In Los Angeles, Lasorda was always more than just the manager of the Dodgers. He became one of the most famous managers in baseball history. He was the face of the Dodgers franchise who hobnobbed with Los Angeles celebrities, managed national teams for the USA and became a roving ambassador for the game in his later years. There is a long tradition of the manager as celebrity. Casey Stengel achieved that during his years with the Yankees. Billy Martin, often for all the wrong reasons, did so as well. John McGraw was probably the first manager to reach that status, but Lasorda may have perfected it.

Since he retired from managing the Dodgers, Lasorda, who died in 2021, has reached a new generation of fans through his colorful use of the English language while managing the Dodgers. Snippets of Lasorda answering a reporter's question about slugger Dave Kingman's performance against the Dodgers, a mound visit with pitcher Doug Rau during the 1977 World Series and various arguments with umpires have gone viral in some corners of the baseball world. These clips all show a furious Lasorda using profane language. He comes off as a vulgarian, but a lovable one.

Baseball is generally seen as a conservative institution, but it is not always altogether clear what is meant by that. Lasorda was not an angry raving right winger like Curt Schilling; nor was he a racist who believed non-white players should be excluded from the Major Leagues. However, Lasorda was a conservative man, like many others, who helped shape baseball into the conservative institution it is today.

The point here is not that Lasorda was a uniquely bad or right-wing figure in baseball. Rather, he was part of a majority at the level and management and ownership who went along with conservative ideas and policies. Because Lasorda was so high profile and mediagenic, he had opportunities that others did not, so not only did Lasorda campaign for an amendment banning desecrating the American flag, but he testified to Congress in support of that idea. While Lasorda was the only baseball celebrity manager to do that, he was hardly alone in his views on the subject.

Both the first Korean born big leaguer and the second Japanese big leaguer played for the Dodgers while Lasorda was the manager, but in 2018 he told a Dodgers fan from Korea "why don't you go back there." That may be one isolated incident, but excusing away racist statements is essentially a defining characteristic of conservative institutions.

The role Lasorda played in Glenn Burke's career is also an important part of the longtime Dodgers manager's legacy. In the late 1970s, it is unlikely that too many big league managers would have been welcoming of a gay player and Burke's trade away from the Dodgers was not the terrible baseball move that it is usually described as being. Nonetheless, Lasorda's intolerance for Burke was a big part of Burke's experience in Los Angeles. This was due both to Lasorda's own homophobia as well as to Lasorda's discomfort over Burke's friendship with his son, Tom Jr.

Like Burke, Tom Jr. was gay, but the senior Lasorda never accepted that and saw Burke as playing a role in Tom Jr. being or becoming gay. That is nonsensical homophobic thinking that may have been relatively common among men of Lasorda's generation, but it still does not excuse it. The late 1970s was a time when anti-gay prejudices were being rethought in many places, but not in the Dodgers clubhouse. Tom Jr. died of AIDS related complications in 1991, while his father continued to deny that he was gay. That is also the legacy of one of baseball's best, funniest, most charming, and most dedicated ambassadors.

Fifty
Dolf Luque

Dolf Luque is one of the most obscure players in this book, but he was a very good pitcher mostly for the Reds, but also for the Boston Braves, New York Giants and Brooklyn Dodgers. Luque was not quite a Hall of Fame caliber player, but his 194-179 record and career ERA+ of 118 are still excellent. In 1919 at age 28 Luque was the top reliever in a pennant winning Reds team and threw five scoreless innings against an ethically compromised White Sox team in the World Series that year. Fourteen years later, at age 42, Luque was one of the top relievers on

Library of Congress, Prints & Photographs Division [Bain News Service - LOC LC-DIG-ggbain-29193]

a pennant winning Giants team and threw 4.1 shutout innings against the Washington Senators in the 1933 World Series, helping his team win again. Luque's best season was 1923 when he went 27-8 with a 1.93 for the Reds, leading the league in wins, winning percentage, and WAR. His ERA+ was an extraordinary 201 that season. There was no Cy Young Award in those days, but if there had been, it is very likely Luque would have won it.

The history of Latinos in baseball is complicated because while there was discrimination against some Latinos, others were allowed to play in the National and American Leagues for much of the twentieth century. One way to see this is through the career of Luque who was born in Havana, Cuba and whose full name was Alolfo Domingo de Guzman Luque. Luque was a very good pitcher, but other Cuban pitchers with comparable ability were excluded from the white big leagues during the years Luque was pitching. While light skinned Cubans like Luque and others such as Rafael Almeida and Mike Gonzalez were allowed to pursue careers in the National League, their compatriots whose skin was darker were excluded until after 1947. Of the handful of light skinned Cuban players who made it to the American or National League during this period, Luque was by far the best and enjoyed by far the longest career. Players like Luque, Guzman and others were generally described as being Spanish, which suggested European origins. In some cases, teams seeking to employ light skinned Latino players had to demonstrate to the that the player in question was sufficiently white.

Over the course of the first half of the twentieth century while what was then understood as the big leagues were deeply segregated, other leagues, particularly in Mexico and the Caribbean, were not. In those Spanish speaking countries, Latinos, African Americans, and white players frequently played with and against each other. While racism exists everywhere, during those years it was codified into law and baseball regulations much more strictly in the US than in the rest of the region.

During his long career in the National League, for example, Luque played with and against only white players and for white managers. However, Luque had career in baseball that included playing and managing in Cuban winter leagues and in the Mexican League. In those settings, the teams were racially diverse.

Luque himself was a complicated figure. He was, on the one hand, one of the most successful managers in the history of the Cuban leagues who mentored many players. However, he was also widely disliked pretty much wherever he played or managed. Although he had a long career in the National League, his experience was not exactly free from bias or stereotype. Luque was viewed as hot-headed and temperamental because of his Cuban heritage rather than because of who he was as an individual. Like a great Dominican pitcher a few decades later, Luque's most remembered on the field moment was a violent one. In 1923, in the middle of his best season, Luque threw a ball in anger at Casey Stengel who was sitting on the New York Giants bench and yelling at Luque.

Luque was allowed to compete against white players in the US, but other Cuban greats from early in the twentieth century including Martin Dihigo and Luis Tiant Sr. played in the Negro Leagues. Even Orestes Minoso, known more widely as Minnie Minoso, began his career in the Negro Leagues before joining the Indians in 1949. In the 1950s several Afro-Latino Cubans including Minoso, Sandy Amoros, and Camilo Pasqual starred in the big leagues. Pasqual was coached by Luque early in his career so the chain of Cubans in baseball runs through him back to Luque. Cubans, including greats like Luis Tiant, Tony Perez, and Bert Campaneris continued to come to the big leagues through the early 1960s, but then that came to an end a few years after the Cuban Revolution. Only beginning in the 1990s was the flow of Cuban players into the major leagues resumed.

Luque's role in the history of Latinos in baseball is central. He was the first Latino player to have a significant career in the National League and still ranks among the greatest Latino pitchers ever.

Fifty-one
Mickey Mantle

Mickey Mantle was the golden boy of postwar baseball. He was the slugging centerfielder on the New York Yankees when the Yankees seemed to win the World Series every year. The switch hitting Mantle hit majestic home runs and, at the beginning of his career, ran as fast as any player in the big leagues. Mantle became the face of the most dominant team in the cultural, financial and baseball capital of the US at the height of the country's global hegemony. In those years, Mantle

Photo courtesy of the National Baseball Hall of Fame and Museum (Mantle Mickey 630.96_HS_NBL)

was not just the face of the game, but in some respects was the face of America. He was a country boy, lost in the big city, but getting by on his good looks and his extraordinary talent. That is not a bad metaphor for the US during much of Mantle's career.

Mantle was one of the first great stars of the post-war era and therefore long been beloved by the baby boomer generation. He began his career in 1951 when the oldest boomers were just becoming aware of baseball, and because he played on the Yankees, was extremely visible throughout the 1950s and into the 1960s. He was better looking and more telegenic than Yogi Berra, the Yankees, other big star of that era. Unlike Berra, Mantle was a white Protestant from the rural heartland, so more marketable nationally in those years than Berra, who was Italian American and Catholic. Mantle aged alongside the boomers ending his career in 1968 just as the oldest boomers were finishing college and the younger ones were in high school.

Paul Simon was nine-year-old, and a big Yankees fan, when Mantle played his first big league game. When Simon wanted to think of a symbol for an America that had somehow lost its way in the 1960s he came up with the line "where have you gone Mickey Mantle," but changed it to "where have you gone Joe DiMaggio" because the rhythm worked better. Mantle was the boomers' guy; DiMaggio was their father's generation.

In recent decades, Mickey Mantle has become remembered less for his play and more for his excessive drinking, difficult personal life and supposed inability to contribute to the team in the last years of his career. There is some truth to all of that, particularly the first two points. Mantle struggled with alcoholism throughout his adult life. While he was playing it was either covered up by the media or treated like some charming boyish excess, but it was neither. Mantle's dependency on alcohol shortened his career, wrought havoc on his personal life and ultimately probably cost him his life. The consensus memory that Mantle was not a very good older player is less accurate because Mantle's final years coincided with a lesser offense rich environment. During his last season, 1968, Mantle's OPS+ was 143 and over his last three seasons it was 153, so he was still among the best hitters in the league and not exactly washed up when he retired at age 36. However, many still look at the .245 and .237 batting average those last two years, as his career batting average fell below .300, and don't see the power, walks or offensive environment of those two years.

This is unfortunate because Mantle was, in fact, one of the greatest players ever. His 110.2 career WAR is the 21st highest in history, which is particularly impressive given that he retired so young. Throughout his career Mantle was compared to Willie Mays as they were both centerfielders born within a few months of each other. Both started their careers in New York in 1951. Willie Mays was the better player in large part because of his superior defense, base running and durability, but Mantle was probably the better hitter. Mantle's career OPS+ of 172 is 10th highest ever and 17 points higher than Mays's. Mantle could hit for average, had power and a great batting eye. He led his league in walks five times which contributed to his remarkable on base percentage of .421. Mantle won the triple crown in 1956 and then came back and had an even better year in 1957, capturing the Most Valuable Player award in both seasons. Eight times during his career Mantle led his league in OPS+. Even in 1967 and 1968 when he was supposedly washed up, Mantle was 7th and 8th respectively in the American League in that category.

There is another side of the Mantle story that fits into the larger context of baseball in America. As many fans know, from a very young age Mantle was pushed and driven to succeed by an intense baseball obsessed father. Mantle's father, who went by Mutt, named his son Mickey after Athletics and Tigers catcher Mickey Cochrane. Mutt taught Mickey how to play, forced him to become a switch hitter, and made him practice until, and sometimes past, the point of exhaustion. When Mantle was discouraged with his play after being sent to the minors, Mutt told him he was a quitter and should go back to the coal mines. Mutt lived long enough to see Mickey make it to the big leagues but died early in the 1952 season.

It is true that Mickey Mantle would have probably not made it without his father, but it is also true that the emotional and family troubles Mickey faced in his life probably had their origins in his relationship with a father who pushed him too hard. Donald Hall wrote baseball is "fathers playing catch with sons." That is true, but baseball is also father's pushing sons in ways that may cross over into verbal and psychological abuse. Mantle was one of those sons, but you can still see that dynamic on too many youth ballfields today.

Fifty-two
Juan Marichal

Juan Marichal was the first great Dominican player in the National League and the first Dominican elected to the Hall of Fame. Marichal was a right-handed pitcher who spent most of his career with the San Francisco Giants. The Giants were the first team to scout the Dominican Republic extensively, signing many very good players from that country, including all three Alou brothers, Manny Mota, and several others during the late 1950s and early 1960s.  © S. F. Giants

Marichal was the best of those players.

Marichal's best years were in the 1960s. Nobody won more games than Marichal's 191 during that ten year period. Bob Gibson was second with 164. Similarly, no pitcher had more WAR than Marichal's 55.3, but during that entire decade Marichal did not get a single vote for the Cy Young Award. Marichal was overshadowed by Sandy Koufax, Bob Gibson, and Don Drysdale who combined for six Cy Young awards. The accomplishments of those pitchers, at the expense of Marichal, was particularly impressive as until 1967, there was only one Cy Young Award for all of MLB. Marichal was different from those hard throwers. He mixed different speeds, pitches, and deliveries, often, but not always, featuring his trademark high leg kick.

Since retiring after during the 1975 season, Marichal has been eclipsed by Pedro Martinez for the title of greatest Dominican pitcher ever, and by Albert Pujols as the greatest Dominican player ever. Nonetheless, Marichal remained a hugely important figure in the Dominican Republic after his retirement, serving as Minister of Sports and Culture from 1996-2000.

There are few truly great players who are remembered primarily for one or two regular season games, but Marichal is an exception. Marichal was of the last generation of big league pitchers who were expected to start what they finished. He threw 244 complete games in his career and twenty or more in a season five times, but on July 2, 1963 Marichal pitched almost two complete games. Marichal, 25-years-old at the time, and Warren Spahn, already 42-years-old and in his last great season, matched each other inning for inning through 15 scoreless frames. Marichal got through the top of the 16th. Finally, with one away in the bottom of the inning Willie Mays hit a solo home run to win the game for the Giants. That game was the subject of a book by Jim Kaplan and may have been the greatest pitching duel ever. It featured two Hall of Famers, one at the beginning of his career, the other at the tail end, shutting down two very strong lineups for almost sixteen full innings.

If that 1963 game was the greatest pitching duel ever, another game, this one about two years later was one of the most interesting, violent, and multi-layered in baseball history. On August 22nd, 1963, Marichal's Giants were half a game out of first place and hosting the league leading Dodgers at Candlestick Park. Both teams had their aces going that day-Koufax for the Dodgers and Marichal for the Giants. The game was also taking place at a time of high racial tension in the US, particularly in Los Angeles where widespread demonstrations in the African American neighborhood of Watts that had led to an uprising, police brutality, violence, arrests, deaths, and the loss of millions of dollars of property, had just wound down. Many African American Dodgers stars, most notably catcher John Roseboro, had gone to Watts to try to reduce tensions. Meanwhile, the Dominican Republic was in the midst of violent political upheaval of its own that came to be known as the April Revolution.

This was a game between two intense rivals occurring against the backdrop of both a very close pennant race and political tensions in two places that were of significant importance to many of the players. Emotions were high before the game began. These political issues would have been irrelevant in baseball even twenty years earlier when only whites were allowed to play in the National League and no Dominican had ever played in that league.

The Dodgers were already angry at Marichal when he came to bat in the bottom of the third believing him to have deliberately thrown at their hitters on that day and in previous games. Sandy Koufax was known for not throwing at opposing hitters and refused to knock Marichal down. This always struck me as vaguely anti-Semitic, suggesting the Jewish guy was not a loyal teammate, and therefore building off other anti-Semitic tropes about Jews being disloyal. Koufax's teammates did not buy into this and believed their star lefty was a good teammate and intense competitor, but he would not throw at Marichal when he led off the bottom of the third. Dodgers star catcher John Roseboro took matters into his own hands throwing close to Marichal's ear, and according to Marichal, clipping his ear as he tossed the ball back to Koufax after the first few pitches.

Marichal responded in one of the worst acts of violence ever to occur on a big league ballfield and clobbered Roseboro over the head with the bat. Roseboro was badly bloodied and almost lost an eye. The ensuing brawl between the two teams only ended when Koufax and Willie Mays managed to calm matters down. Mays was particularly heroic, getting Roseboro off the field and probably saving him from permanent damage to his eye. Mays and Roseboro were on opposing teams, but as the best player and longest serving African American in the game, Mays was respected by Roseboro. The Giants went on to win the game but lost the pennant to the Dodgers by two games. The 1960s were a period of globalization and transition in baseball and that was reflected in this violent and dramatic incident.

Marichal had a very strong 1965 going 22-13 with a 169

ERA+ and remained an effective pitcher into the early 1970s. By 1974 Marichal's career was winding down. Playing for the Boston Red Sox he managed to go 5-1 but had an ERA of 4.87. He was released by Boston at the end of the year. Marichal was almost done as a big league pitcher, but managed to find a team that would take him and made two starts in 1975 for, of all teams, the Dodgers.

That 1965 fight defined Marichal to the media. He was never quite forgiven for it until Roseboro himself explained he had forgiven Marichal and the two men had become friends. By then Marichal had twice failed to get elected to the Hall of Fame, but Roseboro's words opened the doors at Cooperstown and Marichal got in on his next try. Marichal was never involved in another violent incident on or off the field and is widely viewed as both a very decent person and one of the greatest pitchers ever, but that one moment, unfortunately, continues to be how many people remember him.

Fifty-three
Pedro Martinez

It is a nice coincidence of the alphabet that Martinez follows Marichal in this book. While Marichal was the first great Dominican pitcher and the first Dominican Hall of Famer who famously never won a Cy Young Award, Martinez is the first Dominican pitcher to ever win the award. Martinez did not just win one Cy Young Award. He won three and came in second in the voting twice. Martinez viewed Marichal as a role model and a mentor and invited him on stage at the conclusion of his Hall of Fame induction speech in 2015.

Photo 139560034 / Baseball © Sports Images | Dreamstime.com

During the late 1990s and early 21st century when baseball was at the height of its steroid induced homer-mania, Pedro Martinez was almost unhittable, earning his place among the greatest pitchers ever. From 1997-2003, Martinez had 2.20 ERA with an almost unbelievable ERA+ 213 while striking out more than 11 batters per nine innings. His 86.1 career WAR is 15th among pitchers who played most or all of their career after 1900. No starting pitcher who played in the American or National League and is not active, and therefore likely to see their numbers decline, had a lower career ERA+ than Martinez's 154.

At a time when baseball was dominated by huge bloated

looking sluggers and offense was higher than it had been in decades, Martinez was an extraordinary outlier. He was just under six feet tall and weighed only 170 pounds. Unlike some other great pitchers of that time like Randy Johnson or Roger Clemens, Martinez was not the least bit physically intimidating, but for a few years he was completely dominant. Over the course of the 1999-2000 seasons, Martinez led all of baseball, not just pitchers, with 21.5 WAR. His win-loss record over those two seasons was 41-10, but his 1.90 ERA was better than it looked because that was such a high scoring time. That is reflected in his 265 ERA+ for those years. In the 1999 All Star Game, Martinez started for the American League and struck out the first four batters he saw and five of the six he faced in his two innings.

Martinez was more than just a great player. He has played a key role in the growing centrality of Latin Americans in the sport. Beginning in the 1990s, a second wave of Latino player, most visibly from the Dominican Republic, began to make their presence in MLB felt. Players like Albert Pujols, Mariano Rivera and Adrian Beltre are among the best players ever at their positions. Miguel Cabrera, Ivan Rodriguez, Vladimir Guerrero, father and son, and so many others have been high profile big league stars. Even in that group, Martinez has a special place.

Martinez was the most visible Latino star during those years both because of his excellent pitching, but also because of his good media skills. Those skills landed him a post-playing broadcasting career which has kept him visible during recent post-seasons. He was also aware of his place in baseball history and in particular, Dominican baseball history, as demonstrated by not only his relationship with Marichal, but also his pride in his Dominican heritage and his occasional use of Spanish on national English language broadcasts.

Martinez pitched for the Red Sox from 1998-2004 and had his best years there. Those years also coincided with a rejuvenation of the Red Sox rivalry with the Yankees. The two teams met in the ALCS in 1999, 2003 and 2004 with the Yankees winning the first two times and the Red Sox in 2004. The 2004 ALCS was the first time since 1948 that the Red Sox had bested the Yankees in a tough race for anything, although in that year the Red Sox lost a one game playoff and did not win the pennant.

Martinez pitched against the Yankees 32 times during a period when the Bronx Bombers always had a very strong offense. Martinez's numbers against the Yankees, 11-11 with a 3.20 ERA, were subpar, for him. Martinez's frustration with this came through late in the 2004 season when after a poor start against his teams' rivals he commented "what can I say just tip my hat and call the Yankees my daddy." Martinez relationship with the Yankees was not always so light-hearted. During game three of the 2003 ALCS, which the Yankees ended up winning in the eleventh inning of the seventh game, a fight broke out. Martinez, in a pique of anger, threw Yankees coach Don Zimmer, who was 72-years-old to the ground. It was not the great pitcher's finest moment, but fortunately he is remembered for much more than that.

The last time Martinez pitched in a big league game was for the Phillies in the 2009 World Series. With the Yankees leading Philadelphia three games to two, Martinez started game six. He made it through four innings, but was not sharp and gave up four runs. The Yankees won the game and the World Series. For Yankees fans winning the World Series by beating Martinez was particularly sweet because Martinez had been such a big part of the Yankees-Red Sox rivalry.

Pedro Martinez was one of the greatest Latin American players ever, a dominant and fun pitcher when baseball was becoming steroid and home run obsessed, and one of the faces of one of baseball's greatest rivalries.

Fifty-four
Christy Mathewson

This is the third consecutive great right-handed pitcher in this book and part of a series of important Giants that began with Marichal and will continue for a few more players. Christy Mathewson was one of the great pitchers of the early years of the twentieth century. He won thirty games four times and twenty games nine more times on his way to 373 career wins and an ERA+ of 136. His best season was 1908 when he went 37-11 with a 1.43 ERA while pitching 390.2 innings. Matty, as he was widely known, was a big

Library of Congress, Prints & Photographs Division [Bain News Service - LOC LC-DIG-ggbain-22415]

right-handed pitcher whose best pitch was called the fadeaway and would be understood today as something similar to a screwball. He was not renowned for his fastball the way contemporaries like Walter Johnson or Rube Waddell were, but Matty could bring the heat when needed. He had excellent control, averaging just under 1.6 walks per nine innings and seven times lead the league with the fewest walks per nine innings. His longtime catcher Roger Breshnahan once remarked you could "catch Matty in a rocking chair."

Mathewson was not quite the best player of his era. Ty Cobb, Honus Wagner, Joe Jackson, Walter Johnson, Cy Young and others were, at various times, better than Matty, but during this career, Matty seemed to be at the center of many big moments on the field. The 1905 World Series was the second World Series ever, but the previous one in 1903 had not generated any great memories or moments. The first great World Series performance was Matty's in 1905 when he struck out eighteen, walked only one batter and gave up 13 hits while pitching three complete game shutouts. A few years later, Matty was on the mound, and pitched nine innings, during the famous Fred Merkle game (more on that later) and also for the makeup game that decided the pennant on the final game of the season.

Other than Matty's great pitching performance in 1905, and the Hitless Wonder White Sox beating the Cubs, whose 116 regular season wins is still tied for the record, the first few World Series were not very memorable. Today there are many great World Series highlights. They include home runs by Kirk Gibson, Bill Mazeroski and Carlton Fisk, Dale Mitchell looking at strike three from Don Larsen in 1956, Willie Mays's catch or Reggie Jackson's three home runs in the final game of the 1977 World Series, but the first genuinely famous World Series moment was in 1912. Matty was on the mound when it happened.

In the eighth and deciding game of the World Series (game two had ended in a tie) Matty was pitching for the Giants. Always excellent in big games, the great righty limited the Red Sox to one run over nine innings. Unfortunately, the Giants could only get one run across as well. However, in the top of the tenth, the Giants scored to take a 2-1 lead. In the bottom of the tenth, pinch hitter Clyde Engle led off with a fly ball to center but the usually reliable Fred Snodgrass dropped it. Matty battled back, but could not get through the inning. The Red Sox won 3-2 and captured the championship.

Mathewson spent his entire career, other than one game with the Reds, with the New York Giants when they were baseball's marquee franchise, winning the pennant five times during Matty's 17 years with the team. During most of those years neither of New York's other two teams, the Dodgers or the Yankees, then known as the Highlanders, were very good. Before Jeter,

Seaver, Mantle, DiMaggio, and even Ruth, Matty was the original New York baseball legend-the most famous player on the city's most renowned team.

In those early years of the twentieth century, baseball was, in general, a violent game played by rough tempered people like Ty Cobb, ethically challenged players like Hal Chase or players like Rube Waddell whose drinking problem was seen as a source of humor. Matty was different. He was also one of the rare players of that era who had been to college, having attended Bucknell University. He was viewed as a gentleman who treated his team-mates, manager, the media and fans respectfully. Baseball greats have included widely disliked people like Cobb and Rogers Hornsby, lovable rogues such as Mantle or Ruth and players who are role models for young people including Stan Musial, Sandy Koufax, Jackie Robinson, and Roberto Clemente. Matty was the first star who was also a role model. His own awareness of this comes across clearly in his 1912 book *Pitching in a Pinch*. The book combines pitching advice with general guidance on conduct and behavior for boys.

In the early part of the twentieth century a player like Matty was widely admired because of his respectful and decent man-ner. The media was different then and few writers saw this as smarmy or self-righteous. A century later, Derek Jeter, who also was respectful and decent, without ever saying much, and per-haps a little too self-consciously saw himself as a role model, engendered a fair amount of resentment and rancor from some fans. Like Matty, Jeter was a great player, although not quite as great, and played for the most successful franchise in the game. Baseball's enduring popularity, and indeed importance, is due, in part to its ability to create mythic figures, folk heroes, and all role models. Christy Mathewson was all of those things.

Fifty-five
Willie Mays

Willie Mays is on the very short list of players who have crossed over into the status of icons and national treasures. He is also one of the two greatest players ever. Mays's only real competition for that title comes from Babe Ruth, but Ruth never had the opportunity to play against all the best players of his era. A good argument can be made for either player, but nobody ever played base-ball with as much grace, joy,

Library of Congress, Prints & Photographs Division [New York World Telegram & Sun - LOC LC-USZ62-112029]

panache, skill and *joie de vivre* as the Say Hey Kid.

No player in history could do so many things as well as Willie Mays. He was one of the game's great power hitters. His 660 career home runs were the third highest ever when he retired. Today he is sixth on the all-time list, but would have had at least 700 home runs, and possibly have passed Babe Ruth, had he not missed almost two years serving in the military. Mays had close to 3,300 career hits and a .302 batting average despite playing much of his career in the low offense era of the 1960s and playing in Candlestick Park, a terrible park for hitters for much of his ca-reer. He stole over 300 bases and led the National League in that category four times. Nobody ever played centerfield like Mays did. He won twelve consecutive Gold Gloves and would have won more but the award didn't exist until 1957, Mays's fifth full year in the National League. Advanced metrics also demonstrate

Mays's greatness. His 156.1 WAR is the fifth highest ever. In the post-World War II era, only Barry Bonds, bolstered by PED use, has more WAR.

Mays began his professional career with the Birmingham Black Barons in 1948 when he was only 17. He was among the first group of African Americans to make the transition to the American or National League, beginning his long career with the Giants in 1951. Like Mantle, Mays was a very young player when he made it to New York as a big leaguer. New York was a northern city, but racism was present there as well. Mays benefited from the mentorship of Monte Irvin and by being close to the Harlem community near the Polo Grounds. He also broke down barriers and endeared himself to fans, by playing ball on the streets and buying ice cream for young people in his adopted New York neighborhood.

Seven years later, when the Giants moved to San Francisco in 1958, Mays, by then one of the two best and most famous baseball players in the country, was unable to buy the house he wanted in an affluent neighborhood of supposedly liberal San Francisco. Mays outlived all his generation of great players so by the end of his life he was the last connection to the Negro Leagues and the early years of the integration of the formerly all white baseball leagues.

More than any other player, images are a major part of Willie Mays's legacy. Mays making a wonderful catch in the 1954 World Series, playing stickball on the streets of Northern Manhattan or his hat flying off as he runs the bases are part of our collective visual baseball memory. Baseball is rarely thought of as an aesthetic game in the way that basketball is, but it was when Willie Mays was playing.

Mays retired following the 1973 World Series, in which he appeared as a member of the New York Mets. The Giants had traded him back to the Mets midway through the 1972 season, giving Mays an opportunity to finish his career in New York. In the more than half century since then Mays has remained one of America's most famous and beloved people. Mays did not have a long career in baseball after retiring and was even briefly banned from baseball in 1980 by Commissioner Bowie Kuhn for taking a job shaking hands and playing golf with casino patrons. That foolish decision was overturned by Kuhn's successor Peter Ueberroth in 1985. Mays has remained connected to the Giants ever since, at first informally coaching some players, but in more recent decades by coming to the ballpark, attending spring training and just being a presence.

In 2015, Mays was awarded the Medal of Freedom by President Barack Obama. Earlier in Obama's presidency Mays had spoken to the President, eloquently and touchingly, about what it meant to him to see an African American president. Obama responded by telling Mays "you helped us get there." Mays also advised the basketball loving president to be sure to follow through when he threw out the first pitch of the All-Star Game.

The conversation between Mays and Obama on the way to the 2009 All-Star Game, 36 years after Mays retired, reflects not just Mays's greatness as a ballplayer, but the enduring gravity of his baseball career. He has become part of American history and legend not for anything he said or did off the field. In fact, little is known by most fans about Mays's private life or personality. Mays's legend is built almost entirely on his conduct and performance on the field.

Mays has received these accolades in his later years, but he wasn't always as broadly appreciated. In 1969, to celebrate what was supposedly the 100th anniversary of baseball, the baseball writers honored Joe DiMaggio as the greatest living ballplayer. DiMaggio insisted on being introduced with that title until he died thirty years later, but by 1969, Mays was clearly the better player. Mays never was paid on the scale of today's players and when he sought to make some money by working for a casino, he was banned from baseball, despite having played the game with honor and integrity throughout his long career.

Even in San Francisco, Mays was never entirely embraced until late in life. During his first few years with the team, he was occasionally even booed because the Giants didn't win enough, and he was seen as a New York guy. In 1959, during a period when Mays was being unappreciated by Giants fans, Soviet Premier

Nikita Khruschev made a long visit to the US that included a stop in San Francisco. There, labor leader Harry Bridges arranged for the Soviet leader to give a speech to members of Bridges' longshoreman's union. The speech was very well received prompting journalist Frank Coniff to quip "San Francisco is the damnedest city I ever saw in my life. They cheer Khrushchev and boo Willie Mays."

Mays grew up in the segregated deep south, captured the imagination of a country and was honored by an American president for that. Nobody has ever excelled on the ballfield like Willie Mays did while making baseball look so easy and so fun.

Fifty-six
Willie McCovey

It is somehow appropriate that Willie McCovey appears right after his longtime teammate Willie Mays because McCovey spent much of his career in the shadow of the better player with whom he shared a first name and home state. That is unfortunate because McCovey, nicknamed Stretch, was an awesome player in his own right. He  was a frighteningly powerful left-handed slugger who hit long home runs and drew walks in impressive numbers. Even today among National Leaguers only Barry Bonds has more home runs from the left side of the plate.

© S. F. Giants

In San Francisco, well into the 1990s, McCovey was more beloved than Willie Mays. McCovey had a special relationship with that city and with Giants fans there. Unlike Mays, he did not come with the team from New York, so San Franciscans were more quickly drawn to McCovey. Nobody has ever played more games for the San Francisco Giants than McCovey who joined the team in 1959, and other than a three-year period from 1974-1976, played with the Giants until 1980. When McCovey returned to the Giants in 1977, he gave a new generation of Giants fans, including me, who had been too young to have seen Willie Mays, an opportunity to bond with the enormously powerful slugger who had a very strong gentle giant vibe.

During McCovey's second stint with the Giants, San Francisco

Mayor George Moscone, who had been a Giants fan since the team came to San Francisco, described McCovey as being a San Francisco institution like the cable cars or the Golden Gate Bridge. That sounds like an exaggeration by a politician, but it rang true at the time. After all, McCovey hit his first home run for San Francisco, when the Giants were only in their second year in that city, Moscone was just out of law school and George Christopher was mayor. By the time Stretch hit his last home run for the Giants, Dianne Feinstein was mayor, and Moscone had fallen victim to an assassin's bullet. Between 1959 and 1980 a lot changed in San Francisco, but the graceful and powerful McCovey was a constant.

Baseball fans today may be most familiar with McCovey's name from McCovey Cove, the inlet of the San Francisco Bay behind right field at Oracle Park where long home runs sometimes land. That has also helped imprint his name and memory on Giants fans who never got the chance to see him play. It is appropriate that McCovey Cove is behind right field because McCovey was a left-handed pull hitter. For several years before the rules were changed in 2023, defenses shifted against even light-hitting infielders, but for years the shift was only used against the biggest sluggers and most pronounced pull hitters. It was something of a sign of respect. Stretch was one of the few players against whom teams frequently shifted. Once, while managing the Mets playing against McCovey's Giants, Casey Stengel asked his pitcher Roger Craig whether he should position the right-fielder in the upper or lower deck to defend against McCovey.

McCovey may be the only all-time great and first ballot Hall of Famer who was a part time player for most of his career. McCovey played all or part of 22 seasons, but only started in 130 or more games seven times. The presence on the Giants of Orlando Cepeda, who was also a young slugger who could only play first base, McCovey's struggles against left-handed pitching, and knee problems later in his career made it tough for McCovey to get enough playing time. However, he still managed 521 career home runs and an OPS+ of 147.

Despite all his great accomplishments and long home runs,

there is something a bit tragic about McCovey's career. He was overshadowed by Mays throughout his entire prime, played most of his home games at Candlestick Park and spent his prime, like Mays, in a low offense era. That is why, compared to players of the last thirty years, McCovey's numbers do not seem quite as impressive, but in the context of when he played, they are genuinely elite. For example, in 1968, the year of the pitcher, McCovey slashed .293/.378/.545 with 36 home runs. That is a good year but doesn't stand out in today's game. In the context of 1968 it was enough to lead the league in home runs and OPS+, an extraordinary 174, while having the second most WAR for non-pitchers. The next year, also a pitcher's year, McCovey was even better and led the league in home runs, RBIs, slugging, on base percentage and OPS+ while easily capturing the MVP award. Both of those years were, in the context of their time better years than many sluggers with gaudier numbers have had since then.

McCovey's place in baseball lore is also unusual because the most famous play of McCovey's career occurred when, with the tying run on third and the winning run on second and two outs in the bottom of the ninth of game seven of the 1962 World Series, McCovey hit a screaming line drive, but right at Yankees second baseman Bobby Richardson. Richardson caught it for the final out of the game and the World Series. A foot or two either way and McCovey would have been a World Series hero, but he just missed. Charles M. Schultz captured the feelings of Giants fans like himself in a Peanuts comic strip. The first three columns had a glum faced Charlie Brown, head in hands, sitting wordless next to his friend Linus. In the last panel, Charlie Brown blurts out "Why couldn't McCovey have hit the ball just three feet higher." A month or so later, Schultz published an almost identical strip with the word "three" changed to two."

Willie McCovey was one of the most feared sluggers in the game for over twenty years and came within a few inches of being a World Series hero. He retired more than 40 years ago, but in the city where he was beloved, he is remembered every time slugger hits an exceptionally long home run to right field that lands in McCovey cove.

Fifty-seven
John McGraw

John McGraw was a nineteenth century star for the Baltimore Orioles. The Orioles, then in the National League, were the best team in that nascent league during the 1890s. McGraw was their third baseman who excelled at the deadball style of play that defined the game then. McGraw, like most players in the 19th century, had almost no power. However, he was an excellent base stealer who had a career on-base-percentage of .466, still good enough for third highest ever after Ted Williams and Babe Ruth.

Library of Congress, Prints & Photographs Division [Bain News Service - LOC LC-DIG-ggbain-34093]

McGraw ended his playing career with the New York Giants where he was a part time player from 1902-1907.

McGraw was a very good player, but it was as manager that he helped shape baseball in the early years of the 20th century. McGraw began his managing career as a player-manager for the Orioles in 1899, 1901 and 1902, but midway through the 1902 season McGraw moved from the Baltimore Orioles to a pretty bad New York Giants team. The team had been 33 games under .500 in 1901 and was playing even worse than that when McGraw joined the team in July. Shortly after becoming a Giant, McGraw took over as manager, but they still lost more games than they won under his stewardship.

McGraw stayed in New York and would go on to create something of a dynasty there. He managed the Giants until the middle of the 1932 season. During that time the Giants would finish below .500 only three times. McGraw's Giants won the National League pennant ten times during that period and became the best and most well-known team in baseball. As a manager, McGraw was the most famous practitioner of what today would be called small ball. His teams bunted and hit and ran a lot, stole bases, made few mental errors, and pitched well. Until Mel Ott came along in the late 1920s, McGraw's teams never hit for much power. McGraw was the best manager of the deadball era and pioneered baseball strategies that were used for decades. For McGraw, baseball was a thinking game as much as a physical sport. In an era when the ball was harder to hit far or throw fast and when bats were heavier, that approach proved very fruitful for McGraw.

As both a player and a manager, McGraw was fiery, competitive, and often could be nasty. Many people around baseball did not like him, some feuded with him for years. As a player, McGraw had a reputation for playing dirty or, depending how you view it, doing anything to win. He was also an extremely smart baseball man for most of his tenure with the Giants and capable of teaching a great deal about the game to younger players. McGraw managed some very good players-there is no other way to win ten pennants. Among the players McGraw managed were Joe McGinnity, Mel Ott, Bill Terry, Roger Breshnahan, Travis Jackson, and Larry Doyle, but McGraw was almost always seen as the real star of the team.

There was one exception to this. The best player McGraw ever managed was Christy Mathewson. Matty was also the only Giants player who was legitimately a bigger star than manager McGraw. The two men came from very different backgrounds. Mathewson was a college man whose public persona was unblemished. McGraw was from a much more working class and hard-drinking background. McGraw was a New York celebrity who enjoyed the spotlight and the city's nightlife. The two even were also a physical contrast. McGraw was 5'7" while Mathewson stood 6'1". Despite their differences, the manager and pitcher got along well and seemed to respect each other's abilities. McGraw managed Matty for 15 years and the two friends both benefited from each other's good work.

McGraw is still third on the all-time wins list for managers with 2,763 and games managed with 4,769. He was second for years, but Tony LaRussa has recently passed him in both those categories. No manager ever won more pennants than McGraw, but Casey Stengel also won ten.

There is no doubt that McGraw was one of the greatest managers ever, but there are also some very revealing blemishes on his record. Although he won ten pennants, McGraw's teams won only three World Series while losing six. In 1904, the team won the National League pennant, but McGraw viewed the American League as not fit to challenge the National League and refused to play in the World Series. McGraw almost ended the institution of the World Series before it began. McGraw's poor World Series performance is difficult to explain because short series are always hard to predict, but it is also possible that McGraw was not good at adapting when his scientific, as it were, approach to baseball did not work in the World Series.

As the deadball era came to a close in the early 1920s, McGraw was still winning pennants. His Giants won the National League title four years in a row from 1921-24, but after that they were usually good, but not good enough to come in first. The reason for that was that McGraw who had mastered and helped create the dominant strategy of the previous two decades was unable to adapt to the longball. He disdained the home run, seeing it as the antithesis to the kind of baseball he preferred. Until Mel Ott, one of baseball's great sluggers and favorite of McGraw's, hit 42 home runs in 1929, none of McGraw's Giants his as many as 30. By the late 1920s, teams like the Cubs and the Cardinals had adapted more quickly to the new style of play and eclipsed the Giants as the best teams in the league. McGraw's failure in this regard also facilitated the ascendancy of the Yankees as the biggest team in New York and in all of baseball. That ascendancy was accelerated when McGraw kicked the Yankees out of the Polo Grounds, which they had shared with the Giants. This led to the Yankees building Yankee Stadium, a bigger and more beautiful ballpark than the Polo Grounds.

John McGraw built the first great New York baseball teams and was the best and most famous manager of baseball's early years. McGraw's impact on the game and its managers remains profound. In 2022, the Houston Astros, managed by Dusty Baker won the World Series. Baker had been a coach for Roger Craig who played for Casey Stengel who played for McGraw.

Fifty-eight
Fred Merkle

Before we turn to Fred Merkle, take a minute and think of the worst, most embarrassing mistake you ever made. Now imagine you did it in front of a large crowd when you were 19- years-old. That seems pretty bad, but now imagine for the rest of your life people still talked about it. Now it is getting even worse, what if you somehow knew that well over a century later, people who care a lot about your profession, at which you were extremely good, still mentioned your teenage foible. If you can do all that, you may be able to relate to Fred Merkle's story.

Public Domain Photo

Fred Merkle was a solid big leaguer who came to the plate 6,400 times and had a career OPS+ of 109. He appeared in five World Series and received MVP votes in two seasons. Had Giants centerfielder Fred Snodgrass fielded the ball cleanly in the bottom of the tenth inning of the final game of the 1912 World Series, Merkle would have driven in the run that sealed that championship for his Giants. Merkle's teammates over the course of a 16 season big league career included Christy Mathewson, Babe Ruth, Lou Gehrig, and Pete Alexander. Unfortunately, Merkle is not remembered for any of those accomplishments or for any of the other good things he did on the ballfield.

Rather Fred Merkle is remembered even today for something he did not do when he was just starting out in baseball. There are a very small handful of regular season games that are remembered and discussed for decades. The game between Merkle's Giants and the Chicago Cubs on September 23, 1908 was the first game of that kind. Even today, if you mention the Fred Merkle game, many fans will know it.

At the time the Cubs-Giants rivalry was the biggest in baseball. These were the two best teams in the National League; and they played in the country's two biggest cities. The two teams started that day tied for first place in the National League. The Cubs, led by the famous Joe Tinker, Johnny Evers, Frank Chance infield and their great pitcher Mordecai Brown, had won the pennant the two previous years and the Giants were trying to end that streak. The Giants pitcher that day was the great Christy Mathewson. The game was a pitching duel through eight and a half innings.

In the bottom of the ninth with the score tied at 1-1, the Giants put runners on the corners for shortstop Al Bridwell. Bridwell hit a walk-off single and the Giants seemed to have won the game, but then came one of the most famous moments in baseball history. In the excitement and confusion, Merkle, who was on first base, left the field before touching second base as fans rushed onto the field. Cubs second baseman Johnny Evers called for the ball, but never got it as the Giants fans kept it from him. The league eventually ruled that the run didn't count and the game would have to be replayed later. The Cubs won the replay and the pennant. By forgetting to touch second base Merkle cost the Giants the pennant and sealed his place in baseball history.

Like many of baseball's earliest moments, it is not entirely clear what happened that day. Crowds came on the field as soon as Bridwell's hit went through making it tough for Merkle to get to second base. It was also never known for certain what happened to the ball. Evers indeed called for and had a ball thrown to him, but it may have been a different baseball. Moreover, according to many accounts, not touching second base in that situation was not altogether uncommon at that time. We will probably never get answers to these questions, but that mystery contributes both to the mythology around baseball's early years as well as to one of baseball's enduring appeals. Fans can dissect a game from decades, or even a century ago. The final play of that Cubs-Giants game in 1908 is one of the first, and most enduring, examples of this question.

If you took a space alien to a hockey game on a Monday night, a soccer game on Tuesday and a basketball game on Wednesday, each time explaining the rules of the game, by the time you took the alien to the lacrosse game on Thursday, she would be able to understand the rules without any explanation. However, if you took her to a baseball game on Friday, she would be totally confused. Baseball is a game of complicated rules that have an internal logic, but a logic that is frequently impenetrable. Merkle's failure to touch second base, and Evers heads up play, is an example of how understanding rules can be so important.

Fred Merkle is often remembered for what is considered a stupid mistake, but judging him on that one play is unfairly evaluating a good player for his worst moment. None of us would want to be judged that way ourselves. However, Merkle's actions are also a reminder that in baseball, and in life, we should always touch all the bases.

Fifty-nine
Andy Messersmith

Andy Messersmith was the first real free agent who achieved that status not through a technicality, but by challenging the reserve clause and winning. A handful of players in the years leading up to Messersmith's free agency, including Curt Flood and Catfish Hunter, were instrumental in laying the groundwork for free agency, but Messersmith is frequently the forgotten man in that history.

Messersmith was a right-handed pitcher who

Photo courtesy of the National Baseball Hall of Fame and Museum (Messersmith Andy 2909-76_FL_NBL)

began his career with the Angels in 1968 and was traded to the Dodgers following the 1972 season. From 1968-1974, Messersmith was one of the best pitchers in baseball, along the way becoming the first pitcher to win twenty games and be an All-Star for both Los Angeles area teams. Through 1974, Messersmith had won 93 games, with an ERA+ of 123 and 23.9 WAR. Messersmith had one of his best years in 1974 when he finished second in the National League Cy Young voting. His 20-6 record and 2.59 ERA made him the ace of the pennant winning Dodgers pitching staff.

In 1974, Messersmith made $90,000, but after such a great year he believed he deserved a raise. When the Dodgers did not give him the raise he wanted, Messersmith decided to play that season without a contract. Messersmith's plan was to wait until after the season and then argue that he should be a free agent after a full year playing without a new contract. Another pitcher, Dave McNally, pursued a similar strategy, but McNally never played after 1975.

This strategy meant that Messersmith was making a big bet on himself in 1975, but in those pre-free agency years most players had to make that bet pretty much every season, because long term contracts were rare. Messersmith failed to win 20 games in 1975 as he had the previous season, but overall, at the age of 29, he had an even better year going 19-14 with seven shutouts a 2.29 ERA and 6.5 WAR. After the season, Messersmith, and McNally, who was in a similar situation with the Montreal Expos, took their cases to arbitration, arguing that teams only had the right to renew contracts unilaterally for one year. The arbiter, Peter Seitz, ruled for the players and the reserve clause was effectively finished.

The competition for Messersmith, just as it had been a year earlier for Catfish Hunter, was very intense and continued into April of 1976, but finally, after the season had already begun, Messersmith landed a contract with the Braves that would pay him one million dollars over three years. The era of free agency had begun. After Messersmith, it was no longer unusual for a player to be a free agent. For example, following the 1976 season Sal Bando, Bert Campaneris, Joe Rudi, Don Baylor, Bobby Grich and future Hall of Famers Willie McCovey, Reggie Jackson, and Rollie Fingers were all free agents. Every year since then free agency has been an integral part of the game and one of the most exciting parts of the winter hot stove league.

At the time he signed the contract, Messersmith, given the data used by most teams at the time, was a very elite pitcher. He was one of only ten pitchers who had won 100 games with an ERA under 3.00 between 1968-1975. However, he had also thrown almost 2,000 big league innings and like Hunter would encounter arm problems that would limit his days as an effective pitcher. Messersmith had a solid 1976 season, going 11-11 with a 3.04 ERA for a pretty dreadful Braves team. However, after that year he would go on to pitch fewer than 200 innings and win fewer than 10 games. After brief stints with the Yankees in 1978 and the Dodgers in 1979, Messersmith was out of baseball.

Messersmith's willingness to play the 1975 season without a contract and to challenge the reserve clause in arbitration put him unequivocally at the center of the story of free agency and baseball economics. The contract he finally signed with the Braves is also a reminder of how in the early years of free agency many teams didn't quite know what to do. The Braves, following the 1975 season, were in no position to contend for a few years. Even if Messersmith had been healthy and pitching at his best for the length of the contract, the Braves never would have even been a .500 team in any of the three years of his contract.

In those early days teams pursued free agents, if they had the money, with no clear strategy. It was not until years later that free agency became dominated by big market teams. Similarly, teams seemed unaware of how older players were rarely worth signing to big contracts or how switching to a new ballpark could affect a player's performance. Almost any pitcher would see their ERA rise going from Dodger Stadium to Fulton County Stadium as Messersmith did. Throughout the late 1970s, the National League continued to be dominated by the Dodgers, Reds, Pirates and Phillies-all teams that were very cautious in the early days of free agency. Messersmith signing a big contract with a bad team and then suffering arm injuries is a pretty good metaphor for much of free agency in its first few years.

Andy Messersmith broke the dam on free agency and made it much more broadly accessible, forcing baseball to come up with new rules and structures governing the relationship between players and teams.

Sixty
Orestes Minoso

Orestes Minoso, known throughout baseball as Minnie, played a central role in the integration of baseball, particularly the American League. Minoso was born in Cuba and like many great Cuban players, his dark skin kept him out of the white major leagues as a young man. Therefore, Minoso spent the first years of his baseball career playing for the New York Cubans in the Negro Leagues. However, by 1949, he was in the American League, playing for the Indians alongside Larry Doby and Satchel Paige. In those early years of baseball integration, the Indians in the American League, like the Dodgers in the National League, were in the forefront of employing Black players.

Photo courtesy of the National Baseball Hall of Fame and Museum (Minoso_Minnie_BL-575-72_NBL)

When he came to Cleveland in 1949, Minoso became the first Afro-Latino player in the American or National League. Like Clemente, the Alou brothers and so many other Afro-Latino players, Minoso faced prejudice based on his skin color as well barriers because of his initial unfamiliarity with the English language and American culture.

Minoso was traded from Cleveland to the Chicago White Sox early in the 1951 season. In Chicago he developed into a star and became one of the best and most exciting AL outfielders of the 1950s. During his prime years from 1951-1960, Minoso slashed .307/.397/.476 while averaging 16 home runs and 18 stolen bases a year. He made the All-Star team seven times during this period. Those numbers demonstrate that Minoso was the kind of player who could do many things well but did not dominate in any one area.

During the early years of Minoso's career, he was one of the very few Afro-Latino players in the big leagues. By the time other Black Cuban stars like Luis Tiant and Bert Campaneris came along, Minoso's career was winding down.

Jackie Robinson is credited, rightly, with bringing a Negro League style of play to the National League. Robinson reintroduced the running game, leading the league in stolen bases twice and running the bases with a derring-do that had not been seen in decades. Minoso did the same in the American League, leading the league in stolen bases during his first three full years in the league and triples three times during the 1950s. No American League player stole more bases than Minoso in the 1950s. Among all big leaguers, only Willie Mays exceeded Minoso's 167 stolen bases during that decade.

By 1964, Minoso was 40-years-old and no longer a productive player, so the White Sox released him midway through the season. Minoso wasn't quite done with baseball. He had started his career in the Negro Leagues and after he could no longer play in the American League, Minoso spent about another decade playing in the Mexican Leagues where he continued to hit. In 1976, after his Mexican career had wound down when Minoso was 52-years-old, he found his way back to the American League.

The man who brought him back to the White Sox was the same team owner, Bill Veeck, who had first brought him to Cleveland in 1949. Minoso played in three games in September of 1976, all as the designated hitter, and managed to get one hit in eight trips to the plate. Minoso became one of the very few big leaguers to play in four different decades and one of the oldest to ever get a hit. Four years later, Veeck brought Minoso back for two more games at the very end of the 1980 season. At 56-years-old Minoso became a five-decade player as he went hitless in two trips to the plate.

I was just becoming a fan when Minoso played in 1976, but remember his 1980 appearance a bit better. By 1980, when I was boy, Minoso looked positively ancient and from another era. After all, he had been a teammate of Bob Feller and Satchel Paige and had played against Joe DiMaggio and Ted Williams. Both the 1976 and 1980 games felt like stunts, something Veeck did to draw attention and a few more fans. To some extent, Minoso came to be seen through that lens as well, but Minoso was not a stunt or a joke. He was an excellent player and central to the globalization of the game and breaking down of racist barriers.

Minoso was also one of the last players to move between different leagues and different countries to keep playing baseball. Today it is not unusual for players to go to Japan, Korea, Mexico or Taiwan after they can no longer play in the big leagues, but none of those players were excluded from the big leagues because of their racial background as Minoso was. Minoso died in Chicago, the city of his biggest baseball triumphs, in 2015. However, no matter where he played or lived, Minoso was a true citizen of the country of baseball.

In 2022 Minoso was elected to the Hall of Fame. It was a well-deserved honor, but unfortunately one that Minoso did not live to see. Minoso was a major star for a decade, a major figure in the game's history and a man who was capable of getting a hit in the Major Leagues well after his fiftieth birthday.

Sixty-one
Jackie Mitchell

Baseball history is frequently interwoven with myth or mystery that leads to debate among fans and historians that last for decades. Did Babe Ruth really call his shot? Did Johnny Evers have the right ball when he touched second base for the final out of the Fred Merkle game? How much sign stealing did the 1951 Giants do and whatever happened to the ball Bobby Thomson hit for the pennant winning home run? Jackie Mitchell's story is also one that has some of this element of mystery and the unknowable.

Mitchell is known as the young woman, in the media of the time described as a girl, who struck out Babe Ruth and Lou Gehrig in 1931. There is no doubt that this occurred. On April 2, 1931, in an exhibition game between Mitchell's Chattanooga Lookouts and the Yankees, Mitchell entered the game in relief in the first

Library of Congress, Prints & Photographs Division [New York World Telegram & Sun - LOC LC-USZ62-122449]

197

inning to face Ruth and then Gehrig and struck them both out. Ruth looked at strike three and Gehrig swung and missed on all three strikes. The unknown aspect of this is whether the two great sluggers, still in the prime of their careers, were trying their best or were participating in a stunt or show of some kind. Neither Ruth nor Gehrig ever said it was a stunt, but speculation about that has continued for almost a century.

That speculation is evidence of the sexism of the era and how it continues today. At first cut, it may seem extremely unlikely that Ruth and Gehrig, if trying their best, could have struck out against a 17-year-old female pitcher. However, they both struck out in about 8.4% of their plate appearances in 1930 and 1931. The percentage was higher against pitchers who, like Mitchell, were left-handed. While Mitchell was only 17, baseball was different then. A very talented 17-year-old was probably better than many of the older pitchers on the weaker teams. To view it as impossible and therefore obviously a hoax is to believe that it is axiomatic a female pitcher would not have been able to strike out Ruth and Gehrig; and that is where the sexism comes in.

Mitchell was not a local high school student brought in for a single appearance. She was a good pitcher, who by 1931 had been pitching for years, had trained in the Lookouts' system and had the good fortune to have been coached by Dazzy Vance who was a star pitcher with the Brooklyn Dodgers and would later end up in the Hall of Fame. Mitchell would go on to pitch for years in various barnstorming and semi-professional capacities.

Within days of Mitchell's accomplishment, baseball commissioner Kenesaw Mountain Landis voided Mitchell's contract and all but banned her from playing professionally in the minor or major leagues. Landis once again understood his job to be not the promotion of the best possible baseball product, but ensuring the game remain white and male. Instead of seeing Mitchell as somebody who could help draw attention to baseball and bring more women fans and players into the game, Landis saw her as a threat.

Mitchell was one of a small number of women in the 20th century who briefly played professional baseball alongside men.

Today, it seems more likely that a woman will play in the big leagues than a women's baseball league will emerge. Unfortunately, we will never know what Mitchell could have accomplished in baseball had she been allowed to play as far as her talent could take her, but her success against Ruth and Gehrig gives us a different kind of hint. The arguments against women and baseball are no longer the ones that were made at the time, including by Ruth himself, that women were too delicate or would not be able to handle the macho world of baseball. Instead, the more common line is that women are not as big or strong as men. That, in general, is probably true, but Mitchell shows us that is also irrelevant.

Size and strength are important in baseball, but not always. If there is one place on the diamond where these factors are less relevant, it is on the pitcher's mound, particularly for left-handed pitchers. A left-handed pitcher with good control, a tough sidearm delivery and a couple of pitches with some movement on them does not have to be big or throw very hard. This was even more true in the 1930s when not every pitcher had a great fastball. For much of baseball history, many pitchers struck out few batters and pitched to contact. It is certainly possible that Mitchell could have done that at the big league level in the 1930s.

In the early 1930s, barnstorming and semi-professional baseball was an important part of the baseball ecosphere. With no televised baseball and the American and National Leagues limited to 11 cities in essentially the Midwest, northeast and mid-Atlantic regions, for many fans barnstorming was the way the saw the game's best players. There was always an element of barnstorming for Negro League teams as well. Moreover, racial restrictions were not as strict for barnstorming so white and non-white players could compete against each other and demonstrate their skills for fans of all backgrounds.

Mitchell's feat against Ruth and Gehrig underscores the value and excitement of barnstorming. That game was attended by about 4,000 fans, more than the average attendance for four big league teams in 1931. Regardless of if Ruth and Gehrig were trying their best or participating in a stunt, I would have rather been at that game than most of the big league games in that season.

Sixty-two
Joe Morgan

Few players have ever excelled at as many aspects of the game as Joe Morgan did. He was a fine fielding second baseman who won four gold gloves, stole 40 or more bases nine times, hit twenty or more home runs four times and drew 100 or more walks eight times. His career batting average of .271 was not outstanding, but his on base percentage of .392 and OPS+ of 132 were. Morgan was the second baseman on the Big Red Machine in 1975 and 1976 when the team had

Photo 104961456 / Baseball © Jerry Coli | Dreamstime.com

what some consider to be the greatest starting lineup of all-time, including three players, still in their prime, who would end up in the Hall of Fame and a fourth, Pete Rose, who had a clear Hall of Fame career. Morgan was by far the best player on those teams as demonstrated by his MVP awards in 1975 and 1976. In 1975, he got the winning hit in the top of the ninth inning of the seventh game of the World Series.

Morgan was only 5'7" with a slender but athletic build and became one of the greatest players ever. For a long time one of the conceits of baseball was that unlike football or basketball, you didn't have to be extremely tall or even very big to excel at the game. That is much less true now than it was in the past, but it was part of the appeal of the game for many years. It was certainly something older men told me when I was becoming a fan in the late 1970s and early 1980s. Morgan was the proof of that.

One of the more annoying cliches in baseball is to describe somebody as a winner because of some magical and intangible quality. There may be players who can transform their teams and make everybody around them play better. However, those kinds of assertions are very difficult to prove and frequently the team improves for reasons that have little to do with any particular player having mysterious winner qualities, but if there ever was such a player, it was Joe Morgan. Morgan began his career with the Astros, but was traded to the Reds following the 1971 season. After winning two championships with the Reds, Morgan went back to the Astros as a free agent in 1980. He had a very solid year there with a 115 OPS+ and 24 stolen bases in thirty tries. The Astros won the NL West and made their first playoff appearance that year. In 1981 he signed with the Giants and in 1982, at age 38, he had a 136 OPS+ and finished 16th in the MVP balloting. That year, the Giants played their first meaningful late season games in a decade. Morgan even knocked the Dodgers out of the playoffs with a big home run on the last day of the season. The Giants then swapped Morgan to the Phillies. There, he was part of the 1983 pennant winning team known as the Wheeze Kids because Morgan and former teammates Tony Perez and Pete Rose, with whom he was reunited in Philadelphia, were all at least 39 years of age.

After he retired Joe Morgan had a second career as an announcer for ESPN where he regularly criticized advanced metrics and new ways of understanding the game. Morgan became the straw man to whom more analytically minded fans and writers pointed when they wanted to show an out of touch announcer who did not understand the new approach to the game. A popular iconoclastic website that criticized announcers and conventional baseball thinking at the time was called Fire Joe Morgan.

In this regard, Morgan is a symbol of how ballplayers have long been resistant to changes in how the game is understood and approached and have, either explicitly or implicitly, sought to stifle debate about the game with some variation of the line "you didn't play the game so you can't understand it." This was deeply ironic because Morgan's style of play, power, patience, and offensive value that far exceeds batting average, was precisely the kind of play that advanced metrics loved. Morgan walked a lot, had a high base stealing success rate, and rarely made mistakes on the bases. Those were all things that advanced metrics capture better than conventional measures.

The Fire Joe Morgan website was not fair to Morgan who always played the game with intensity and intelligence, but it reflected the changing relationship between fans and baseball's gatekeepers. Today, anybody can start a podcast, create a popular Twitter account, or write a blog about baseball. That was not true when Morgan was playing, but it was starting to change when he began announcing. The gatekeepers were decreasingly relevant and even out of touch with how the game was changing. Morgan became a target because of that.

Morgan's career batting average of .271 is good but not top tier. Of the 115 players who played more than 1,000 games at second base since 1900, Morgan is tied for 56th in batting average with Tom Herr. However, he is 7th in on base percentage and 26th in slugging percentage. When ballpark and era are factored in, his OPS+ of 132 is 4th ever for his position and best of any second baseman who played in an integrated league. Advanced metrics do not usually like base stealers, but Morgan's success rate was an astounding 80%, so his 689 career stolen bases brought real value to his team. Today Morgan is regarded as one of the top two second baseman ever. His only real competition is Rogers Hornsby, who was a better hitter but played in a segregated league and was never the defender that Morgan was.

Joe Morgan could do everything on the ballfield. He was a wonderful and complete player, who seemed to always come up with the big hit. Today his standing among the game's greats has improved due in large part to the changes in understanding the game brought about by advanced metrics, the same ones that Joe Morgan, the announcer, seemed to oppose.

Sixty-three
Masanori Murakami

The 1965 game where the fight between John Roseboro and Juan Marichal occurred, described in the Juan Marichal section of this book, was one of the most significant events in baseball history. After that fight, Marichal was ejected from the game. Koufax got the first two outs of the inning, but then, probably distracted by the events earlier in the inning, walked Jim Davenport and Willie McCovey. This brought Willie Mays to the plate who hit a three run home run giving the Giants a 4-2 lead. Ron Herbel, a journeyman Giants pitcher, relieved Marichal and held the Dodgers scoreless into the ninth inning. He got the first out of that inning, but put the next two runners on. Giants manager Herman Franks had seen enough and brought in a lefty to get the final two outs. The new pitcher got the next batter to fly out, but

© S. F. Giants

203

second baseman Hal Lanier made an error and a run scored. The lefty then got the next two outs and the Giants won 4-3.

That left-handed reliever, Masanori Murakami, who picked up the save in that game, was no ordinary big league pitcher. Murakami was the first Japanese player ever to play in the Major Leagues. It has long struck me a great quirk of history that in that famous game, laden with national and even international political drama, Murakami got the save. While big league baseball was finally recognizing and using talent from the Caribbean and Mexico, baseball in Asia was still not on the minds of most American fans. Murakami changed that, albeit briefly.

Murakami only played for the Giants in 1964 and 1965, appearing in 54 games, all but one in relief. After the 1965 season, Murakami went back to Japan where he continued to pitch until 1982. Because his US career was so brief and he never played in an All-Star Game or World Series, he was quickly forgotten. By the late 1970s, Murakami was rarely mentioned. While some fans knew his name and that he was Japanese, they didn't seem to know much more about him. His time with the Giants was so brief that many fans, when they learned about Murakami, probably assumed he was not effective enough to remain in the big leagues.

One thing we know about the left-handed reliever was that he could get big league batters out. In 1964, when Murakami was 20-years-old, he pitched 15 innings with a 1.80 ERA, striking out 15 while issuing only one walk. The following year Murakami saw much more playing time going 4-1 with eight saves and an ERA of 3.75, about league average. However, his 85 strikeouts in only 74.1 innings were extremely impressive for the era. In 1965, Murakami had more strikeouts per nine innings than Sandy Koufax or Bob Gibson. Murakami was not a star, but he was a valuable reliever on a contending team.

In the mid-1960s, World War II was not the distant memory it is today. Japan was becoming a key Cold War ally of the US, but many Americans still harbored great hatred toward the country. At many baseball games in 1964 or 1965, there would have been thousands of fans in the seats who fought against Japan or had a close relative who did. Moreover, there were tens of thousands of Japanese Americans for whom internment during World War II, simply because of their ethnic background, was a very real memory, rather than something that had been told to them by their parents or grandparents. In other words, Murakami encountered prejudice and anger from some fans, while for a small minority he was a symbol that represented hope and showed what Japanese people could do and how they could excel at America's game.

It is no accident that Murakami played for the Giants. In the mid-1960s, the team was on the forefront of the globalization of baseball and had benefited because of players like Marichal, Murakami, the Alou brothers, and Orlando Cepeda. However, there was also a large Japanese American population in San Francisco as well as other parts of northern California, so the experience was less isolating for Murakami than it might have been if he'd played in Philadelphia, St. Louis, or some other non-coastal city.

When Murakami went back to Japan he continued to primarily pitch in relief and had a solid career going 103-82 with a 3.64 ERA. However, he was a middle reliever and occasional starter, so not a big star. In his very early 20s, Murakami was an effective big league pitcher, but was certainly not a standout or exceptional talent in Japan. Although this is only one case, it is strong evidence that Japanese players by the mid-1960s and certainly into the 1970s and 1980s were good enough to contribute to big league teams in the US.

Unfortunately, after Murakami went back to Japan it would be three decades before another Japanese player would make to the big leagues in the US. Since the mid-1990s there have been many Japanese playing in the US including some of baseball's biggest stars. This is one of the unequivocally positive changes in the game-and it began with Murakami.

Sixty-four
Stan Musial

In 2014, shortly before he turned 80, my father was hit by a car and badly injured. On one of my visits to the hospital where he was recovering from his injuries and gradually learning to walk again, I mentioned Stan Musial. Musial had been my father's favorite baseball player, but my father paid little attention to sports in his adult life. As soon as I said Musial's name, my father responded "Stan the Man" and immediately tried to imitate Musial's very distinctive batting stance.

Photo courtesy of the National Baseball Hall of Fame and Museum (Musial Stan 4466-70_FL_NBL)

Musial is not an important player because he was the author's father's favorite player, but because he was one of those players with a very strong connection to a city and a team, perhaps the most underrated of any truly all-time great and because at a key moment in his career, when faced with a clear moral decision, Musial chose to side with progress rather than racism.

Musial is the only player in National League history to play over 3,000 games for the same team in the same city. Carl Yastrzemski and Cal Ripken, Jr did it in the American League. Musial was not only by far the greatest Cardinal player ever, who played many more games for that team than anybody else, but remained part of the Cardinals family and a presence in St. Louis for decades after retiring.

Most fans understand Musial as having been a great player, but he is still not fully appreciated. An overview of his numbers quickly demonstrates his greatness. Musial won three MVP awards, finished in the top ten in MVP voting 13 times, including every year from 1948-1957 and was on the all-star team in 20 seasons. His 475 career home runs and .331 batting average put him in a group with Babe Ruth, Lou Gehrig, and Ted Williams as the only players to hit 400 home runs with a batting average of .330 or better. Advanced metrics are even kinder to Musial. His OPS+ of 159 is tied with Hank Greenberg for 19th. Despite missing a year serving in the military during World War II among position players who began their careers after 1920, only Henry Aaron, Barry Bonds and Willie Mays have more WAR than Musial's 128.

The years from 1947, Jackie Robinson's first with the Dodgers, and 1957, the Giants and Dodgers last in New York, are broadly understood as the golden age of New York baseball. In each of those years, other than 1948, a New York team was in the World Series. The World Series was played entirely in New York City in seven of those years. New York players dominated MVP voting and were the most visible stars in the game. However, the best player in baseball during that period was Musial, and it wasn't particularly close. His 81 WAR were ten more than any other player. His OPS+ of 167 was exceeded only by Ted Williams and Mickey Mantle. Only Ralph Kiner hit more home runs; only Ted Williams had a higher batting average. For over a decade, when the baseball world was watching New York, Musial was not getting as much attention, but he was the best player around. Joe DiMaggio is much more remembered today than Stan Musial, but Musial was the better player.

By 1942, Musial's second year in the big leagues, the Cardinals had become the best team in the National League and had eclipsed the Yankees as the best team in baseball. The Cardinals won four pennants and three World Series between 1942-1946. Stars like Enos Slaughter, Harry Brecheen, and Marty Marion were valuable members of those teams, but there was no question who the best player on the team and the league.

Musial missed all of the 1945 season due to military service, but in 1946, Musial, back from the war, was the National League MVP. He got off to a slow start in 1947 and was hitting under .200 through the first fourteen games of the season. On May 6th, the Cardinals, who were in last place, went to Brooklyn to play the first place Dodgers. In those days St. Louis was the southernmost and westernmost big league city. Naturally, the Cardinals took advantage of that and scouted the south extensively. Players like Dizzy Dean and Enos Slaughter were among the fruits of that approach.

The struggling Cardinals soon had another problem on their hands as several of their players indicated that they would not take the field if the Dodgers were going to play their rookie first baseman Jackie Robinson. These players wanted to keep the National League white and refused to play against an African American. Or at least that is how the story goes. This is another one of those baseball myths that may be true, untrue, or partially true. One thing we know is that the Cardinals best player refused to have anything to do with that racism and made it clear that he intended to play against the Dodgers. Without Musial's support, the racists abandoned their position and played. Musial's decision sent a clear message to his teammates, thus quieting the Cardinals threats and indignation aimed at Robinson.

In one of those wonderful and weird baseball coincidences, Musial had grown up in Donora, Pennsylvania playing alongside African Americans on the baseball field and basketball court. One of those players was Joseph Griffey, known as Buddy, whose son and grandson were Ken Griffey Sr. and Ken Griffey Jr.

Sixty-five
Alyssa Nakken

On April 12, 2022, San Francisco Giants first base coach Antoan Richardson was ejected from a game between the Giants and the Padres because he took umbrage at what he viewed as racist language from Padres coach Mike Schildt. Schildt, speaking of Richardson with whom he had already exchanged words, turned to the Giants bench, and Giants manager Gabe Kapler and said, "you need to control

© S. F. Giants

that mother#cker." Richardson did not like the suggestion that a white manager needed to control a Black coach. He made that view known and was ejected from the game.

Kapler then sent Alyssa Nakken to replace Richardson as the first base coach. At first cut, this does not seem like a big deal. Base coaches get ejected, hurt or need time off from time to time and are temporarily replaced. However, this was not an ordinary coaching change. When Nakken took her spot behind first place she became the first woman to be on the field and in uniform in an official capacity during a big league game.

Again, this happened in 2022. While it is important to recognize Nakken and her accomplishment, it is also appalling that this did not happen sooner. Until very recently, the complete exclusion of women from big league baseball fields was rarely mentioned by most of the baseball world. The absence of women playing for Major League teams may be, partially, if unsatisfactorily, explained by differences in size and strength of men and women, but that rationale does not apply to managers, coaches, umpires, or front office executives. Nakken coached first base for the Giants about a year and a half after Kim Ng became the first female general manager of a team, but there have been very few other women coaches, general managers, umpires, or managers since then. Nakken and Ng are therefore members of a very small sorority.

Nakken has the most tenuous claim of being a baseball player of anybody in this book. She never played the game professionally, and like most girls, focused on softball rather than baseball when she was growing up. A native Californian, Nakken was a standout softball player at Sacramento State University. Like many good college softball players, after graduation there was little future for Nakken had she wanted to continue playing softball or baseball.

In 2012, the year Nakken graduated from college, some attitudes in baseball were beginning to change around gender but also around coaching in general. The idea that a coach was, with very few exceptions, required to be a former player was beginning to fade away. As new technologies and teaching techniques were being introduced to the game, on the field experience, while still preferred, was less important. People who knew baseball and were willing to embrace the newer ideas were given more opportunities. Nakken, who had begun her professional baseball career as an intern with the Giants shortly after graduating from college, took advantage of this new development and became a coach in the Giants system. Her first year with the big league team was 2020, the Covid shortened year, but it was not until 2022 that she coached at first base.

It should be noted that coaching first or third base is more visible than other coaching roles, but is not necessarily the most important. There is also some irony that her opportunity to coach first base arose because of an ugly racial incident. The decision to send Nakken to replace Richardson at first base was made by Giants manager Gabe Kapler, who is also a bit of an iconoclast and one of the few baseball managers or players who has generally taken progressive positions on a range of political issues. Kapler went on to back Richardson and defend his reaction to the racist language.

Additionally, the Giants were a good organization for Nakken, because, by 2022, they had a very large coaching staff. This meant that there were more opportunities for Nakken with the big league team. The Giants had also become one of the more innovative teams in the game, fully embracing a heavily quantitative understanding of baseball as well as the idea that players need coaching during the season so they can continue to improve and adapt.

Nakken was the first woman to coach on the field for a big league team, but she is one of a small group of women who have coached or managed in professional baseball that includes Justine Siegal, Rachel Balkovec, and Bianca Smith. Siegal preceded Nakken in becoming the first female coach in professional baseball. Balkovec was hired to manage in the Yankees farm system in 2022, becoming the first female manager in professional baseball. Smith, who coaches in the Red Sox system, was the first African American female coach in professional baseball.

The prejudices against women in baseball have been extremely enduring, but there is reason to think this is very slowly changing. It is possible that Nakken, Siegal, Smith, Ng and Balkovec will be trailblazers who will open to baseball to many more women. They have all demonstrated the rather obvious point that it is not necessary to be a man to be a good baseball executive, coach, or manager.

There has been no female equivalent to Jackie Robinson, but that day may come. When it does, that woman will have the advantage of a foundation built by women like Nakken.

Sixty-six
Hideo Nomo

One of the key events of the second wave of globalization of MLB began on May 2nd, 1995 at Candlestick Park. Because of the late start of the 1995 season due to a labor dispute, it was only the eighth game of the season for both the Giants and the visiting Dodgers. After fourteen innings, neither the Giants nor the Dodgers had scored. The Dodgers then scored three in the top of the fifteenth, but the Giants came back with four in the bottom half of the inning to win the game.

Photo 173385954 © Jerry Coli | Dreamstime.com

The Dodgers starting pitcher that day was a rookie from Japan named Hideo Nomo. Nomo struck out seven while allowing no runs and only one hit over five innings in his big league debut. Almost thirty years after Masanori Murakami's final game with the Giants, a second Japanese player finally made it to the big leagues. Nomo was a pitcher like Murakami, but was a right-handed starter rather than a left-handed reliever. Nomo had pitched five full years in Japan and was already 26-years-old by the time he made his Dodgers debut.

In Nomo's second start, on May 7th in Colorado, Nomo did not fare as well giving up seven earned runs and not making it out of the fifth inning. Then from mid-May until early August, everything fell into place and Nomo was the best and most exciting pitcher in baseball. He had eight starts in which he struck out at least ten batters including striking out 14 Pirates in seven innings on May 17th. A month later on June 14th, Nomo struck out and 16 batters, also against the Pirates.

Nomo had a distinctive windup, sometimes referred to as the Tornado, where he raised his arms high above and behind his head, turned his entire body away from the batter, and then took a very long stride to the plate. By mid-summer of 1995, Nomo was a major baseball sensation. Nomomania swept the baseball world, particularly in Los Angeles where there was a sizeable Japanese American population.

Nomo was starting the All-Star game for the National League in 1995. He threw two scoreless innings while striking out Kenny Lofton, Edgar Martinez and Albert Belle. During that first season with the Dodgers, Nomo went 13-6 with a 2.54 ERA. He led the league in strikeouts and shutouts while finishing fourth in the Cy Young balloting and taking home Rookie of the Year honors. Nomo's second year was almost as strong as he went 16-11 with 3.19 ERA and only two fewer strikeouts than in the previous season. Again, he finished fourth in the voting for the Cy Young Award. Nomo played in the big leagues for 12 years including two stints with the Dodgers as well as time with six other teams. He was never as good as he was during his first two years, but was a solid and reliable starter for most of his career, finishing with 123 wins and 20.9 WAR.

Nomo was the second Japanese player in the big leagues, but after him there was no turning back. For much of this century Japanese players have been an integral part of big league baseball as many of the game's biggest stars including Ichiro Suzuki, Shohei Ohtani, Yu Darvish and many others come from Japan. Younger fans may think of this as completely normal, because in this era it is. Before Nomo, the view around much of baseball was different. Japanese players were thought to be almost inherently inferior and the Japanese league, Nippon Professional Baseball (NPB) was viewed as almost a minor league-a place for those who couldn't quite make it in the Major Leagues to make a few dollars at the end of their career. Nomo changed all that. He was not only a very good player, capable of winning Cy Young votes and starting in an All-Star Game, but he showed that Japanese players could generate a different kind of excitement in baseball, bring new fans into the game and break through as major stars.

The timing of Nomo's career also lent it greater significance. Nomo began his career the season after the major strike of 1994 that led to the cancellation of the final third of the regular season as well as the entire post-season. Players and management finally came to an agreement, more accurately a federal judge in Manhattan made a ruling that ended the strike, on March 31 of 1995. The 1995 season was saved, but it did not start on time and teams only played 144 games that year. That judge was Sonia Sotomayor who was a big baseball fan and would later be appointed to the Supreme Court by President Barack Obama.

As the 1995 season began, baseball desperately needed good news stories that would take the fans' minds off of labor issues and salary caps and refocus them on the positives that baseball offers. By mid-season Cal Ripken's consecutive game streak became that story. A few years later Sammy Sosa and Mark McGwire's steroid infused home run chase played that role. However, in the first weeks after baseball resumed, Nomomania was the biggest story in baseball and a uniquely positive one, an unknown rookie taking the league by storm, but this time with a global twist that would forever change baseball.

Sixty-seven
Lefty O'Doul

Lefty O'Doul was one of the best hitters in baseball history about whom most fans have never heard. Just over 2,000 players have come to the plate 3,000 or more times in their big league career. Of those, only five, Ty Cobb, Rogers Hornsby, Joe Jackson and Negro Leaguers, Oscar Charleston and Jud Wilson, had a higher batting average than O'Doul's .349. A sixth, Turkey Stearnes, is tied with O'Doul. O'Doul rounded out that batting average with an OPS+ of 143, the same as Hall of Famers Harmon

Library of Congress, Prints & Photographs Division [Bain News Service - LOC LC-DIG-ggbain-28601]

Killebrew, Eddie Matthews, and Mike Piazza, over parts of 11 big league seasons. O'Doul, along with Bill Terry, still holds the record of hits in a single National League season with 254.

There is no doubt that O'Doul, who was an outfielder and occasional pitcher, was good enough to be among the very best players in the game during the 1920s and 1930s when he was an active player, but he only played 11 years in the big leagues and only came to bat a total of 3,660 times. The reason for that is that O'Doul spent part or all of many seasons playing in the Pacific Coast League (PCL). The PCL was, naturally, based in the west coast with teams in San Francisco, Oakland, Los Angeles, and other major western cities. Many great players including Ted Williams, Joe DiMaggio and Earl Averill got their start in the PCL. In the days before the Dodgers and Giants moved to California, the PCL was considered by many fans in the west coast to be a third major league.

No player reflects the significance of the PCL as well as Lefty O'Doul precisely because he went back and forth between teams like the Boston Red Sox and New York Giants and then the Salt Lake City Bees and the San Francisco Seals. O'Doul hit wherever he went-and even pitched a bit too, but he chose to stay in the PCL because he could make almost as much money, travel less and be closer to home. We think of the American and National Leagues as the big leagues for most of the twentieth century, but we know that the best non-white players were not allowed to compete in those leagues. O'Doul reminds us that some of the best white players also decided they had better options. The Seals were the preeminent PCL team, and for most of the 1930s probably could have beaten most of the weaker big league teams. They generally played in front of bigger crowds than teams like the Phillies or Browns. It was therefore very reasonable for players like O'Doul to stay in the west coast.

A native of San Francisco, O'Doul is the player most identified with the Seals because he managed the team from 1935-1951. During those years, he was one of the most famous and recognized sports figures in San Francisco. The old PCL is mostly forgotten now, but the league is a hugely significant part of baseball history. It is one of the many streams that led to the baseball we have today.

O'Doul's movement back and forth between the PCL and the big leagues also demonstrates how, to many people at the time, the lines between major and minor leagues were not as clear as they are today. However, that was not O'Doul's biggest contribution to the game. O'Doul also contributed a great deal to the popularity of baseball in Japan and to ties between baseball communities in the US and Japan.

O'Doul made his first trip to Japan as part of a baseball tour in 1931. By then baseball had been played in Japan for decades, but that tour helped generate attention in Japan to the first professional baseball league there. O'Doul was joined on that trip by stars including Lou Gehrig, Mickey Cochrane, and Al Simmons. O'Doul returned to Japan several times in the 1930s to try and build up the game in Japan. Sometimes O'Doul went to Japan as part of a barnstorming team including in 1934 when Moe Berg was one of the American players on the trip. During other trips to Japan O'Doul, along with other big league players, conducted clinics to help develop young Japanese ballplayers. Those visits stopped during the war, but began again in 1949 and the 1950s. On those trips, O'Doul led delegations of big league players that included Yogi Berra, Joe DiMaggio and other stars. In those years, the trips were meant to strengthen relations between the two countries who had fought each other during World War II. These kinds of soft power tactics were an important part of US Cold War strategy.

No American player did nearly as much for baseball in Japan. The Japanese baseball world recognized this by making O'Doul the first American to be enshrined in Japan's Baseball Hall of Fame. O'Doul's life in baseball, more than any other player, sheds light on the importance of the PCL, the position of the American and National League relative to the rest of the baseball world in the first part of the twentieth century and the globalization of the game. The Japanese have recognized this. Someday Cooperstown might find room for a player whose impact on baseball was so large and who hit for a higher batting average than Babe Ruth or Ted Williams.

Sixty-eight
Sadaharu Oh

Players like Masanori Murakami, Hideo Nomo and Ichiro Suzuki have shown how Japan is central to the continuing history of MLB, but the greatest player in Japanese history was Sadaharu Oh. Oh never played in the US, but was the biggest baseball star in Japan for a generation and remains the most famous Japanese player ever.

Oh spent his entire career with the Yomiuri Giants, Japan's most famous, and frequently best, team. Like Ruth, Mantle, DiMaggio, Mathewson and Jeter in the US, Oh benefited from playing for a team that was at the center of his country's baseball universe. A left-handed hitter and throw-

Photo courtesy of the National Baseball Hall of Fame and Museum
(Oh Sadaharu 3183.77b_BAT_NBL)

er, Oh played from 1959-1980. After his playing career ended, Oh spent 19 years managing in Japan including five with the Yomiuri Giants.

Oh was a first baseman, but much better known for his hitting. He was small compared to American sluggers, standing only 5'10" but he generated power with an unusual swing that began by lifting up his right leg as the pitch approached. Over the course of his 22 year career with the Giants, Oh slashed .301/.446/.634. Oh is most remembered for smashing 868 home runs, the most ever of any player in Japan. Oh's home run total exceeds that of Barry Bonds by over 100. There are still those in the US who think Henry Aaron, not Bonds, is the all-time home run leader, but any debate over who is the all-time leader in home runs must include Oh.

It is difficult comparing great sluggers across eras and even more so across continents and oceans. And, if that comparison is going to be made, Josh Gibson deserves some mention as well. Oh's home runs were better documented than Gibson's for whom the data is incomplete. The question with regards to Oh is whether the pitching in Japan was comparable to big league pitching in the US at the time. Unlike later Japanese stars, Oh never played in the US. In general, during most of Oh's career, Japanese baseball was probably, with regards to level of play, somewhere between AAA and the Major Leagues, but there is no way to prove that. In many respects, the comparison is irrelevant, particularly in Japan. Oh was one of the greatest home run hitters ever and his 868 home runs are as important to his country as Bonds or Aaron's are to the US.

Oh remains a folk here in Japan comparable to Babe Ruth in the US. In addition to his great play, Oh also articulated a Japanese approach to the game, drawing on Japanese practices of Zen and martial arts to improve his hitting as a young player. Oh's 1984 memoir was titled *A Zen Way of Baseball*. One of the reasons Oh is so beloved in Japan is that he played an American game with a distinctly Japanese perspective and approach.

Baseball in Japan has always had a complex relationship to baseball in the US. Unlike in Mexico or various Caribbean countries, Japanese baseball was not closely tied to American baseball. Japanese baseball was much more of a separate entity with, beginning in the 1930s, consistently structured leagues, little contact other with American baseball, other than exhibitions, and fewer players going back and forth.

Since the early 1950s, the best players in Mexico and the Caribbean made their way to the big leagues. The exception to that was Cuba after the revolution. Even before the 1950s, it was not unusual for American or National League players to play in that region during the winter. Before 1947, African American players who were excluded from what was then considered the Major Leagues frequently played in the Caribbean or Mexico. Japanese players started coming to the US in significant numbers in the late 1990s, but even since then it is not a given that the best players from that country will make their way to the US.

One of the reasons Oh is so fascinating is that he was such a great player about whom we have a very thorough statistical record, some video, troves of articles and other resources, but we cannot fully answer the question of how good he would have been had he played in the US. Several great American players played against Oh in exhibition or other settings and were impressed by him. Tom Seaver said, "if he played in the United States, he would have hit 20-25 home runs a year and, what's more, he'd hit .300." Frank Howard, who hit 382 big league home runs from the late 1950s to the early 1970s, summed up his view of Oh. "He would play in any league, any time, including our own major leagues, and he would be a star in any league. Make no mistake about it." Frank Robinson estimated how many home runs Oh would have hit in the big leagues. "I'm sure he would have hit in the thirties and probably the low forties (home runs per year)."

As baseball seeks to include all its history, it should recognize the contributions of Oh not just on the field, but as a hero in Japan who helped deepen the globalization of the game. Oh did that in part by marrying a deeply American game to his own Japanese culture-and excelling for over twenty years. A good place to start would be to enshrine Oh in the Baseball Hall of Fame in Cooperstown.

Sixty-nine
Buck O'Neil

Buck O'Neil played in the Negro Leagues in the 1930s and 1940s. O'Neill was a solid ballplayer-a good fielding first baseman who could hit, but had limited power. O'Neil spent most of his career with the Kansas City Monarchs. While with the Monarchs, he played alongside Satchel Paige for several years in the 1940s. O'Neil also served as manager of the Monarchs in 1948. Like many of his generation, he missed some playing time, in O'Neil's case the 1944 and 1945 seasons, because he was serving in the military during World War II.

Photo courtesy of the National Baseball Hall of Fame and Museum (O'Neil Buck 7174-72_FL_NBL)

O'Neil was not a Negro League legend like Josh Gibson or Paige, who were superior players, but he was uniquely important in both deepening the integration of the National and American Leagues as well as in keeping the history of the Negro Leagues alive. After Jackie Robinson, and then Larry Doby and others began playing for the Dodgers, Indians and other teams, the Negro Leagues continued for a few more years, but then faded away due to the hegemony of the larger and wealthier newly integrated leagues.

Into the 1950s, some white team executives still knew little about the Negro Leagues or the Caribbean, who the best young non-white players were, how to see them or the best way to contact them. Several people played key behind the scenes roles in getting these players signed and brought into the big leagues. The legendary scout Alex Pompez was the most prominent person doing this in the Caribbean. O'Neil played a similar role with African American players in the final days of the Negro Leagues and afterwards. During the 1950s, after his playing career wound down, O'Neil was able to identify African American players through a network of baseball relationships that no white baseball executive had. He earned a reputation as a very keen evaluator of talent and helped discover stars like Elston Howard, Ernie Banks, Lou Brock, and Oscar Gamble. The latter three players all signed with the Cubs where O'Neil served as a scout beginning in 1955. In 1962, O'Neil, still with the Cubs, became the first African American coach in the American or National League. He remained part of the Cubs organization through the 1988 season.

Today most fans are aware of the Negro Leagues. In 2021 MLB decided to recognize some of the Negro Leagues as official Major Leagues; and teams now have throwback days where they celebrate Negro League teams that played in their cities. However, during the 1950s through about the 1980s, few fans, particularly white fans, knew much about the Negro Leagues as MLB paid barely any attention at all to that history. A handful of African American players from the era before Jackie Robinson were inducted into the Hall of Fame beginning in the early 1970s, but in general this aspect of baseball history was ignored by MLB.

More than any other former player, O'Neil was committed to keeping the Negro League legacy alive, even during the years when the Negro Leagues were forgotten by many. O'Neil, who was telegenic, charming and a gifted raconteur, never stopped telling stories about those days or talking about great Negro League players. He helped keep the memories of players like Josh Gibson, Cool Papa Bell, and Satchel Paige alive long after they had retired and passed away. O'Neil shared recollections not just of these men's exploits on the ballfield, but of who they were as people and the struggles they faced playing baseball in a largely segregated country.

O'Neil spent much of the last third of his life traveling and speaking about the history of the Negro Leagues. He was one of the major engines behind the creation of the Negro League Baseball Museum. The museum, located in Kansas City, has preserved an important part of baseball's, and America's, history, educated many continues to show the connections between the different eras of African American baseball through to the present day. O'Neil was one of the initial board members of the museum and remained deeply involved there until his death.

One of the reasons O'Neil was a bridge across so much of the African American baseball experience was because he lived a very long life. He was born in 1911 in Florida when apartheid still ruled the American south and died in 2006 a few months before his 95th birthday. There were not too many people in the early 21st century who had seen or played with most of the great Negro League players, had scouted several future Hall of Famers and could speak so compellingly about the game. In his later years, O'Neil was a living reminder of a period in the history of baseball, and the US, that seemed unimaginably far away to many fans.

In 1994, film maker Ken Burns recognized what a gifted communicator O'Neil was and how much baseball history he had seen. Burns gave O'Neil a lot of time throughout his 1994 multipart documentary about baseball. That film gave O'Neil more exposure and his biggest platform for telling fans about the Negro Leagues. O'Neil later served on the Veterans Committee of the Hall of Fame and helped preserve the memory of the Negro Leagues, and many of its stars, in Cooperstown. O'Neil himself was finally inducted into the Hall of Fame in 2022, more than fifteen years after his death. This honor came at least fifteen years too late for a man who was a keeper of so much of baseball's history.

Seventy
Shohei Ohtani

Shohei Ohtani is the most fascinating, exciting, and unusual player in baseball today, and one of the best baseball stories in years. If you don't appreciate Ohtani, you are either not a baseball person or have achieved exalted heights of baseball grumpiness.

Before Ohtani, the last player to excel as both a hitter and a pitcher was Babe Ruth. Ruth started as a pitcher and moved to the outfield, but even the Babe only spent two years, 1918 and 1919, as a true two-way player. Ohtani has already had four seasons in Japan and four with the Angels where he was both a hitter and a pitcher. Barring injury, he will continue to do that for several more years. Between the Babe and Ohtani, not only did no player excel in both these roles, but very few were even given the chance.

Creative Commons - Mogami Kariya https://flickr.com/photos/kariyamogami/52252188505/

In 2018, Ohtani won the Rookie of the Year, hitting 22 home runs with a 151 OPS+ while pitching 51.2 innings with a 127 ERA+. In his 2021 MVP season, Ohtani hit 46 home runs, had an OPS+ of 157, stole 26 bases and had an ERA+ of 141 over 130.1 innings. No player ever had a year like that. The following year, 2022, Ohtani was almost as good. His OPS+ dropped to 144, but he had a better year as a pitcher. In 2022, Ohtani had an ERA+ of 172 over 166 innings. His 9.6 WAR in 2022 was slightly higher than his nine WAR in 2021. Ohtani has even forced a rule change that now allows a DH to stay in the game even after he has been removed as a pitcher. This rule was never considered before Ohtani because no pitcher was ever a good enough hitter to be a real DH.

For over a century it was understood in baseball that being a good hitter and a good pitcher was almost impossible because both crafts require so much work and practice that nobody could do both well. As baseball became more specialized, this became even more concretized. The adoption of the designated hitter rule in the American League in 1973 and then the National League in 2022 occurred because everybody knows that pitchers cannot hit.

One of the most fascinating things about Ohtani is he forces us to rethink what we thought we knew about baseball. Ohtani's success should lead other teams to revisit some of their strategic assumptions. The question is not one of finding another Ohtani, although most teams would like that. Rather, smart teams could look at what Ohtani has done and realize that pitchers, even with a universal DH, who can hit a little bit, run well or field a position decently have substantial value beyond their pitching. This is particularly true of back end of the bullpen type pitchers who most teams cycle through quickly. For example, the fourth righty out of the bullpen would be more valuable if he could pinch run sometimes or play a passable outfield.

Another way that Ohtani may lead teams to think differently is by having position players pitch more. We have already seen this with the uptick in position players pitching in recent years, but this could be taken even further with fourth outfielders and backup infielders working on their pitching not with a hope of being an ace starter like Ohtani, but of becoming a back end of the bullpen reliever. This would also force baseball to alter its new rules that limit when teams can use position players as pitchers.

By the time Ohtani played his first game for the Angels in 2018, it was no longer a big deal for a Japanese player to be starring in the US. Nonetheless, Ohtani is part of the ongoing story of globalization in big league baseball. When Ohtani was preparing to come to the US, the bidding was intense with several teams hoping to land the young pitcher and outfielder. Bidding for Japanese stars has become part of baseball in the 21st century. This occurs during the off-season and is part of the larger free agent market. Over the years players including Yu Darvish, Daisuke Matsuzuka, Ichiro Suzuki, and Seiya Suzuki have been part of that process.

Throughout its history there have always been fans and others who believe baseball has lost its appeal and become worse than it was in previous years. The PED era, ongoing labor issues, cheating scandals and concerns about pace of play and a game that has become too dependent on home runs, strikeouts and walks have led many to believe that baseball today is in a crisis of some kind. There is something to that. Attendance is down from where it was even a few years ago. The 2022 lockout, unresolved issues from the PED era, mid-June games between non-contenders that last almost four hours—an issue that MLB addressed in 2023 with the introduction of the pitch clock—and starting pitchers that seem to rarely pitch even five innings are all evidence of baseball's current crisis.

Ohtani is the rebuttal to the idea that baseball has lost its appeal. Despite all the problems many see in baseball, it is still possible for a player to arrive from another country and do something that nobody thought could be done and earn comparisons to the Babe Ruth. Ohtani is the ultimate baseball feel good story at a time when the game needs one.

Seventy-one
David Ortiz

Few players capture the contradictions of baseball in the 21st century as well as David Oritz does. Ortiz was a slugging designated hitter, beloved by Red Sox fans, but less so in the Bronx. He was an extraordinary clutch hitter who led his team to three World Series championships. Ortiz was great with the media and seemed like a friendly easygoing man who was good to the fans as well.

Ortiz began his career with the Twins, where he played from 1997-2002, but it was in Boston where his career took off. Ortiz went to the Red Sox in 2003 and remained there until the end

Photo 139037684 / Baseball © Dreammediapeel | Dreamstime. com

of his career in 2016. During those years, the Red Sox won their first World Series since 1918 in 2004, and then won it all again in 2007 and 2013. In those years, they were the biggest team in the game and Ortiz was their most famous player. Ortiz became a Red Sox legend in game four of the 2004 ALCS. The Red Sox were trailing the Yankees three games to zero and were tied in the bottom of the 12th inning of game four when Ortiz hit a two-run walk-off home run.

The Red Sox won the next three games and the American League championship, and then swept the Cardinals in the World Series. Ortiz was named the MVP for that ALCS having slashed .387/.475/.742 in the seven game series. Over the course of his career Ortiz was an astounding post-season performer. In 369 post-season plate appearances, all with the Red Sox, Ortiz slashed .289/.404/.543 with 17 home runs.

In this century, the Red Sox have dramatically remade their image. They have become a very well-funded powerhouse like the Dodgers or the Yankees. However, when Ortiz joined the team, the Red Sox seemed almost cursed. The ground ball that went through Bill Buckner's legs in 1986, Bucky Dent's home run, the bloop single by Joe Morgan in 1975, and going back to the 1940s, losing a one game playoff in 1948 and losing the World Series two years before that, in part because star shortstop Johnny Pesky didn't throw the ball to the plate quickly enough, were all evidence that the Red Sox just couldn't win a championship. Ortiz was instrumental in changing that narrative in 2004.

There is another more complex side to David Ortiz's career. Ortiz is a reminder that MLB never genuinely resolved the PED issue and that punishment and consequences have always been meted out inconsistently or capriciously. We don't know with complete certainty whether, or how frequently, Ortiz used PEDs, but there is some evidence that he did. First, in 2003 Ortiz tested positive for PEDs. That information was leaked much later because that test was supposed to be anonymous. The 2006 report on PED use, led by former US Senator George Mitchell did not mention Ortiz, but there is more to that story as well. Mitchell was a director, and part owner of, you guessed it, the Boston Red Sox. Lastly, during Ortiz's career any player whose body type and power numbers changed as much as Ortiz's did between 2002 and 2004 was thought to be using steroids. It is possible that Ortiz was the unusual player who came by those changes naturally, but that seems unlikely.

I don't know the full story about Ortiz and PEDs, but it does not seem right that Barry Bonds, Roger Clemens, and others have been all but formally banned from the game while Ortiz gets seems to get a pass. Nowhere has that been more apparent than with regards to Hall of Fame voting. Ortiz, as widely expected, got elected to the Hall of Fame on his first try. Putting the PED question aside for a moment, Ortiz benefited more from home ballpark and the era in which he played than almost any other recent Hall of Famer. Ortiz's Hall of Fame candidacy rested on a belief that those things did not matter, that 45 home runs in 2005 was the same as 47 home runs in 1969, that defense was irrelevant, and RBIs were still a useful indicator of ability. But really, Ortiz got into the Hall of Fame because of his well-earned reputation as a clutch hitter and because he was likeable.

One quick way to see this is to compare Ortiz to another left-handed hitting first baseman who had great power and did not contribute much with the glove. Ortiz had 20 more home runs than Willie McCovey as well as a higher batting average, slugging percentage and on-base percentage. Ortiz slashed .286/.380/.552 while McCovey slashed .270/.374/.515. However, to believe Ortiz, who played most of his career in Fenway Park during a high offense era, was better than McCovey, who played at Candlestick Park, mostly during a low offense era, is to refuse to understand anything about context. This is seen in McCovey's OPS+ of 147, which is higher than Ortiz's 141. Similarly, McCovey had almost 10 more career WAR than Ortiz's 55.3 WAR.

McCovey and Ortiz are both Hall of Famers, but there are many players who have received little or no Hall of Fame consideration who were better than Ortiz. Will Clark had almost 56.5 WAR, and an OPS+ of 137, only four points lower than Ortiz. Norm Cash, who is almost entirely forgotten now, had 52 WAR and an OPS+ of 139. Reggie Smith had 64.7 WAR and an OPS+ of 137.

The point here is not that Ortiz is undeserving of being in the Hall of Fame. If I had a vote, I probably would have voted for him because his post-season numbers strengthen an otherwise borderline candidacy. However, Ortiz's legacy is a reminder that the steroid era has not gone away, and that the Hall of Fame and so much of the historiography of baseball is personal.

Seventy-two
Satchel Paige

In October of 2021, President Joe Biden met with Pope Francis. This meeting was of particular significance because Biden is only the second American president who is Catholic. During that meeting, Biden, seeking to build a bond with the Pope, told a story about Satchel Paige. The video of the inter-action reveals an enthusiastic Biden and a puzzled Pope and translator. At one point, Biden seeks to explain that Paige was a pitcher and makes a pitching motion. Paige him-

Photo courtesy of the National Baseball Hall of Fame and Museum (Paige Satchel 715.72 NBL)

self had been dead for almost forty years, but this demonstrates Paige's status as a folk hero who, even in death remains relevant today. Paige became bigger than the game he played through his deeds, his legend, and his eternal sayings.

Satchel Paige was an American archetype whose life seems more mythical than real, as if a Hollywood filmmaker decided to create a person drawing on several different legends. Paige, born in the early years of the twentieth century in the segregated south, became the best pitcher in the country, but was kept out of what was then considered the big leagues because he was African American. While playing in the Negro Leagues he was a hugely popular attraction in regular season games and as a barnstormer.

He finally got his chance to play in the American League when he was in his early 40s and excelled despite his age. Then, after pitching for a few years there, Paige continued to barnstorm and pitch in other capacities, but in his 50s was brought back into the American League in what looked like a cheap stunt, but managed to pitch three scoreless innings.

The folk legend that was Satchel Paige was burnished by a flair and panache that would have seemed like bluster if Paige had not been so likeable. He gave his pitches goofy nicknames, sometimes walked batters on purpose to load the bases just to create a bigger challenge for himself and on occasion told the outfielders-and sometimes the infielders too-to sit down because he was going to strike the side out. He usually made good on that promise.

The legend was enriched by Paige's nickname, which he came by honestly. As a boy Leroy Paige made extra money shlepping travelers' bags, or satchels, at the Mobile, Alabama train station, and soon became known as Satchel. Paige told colorful anecdotes and dispensed wisdom. When asked how where he got his fastball, Paige usually told people he acquired that skill from "throwing rocks at white boys" when he was a youth. When he got older, Paige offered six rules for staying young. The final one was "don't look back. Something might be gaining on you."

The mythology around Paige, most of which is true, make him massively important to baseball's position as an American cultural institution. Moreover, Paige's life story cannot be separated from America's racist history. Paige began pitching with the Birmingham Black Barons in 1927. Paige pitched regularly in the Negro Leagues for the next twenty years, but also barnstormed, played in the Caribbean and pitched in other settings.

The statistical record for Paige is incomplete because reliable records do not exist for much of his career. However, we know that many players, from all backgrounds, who played with or against Paige, describe him as the greatest pitcher they ever saw. The Negro League records for Paige show his to be the best pitcher in the league for most of the 15 years he played there. Paige led the Negro League in strikeouts six times and strikeouts per nine innings eight times. His Negro League ERA+ was a spectacular 166. Paige was the ace pitcher on the 1934 Pittsburgh Crawfords which may have been the best Negro League team ever assembled. Josh Gibson, Oscar Charleston, Judy Johnson and Cool Papa Bell were among Paige's teammates. Paige led the team going 13-3 with a 1.54 ERA.

Paige was already 40-years-old when Jackie Robinson made it to the Brooklyn Dodgers, so was thought to be too old to play in the big leagues. That did not stop him. Midway through the 1948 season, Paige joined the Cleveland Indians. From July through the end of the season, Paige went 6-1 with a 2.48 ERA. He started and pitched out of the bullpen, and even threw two shutouts. Cleveland would not have won the pennant that year without him. Paige stayed in the American League with Cleveland and then the St. Louis Browns through the 1953 season, finally retiring when he was 47-years-old. Over the course of those years, he pitched 473 innings with an ERA+ of 124. His best year was 1952 when he went 12-10 with a 127 ERA+ for a dreadful St. Louis Browns team. Only seven other pitchers have pitched more than 400 innings with an ERA+ of 120 or better after the age of forty. Among them are Roger Clemens, Cy Young, Pete Alexander, and Tom Seaver.

Paige wasn't finished pitching yet. After leaving the Browns in 1953, Paige continued to barnstorm and in 1965, when he was 59 years old, Paige was brought back to the big leagues by Kansas City Athletics owner Charlie O. Finley. On September 25th of that year, Paige started against the Boston Red Sox and pitched three scoreless innings. The only hit he surrendered was a double to Red Sox star Carl Yastrzemski. It was an amazing pitching performance that sounds more like the stuff of barnstorming legend than of official American League baseball, but that is how good Paige was.

Seventy-three
Chan Ho Park

Any American baseball fan who has spent time in Europe or other parts of the world where baseball is not popular has been asked a variation of the question "why do Americans play baseball when the rest of the world plays football (meaning soccer)." This is one of those questions that reveals the ignorance of the questioner. First, much of the world does not play either sport. In countries like India, Pakistan, Bangladesh and many others, cricket, not soccer, is the most popular sport. Moreover, the idea that baseball is only played in the US reveals a very Euro-centric world view, suggesting that countries like Cuba, the Dominican Republic, Venezuela and several Asian countries simply do not exist.

One of those countries where Europeans may not be aware

Photo 73495778 / Baseball © Jerry Coli | Dreamstime.com

of the popularity of baseball is South Korea. Until Chan Ho Park, many American baseball fans were probably not aware of that either. Baseball was never quite as popular in Korea as in Japan, but the game has been played there for over a century. Similarly, although there have not been as many Korean as Japanese players in the big leagues, there have been quite a few including some well-known stars such as Shin Soo Choo, Byung Hyun Kim, and Hee Seop Choi over the last 25 years.

Chan Ho Park was the first Korean to play in the big leagues. He appeared in a few games in April of 1994 with the Dodgers before being sent down and two more as a September call up in 1995. Because of those 1994 games, Park was the second Asian player, after Masanori Murakami, to play in the US. Unlike Murakami or most of the other Japanese players, Park began his professional career in the US, signing with the Dodgers as an amateur free agent out of high school. However, after his playing days in the US were over, Park returned to Asia and pitched in both Japan and Korea.

Unlike Hideo Nomo, Park was never a big star, nor did Park ever generate media coverage comparable to Nomomania. Park established himself in 1996 as a second-tier pitcher on the Dodgers, but between 1997 and 2001, was a very solid starter going a combined 75-49 with an ERA+ of 108. After that, Park bounced around playing with the Rangers, Padres, Mets, Dodgers again, Phillies, Yankees, and Pirates. Park's peak was in 2000-2001. Over those two years he combined for a 33-21 record and a 122 ERA+ and made the All-Star team in 2001. Park was not particularly effective after 2001, but remained in the league through 2010. On balance, Park was a journeyman pitcher who had a solid big league career, and in doing that, he demonstrated that Koreans were clearly good enough to play in the big leagues. In 1994, there were no other Koreans playing in the big leagues, by Park's last year there had been thirteen. By the 2022 season that number had grown to 27.

Koreans like Park have contributed to the globalization of big league baseball in this century. Today, MLB draws elite from not just the US, but from the world. That is a new development and has made MLB a better product. Fans know that the players they are watching are, with fewer exceptions than at any time in the past, the best players in the world.

Players like Park also bring up a different set of questions about globalized baseball. In recent decades, MLB has accelerated its efforts to increase the popularity of baseball in various parts of the world. This has included playing games overseas, establishing clinics in foreign countries and, most notably, the World Baseball Classic. The success of Asian players from Japan, Korea and Taiwan have strengthened that effort. However, there is also the possibility that as MLB becomes a bigger draw for Asian players, leagues in Asian countries will become less popular. Baseball fans in Japan and Korea have team loyalties and baseball lore of their own. If the best players in those countries continue to make their way to the US, those leagues could become de facto minor leagues. Their focus, and purpose, would be to produce talent for the US rather than to provide baseball for local fans.

This has not happened yet, but the tendency is there. Many of the best players in Japan and Korea want to test themselves against the best players in the world, who are overwhelmingly to be found playing in the US. It is possible that leagues in affluent countries like Korea and Japan will create structures that make it more difficult for players to go to the US, but players in those countries might not be comfortable with that.

Ultimately MLB will have to plan for the next phase of globalization. Simply bringing the best players to the US was phase one, but there needs to be something more. Some possibilities include playing more games in Asia, finding a way to add teams in other countries, expanding the World Baseball Classic so it is played more frequently or other means of bringing more baseball to more fans outside the US.

Seventy-four
Buster Posey

Buster Posey was one of the last players I included in this book. I am aware that as a longtime Giants fan, I may not be entirely objective about Posey, but his career tells us a lot about baseball in recent years. Posey was a great player who retired following a very strong 2021 season at 34-years-old with 44.8 WAR in ten full seasons and parts of two others. Posey was the best catcher in the National League for most of his career. He was an excellent defender and handler of pitchers and slashed .302/.372/.460 for an OPS+ of

© S. F. Giants

129. He was the starting catcher and one of the best hitters on three Giants World Series winning teams. Because of his short career, his spot in Cooperstown is, while deserved, not quite assured.

Posey is important for two reasons beyond simply his record as a player and the role he played in helping the Giants win their first World Series since moving to San Francisco, and in the Giants mini-dynasty from 2010-2014. Posey's larger significance to baseball began to take shape early in the 2011 season, a few months after the Giants won the 2010 World Series. On May 25th of that year, the Giants were hosting the Marlins in San Francisco.

In the top of the 12th, with the score tied 6-6, Marlins shortstop Emilio Bonifacio hit a long fly ball. Scott Cousins, the Marlins centerfielder tried to tag up and score from third. The play at the plate was close, but Cousins aggressively ran over Posey and was called safe. Posey's leg was broken in the collision and one of baseball's best, and most marketable young players, was out for the season. Many were concerned he wouldn't return to the level of play he had established in his rookie year.

Giants fans, and many around baseball, were outraged. It was one of those sports injuries that anybody at the ballpark or watching on television could see was painful and destructive. There was a real possibility that Posey would never be the same player again. This led to a discussion around baseball about whether there needed to be a rule change to protect catchers from plays at the plate like the one that almost derailed Posey's career. Because the collision at the plate with the runner seeking to knock over the catcher and jar the ball loose had long been part of the game, some argued that to change that would be to make the game too soft and take away an essential baseball play. Others argued that the risk of injury to the catcher, and potentially the baserunner, was too high and a rule change was overdue. The latter argument won out.

It took baseball some time and a few more catchers being injured in home plate collisions, but, beginning in 2014, after Alex Avila the Tigers catcher, was injured in a similar play in the 2013 ALCS, a new rule was implemented. The rule had two main components. First, runners were forbidden to deviate from their path to run into a catcher. This meant that unless the catcher was directly in front of home plate, the runner could not try to knock the ball loose. Second, catchers were forbidden to stand in front of the plate unless they had possession of the ball. This rule is widely known as the Buster Posey rule. Few players have a rule named after them, but Posey does. The Buster Posey rule is a sensible policy to keep catchers safer and to eliminate a play that always struck me as incongruous, like a small bit of football in the middle of a baseball game.

For many years an old friend of my step-father's was one

of the Giants team doctors who was frequently able to get my sons and I tickets to games when we were in San Francisco. The tickets were sometimes in the family section where we sat next to the wives, children and occasionally parents, of the players. During the pre-season 2013 series between the Giants and the A's, we were in those seats a few rows behind Buster Posey's wife and their two young children. I remember watching Mrs. Posey interact with the other wives that day because it had just been announced that Posey had signed an eight year $168 million contract. I tried to imagine what was going through her head.

Posey played well for most of that contract, but by the end of 2019 was showing signs of slowing down. Over the next three seasons, Posey made several decisions that are very unusual for a baseball player, but very rational for a human being. First, Posey decided to sit out the 2020 season because he was concerned about Covid. Specifically, he did not want to either spend the entire shortened season away from his family or risk bringing the virus home to his four children, including two recently adopted babies. That decision cost Posey $8 million 2020.

In 2021 Posey returned and had a fantastic season slashing .304/.390/.499, making the All-Star Team and receiving some MVP votes as he led the Giants to a franchise record 107 wins. Then, after the season, Posey announced his retirement. Had he not retired, the Giants most likely would have exercised their option and paid him $22 million for the 2022 season.

Between 2020 and 2022, Posey made decisions that cost him $30 million in salary but protected the health of his family. There are countless stories of athletes who hung around too long even though their skills were deteriorating. Posey is the opposite. He genuinely believed that there is more to life than baseball and that there is such a thing as enough money. That is extremely unusual, but it could be precedent setting. Now that Posey has done it, other players may begin to see the game through that lens as well.

Seventy-five
Pee Wee Reese

No team holds a place in the collective baseball and cultural memory quite like the Brooklyn Dodgers. The Dodgers were more or less a laughing-stock for most of their existence until about 1941 when they won their first pennant in over twenty years. They would win six more before moving to Los Angeles in 1958. The most famous franchise in baseball is the Yankees, but the most famous team over a specific period was the Dodgers of that era. Those Dodgers teams had a character, in stark contrast to the Yankees who beat them in six of seven World Series during those years, that was something of the gruff, loveable, and distinctly human underdog. If in the 1950s, as the saying went, rooting for the Yankees was like rooting for US Steel, then rooting for the Brooklyn Dodgers was like rooting for a beloved neighborhood café that is in danger of being squeezed out by yet another Starbucks.

Photo courtesy of the National Baseball Hall of Fame and Museum (Reese Pee Wee 3544.63_FL_NBL)

Those Dodgers had colorful nicknames: The Duke, Campy, Oisk, The Reading Rifle, and Preacher. The team had African American stars such as Jackie Robinson, Roy Campanella and Don Newcombe well before most other teams. The Dodgers even had a Brooklyn born Jewish southpaw, Sandy Koufax, on their pitching staff during their last few years in that borough. However, no Dodger embodied the spirit of that *Boys of Summer* era more than Harold Reese, known by the best nickname of any of those Dodgers, Pee Wee. Reese became the Brooklyn Dodgers shortstop midway through the 1940 season. The team finished second that year and were never again a bad team or a laughingstock. One player cannot turn a franchise around, but Reese's ascent dovetailed almost exactly with the Dodgers becoming a very good team for a very long time.

Jackie Robinson, Gil Hodges and Duke Snider were bigger stars, but Pee Wee Reese was the constant and the team captain. He was the starting shortstop on every one of those seven Dodgers pennant winning teams and played in every one of those World Series games. Reese is often remembered as being part of that team and for his relationship with Jackie Robinson but some overlook just how good a player he was.

Reese was a standout defender. His 25.6 career defensive WAR is 13th highest among shortstops. Had the Gold Glove award existed when Reese was playing, he would have won several. Reese was not a great offensive player. His career OPS+ was only 99, meaning his production was about league average, but combined with great defense at shortstop, Reese was a very valuable player. His .366 career on base percentage was very good for a shortstop for that era and brought value to the top of powerful Dodgers lineups. Reese's 68.4 career WAR is 14th highest among shortstops, but was eighth best when Reese retired. That number would have been at least 75 had Reese not spent three years of his prime serving in the military in World War II. Reese spent his entire career with the Dodgers and went with the team to Los Angeles. He was the starting shortstop in the first big league game ever played in California. The Dodgers were drubbed by the Giants in San Francisco that day by a score of 8-0.

In 1947, when Jackie Robinson broke into the National League, Reese was not yet the Dodgers captain, but he was one of the team's veteran stars and the best shortstop in the league. He was also from the South. Reese had grown up in Louisville, Kentucky, the northern part of a border state, but still very southern feeling. There were a small handful of National League stars, such as Hank Greenberg and Stan Musial, who when confronted with an African American opponent, chose to place themselves on the right side of history. Musial and Greenberg were better players than Reese, but they were both from the north. Musial was Catholic and Greenberg was a Jew from New York. This did not make their sentiments any less sincere, but to the racists, what people like Greenberg and Musial did had less meaning.

Unlike those players, Reese was Robinson's teammate. Reese's friendship and support of Robinson was critical both in making Robinson's life in the National League easier, but also in sending the message to other southerners, particularly on the Dodgers, that Robinson was there to stay.

The most famous example of Reese's support on a May 13th, 1947 game against the Reds in Cincinnati. At that time, Cincinnati was the southernmost city in the National League and stone's throw from Reese's hometown in Kentucky. Fans at that game booed and jeered Robinson while yelling racial epithets at him. In the face of this, Reese showed solidarity with Robinson by putting his arm around his teammate. Although we think of Reese and Robinson as making up one of the best middle infields in baseball history, Robinson spent his first year with the Dodgers as a first baseman, so Reese had to walk across the field to embrace Robinson. This was, again, one of those famous baseball events that remains shrouded in mystery with the details not entirely clear. However, the point of that story remains evident. Reese was a team leader who sided with Robinson rather than the racists.

Pee Wee Reese was a central player in the transformation of the Brooklyn Dodgers from a laughingstock into one of the most celebrated teams in baseball history and helped that happen through his support for Jackie Robinson.

Seventy-six
Branch Rickey

Branch Rickey only played in a total 118 games for the St. Louis Browns and New York Yankees, then known as the Highlanders, between 1905 and 1907, and two more games with the Browns in 1914. He was a catcher who hit well in 1906, but not in any other year. Rickey, like the great Christy Mathewson, was among the few players of their generation to have attended college, having graduated from Ohio Wesleyan. He was

Library of Congress, Prints & Photographs Division [LOC LC-DIG-npcc-19279]

a deeply religious man who quoted scripture frequently and, according to many observers at the time, was somewhat on the self-righteous side.

After his playing days wound down, Rickey then spent ten years managing the Browns and later the Cardinals between 1913-1925, but did not make much of a mark there either. Rickey was not particularly successful as a manager and soon moved up to the front office full time in 1925, after having been involved in the running of the team for several year before that. Rickey remained a baseball executive for most of the rest of his life. During his first two decades in the front office, first with the Cardinals and then with the Dodgers, Rickey had an enormous impact on baseball. It is not an overstatement to say that in those twenty years, Rickey helped create big league baseball as we know it.

The first major innovation Rickey made was the creation of an affiliated minor league system. For the first few decades of the twentieth century, there were extensive networks of minor league teams throughout the country. Some big league teams had informal arrangements with some minor league teams, but they did not directly control those teams. This made it difficult for big league clubs to develop talent on their own terms or to keep a substantial number of prospects under their control at any time.

The Cardinals, under Rickey's leadership were the first team to have minor league teams that they controlled directly. The Cardinals farm system was extensive. In some cases they controlled entire minor leagues. This gave the Cardinals a big advantage over the other teams. Eventually the rest of the American and National League caught up, but for a generation the Cardinals were the best team in the National League. That farm system helped the Cardinals develop stars like Dizzy Dean, Stan Musial, Joe Medwick, and Enos Slaughter. The Cardinals won the World Series in 1931, and repeated in 1934, 1942, 1944 and 1946. During the 21 years from 1926-1946, the Cardinals won nine pennants and five World Series. Rickey had left the Cardinals by the end of 1942, but his system kept on creating winning Cardinals teams for a few years. That was a nice run, made possible by the Cardinals' innovative minor league structures.

The contribution Rickey made by creating the farm system that teams would follow well into the 21st century is only the second most important thing he did as a baseball executive. After leaving the Cardinals, Rickey moved to Brooklyn where once again he helped build a team that would be the best in the National League for a generation. However, Rickey made an even bolder move in October of 1945, when he signed Jackie Robinson to a contract to play with the Dodgers farm team in Montreal. A year and a half later, Robinson was playing in Brooklyn.

Rickey's role in integrating baseball is sometimes overstated. By the mid-1940s, there were many activists, journalists and baseball people who had been seeking to break down baseball's color line for years. Most of these people were African American, but there were some white people as well, mostly on the far political left, who advocated for this change as well. Notably, Rickey did not purchase Robinson's contract, but simply signed him to a new one with the Dodgers. This suggested a lack of either understanding of or respect for the Negro Leagues. However, there were sixteen teams in the white major leagues in 1945. None of the executives from those teams had the courage to be the first to sign an African American player other than Rickey-and for that he deserves the credit.

The project of integrating the National and American Leagues, as Rickey understood, was not a simple or easy one. Rickey famously sought to address this by identifying not only a player who could contribute on the field, but who had the right temperament as well. Baseball history might have been quite different if Jackie Robinson had hit .243 with 6 home runs and not been able to learn first base, a new position for him, in 1947. The widely told version of the temperament question is that Rickey sought an African American player who could handle the pressure and who could be counted on to remain calm in the face of bigotry, harassment or worse. Given the time, this was an understandable approach, but it also suggests that Rickey had a patronizing attitude towards African American players and wanted the "right kind" of African American to break to color line.

There is a coda to Rickey's career that is also relevant to baseball history. In 1958, after the Dodgers had left Brooklyn for Los Angeles, Rickey became president of the Continental League. The Continental League was a proposed third major league that never came into existence. The league would have been anchored by a team in New York, which was down to only one team in 1958 as the Giants and Dodgers had moved to California. The National League saw this as a threat and substantially accelerated their expansion efforts, leading to the creation of the New York Mets.

Branch Rickey was not a great player, but almost nobody was as directly responsible for the shape of Major League Baseball today as Rickey. Rickey was central to the integration of the game, the evolution of the minor leagues and maybe even New York getting a second team in 1962.

Seventy-seven
Cal Ripken Jr.

Because baseball is such a statistically oriented game, records are particularly central to its lore. The PED era has changed
that somewhat, particularly with regards to home run totals.
Nonetheless, there are several records that most baseball fans
agree will never be broken. Some like Cy Young's 511 wins, or
his 315 losses, are from an era when the game was completely
different than what it is today. Others are relatively obscure. Sam
Crawford's record of 309 triples, which has stood for over 100
years, is pretty safe, but nobody cares too much about that.

There are two record that, for most of the middle of the twentieth century, seemed unbreakable. The first was Joe DiMaggio's
56 game hitting streak. That record was set in 1941 and still

Photo 28115536 / Baseball © Jerry Coli | Dreamstime.com

stands today. In the 80 years since DiMaggio's streak, only one player, Pete Rose in 1978, had a hitting streak of more than 40 games. The other record that seemed secure was Lou Gehrig's consecutive game streak. From June 1, 1925 through April 30, 1939, Gehrig played in every Yankees game, a total of 2,130 consecutive games. In 1983, Steve Garvey's streak of 1,207 games came to an end. Nobody else had come that close in the years since Gehrig retired.

Then Cal Ripken Jr. came along. Ripken began his streak on May 30, 1982. Ripken went on to win the Rookie of the Year award that year and was the American League Most Valuable Player the following season. Ripken then played every Orioles game for over a decade. In some years, he played every inning of every game. On September 6, 1995, Ripken played in his 2,131st consecutive game and broke Gehrig's record. Ripken went on to play 500 more consecutive games. His record of 2,632 consecutive games played ended in 1998 and looks as unbreakable as Gehrig's once did. By breaking the record, Ripken also again connected baseball with its own history and demonstrated the ability of the game, at its very best, to reach across decades and generations.

The record itself was remarkable, but what made it even more significant was that it occurred in the season following the 1994 strike. Like Hideo Nomo earlier in the year, Ripken's streak was a feel good story that helped baseball bring fans back and have positive associations with big league baseball again. Moreover, unlike Nomo's great rookie year, which was unexpected, the streak was an easy thing to promote because it was clear what game would be the record breaker. This allowed MLB to have a summer long focus on the streak and a major celebration on the day Ripken broke the record.

It also helped that Ripken was such a likeable person. Ripken avoided controversy, seemed to get along with his teammates, played his entire career with one team and although he was very well paid, managed to avoid stories about his contract negotiations. Because of the record itself, Ripken was seen as a workmanlike player who simply did his job every day. Many saw him as something of a throwback-a player who embodied the imaginary values of an imaginary era.

Ripken is also one of those players with an extraordinarily deep tie to his only team. He is one of the four players to play in 3,000 or more games with one team. The others are Henry Aaron, Carl Yastrzemski, and Stan Musial. Ripken was also born in Maryland and grew up in the Orioles system because his father was a longtime coach and manager with the organization. His younger brother Billy even played a few years alongside Cal in the big leagues. For two years, Cal and Billy made up the Orioles middle infield, while their father managed the team.

Only a very good player can stay in the lineup every day for well over a decade. Ripken was one of the two greatest short-stops of the modern era. The only real competitor for this title is Alex Rodriguez who spent about half his career at third base, and like many stars of his era, used PEDs. Ripken was a slugging shortstop who played great defense as well. His defense was sometimes unrecognized because he didn't profile as a great de-fender, so he only won two Gold Gloves. However, his 35.7 career defensive WAR is the third highest of any shortstop.

To a large extent, Ripken remade the shortstop position. Until 1980 shortstops were expected to field their position well, but not to hit much. In general, those shortstops who could hit had very little power. Of the 15 seasons through 1980 in which a shortstop hit twenty or more home runs, seven belonged to Ernie Banks. Banks was a better power hitter than Ripken, but couldn't stick at shortstop and moved to first base midway through his career. Ripken had eight seasons with 25 or more home runs. Beginning in the late 1990s, when Ripken's career was winding down, it was not unusual to have several shortstops a year reach-ing that milestone. In both 2019 and 2021, seven shortstops had 25 or more home runs. In 2022, that number fell to four.

Cal Ripken Jr. broke one of baseball's most sacred records and did it in a way that made it possible for all baseball fans to celebrate his success. Along the way, he revolutionized the short-stop position and helped usher in today's game.

Seventy-eight
Mariano Rivera

Mariano Rivera is the greatest closer in baseball history and the only player ever unanimously elected to the Hall of Fame. Rivera has 50 more saves than any other pitcher, a career ERA+ of 205, the highest of any pitcher ever, and 56.3 career WAR, about 20 more than any other pitcher amassed out of the bullpen. For good measure, Rivera threw 141 innings in the post

Photo 93914023 / Baseball © Jerry Coli | Dreamstime.com

season in which he went 8-1 with a 0.70 ERA and 42 saves. During an era when players were bulking up, often with the help of PEDs, Rivera was smaller than most pitchers, but better than almost all of them. Rivera is one of the few pitchers in baseball history to get by almost entirely on, one special pitch, a cutter that mixed with a decent fastball, and thrown with excellent control, baffled a generation of hitters. Rivera played his entire career with the Yankees and was the closer on four of their championship teams and the setup man on a fifth.

Rivera was one of those great players who made it look easy, in part because he did not look the part of a star athlete. There are some players including Aaron Judge, Randy Johnson, or Rickey Henderson who look exceptionally athletic either because of their build or size, but Rivera looked like a pretty ordinary guy. His pitching also had a smooth, almost effortless feel to it. Rivera always seemed completely unfazed and unstressed as he threw

91 mile per hour cutters past batters, occasionally jamming them and inducing a popup to second base or shortstop.

The evolution of how pitchers are used is one of the strategies that continues to change substantially and to have dramatic effects on the game. The journey from complete games being the norm and the expectation to today's strategies of openers, and many games where six or seven pitchers are used, would be a good subject for a book. There are several people who have played a role in those changes, but Rivera is a good place to start.

First, while Rivera is the greatest closer ever, the position itself only became a distinct role in the late 1980s and may already be fading away. The job of the closer is to pitch the ninth inning and finish, or close out, the victory for his team. Many closers usually pitch only one inning. This makes them distinct from an early iteration of relief stars who were frequently asked to stop an opposing team's rally in the sixth, seventh or eighth inning and remain in the game until it was over. Those pitchers were known as firemen because they extinguished rallies.

The closer evolved in the late 1980s. The first famous dominant closer who generally pitched only one inning was Dennis Eckersley beginning in 1988. Within a few years most teams had one pitcher to whom they gave the ball in the ninth inning if they had a lead. There have been several excellent closers including Eckersley, Lee Smith, Billy Wagner, Craig Kimbrel, and Trevor Hoffman, but Rivera was better than any of them. Rivera was also uniquely consistent, saving 25 or more games in 16 seasons. Only fellow Hall of Famers Trevor Hoffman with 14 seasons with 25 or more saves and Lee Smith with 13 came close to that.

There is something odd about the closer position. First, it rests on the idea that there is something special about the ninth inning that requires a particular kind of pitcher. Many closers only pitch in the ninth inning, rather than earlier innings when, for example, better hitters are due up for the opposing team. The idea of the closer also suggests that some pitchers are, for whatever reason, not suited to pitch the ninth inning and are better off as setup men, pitching the sixth, seventh or eighth inning. While this is a reasonably widespread perception, there is little data to support either of these positions.

It is not clear whether the closer position will remain a central part of the game. While there are many teams that still use a conventional closer, many teams utilize their pitching staff in ways that are very different from a few years ago. The starting pitcher role is changing as teams use openers and expect fewer innings from starters. It seems that the conventional closer role may be the next to go.

Like many closers, Rivera was originally a starting pitcher. He was primarily a starter in the minors and struggled while starting ten games for the Yankees in 1995. Conventional wisdom suggests that pitchers who rely heavily on one pitch are better off in the bullpen, although Phil Niekro's career suggests there are exceptions. Most relievers couldn't make it, or could not be quite as successful as starting pitchers. That seems to be true of Rivera, but this also raises the question of how valuable closers are. If almost all closers are failed starters, then how much should a great closer be valued? Most teams would not think of turning a competent number three starter into a closer, but when it has been tried it has usually worked.

The closer role had been broadly accepted when Mariano Rivera began his career, but he quickly became, and remains, the standard against which all others are measured. No role in baseball is as consistently high pressure as the closer; and Rivera excelled under that pressure for a generation.

Seventy-nine
Frank Robinson

Frank Robinson had a very long and extraordinary, career in Major League Baseball, beginning as a 20-year-old rookie with the Cincinnati Reds in 1956 when he hit 38 home runs and slashed .290/.379/.558 for an OPS+ of 143. By the time his career was over, Robinson had accumulated 107.3 WAR, still the seventeenth most of any position player in history. Robinson was one of the first African American players, and the first great African American player, who never played in the Negro Leagues.

Robinson, who played from 1956-1976 is also one

Photo 74066574 / Frank Robinson © Jerry Coli | Dreamstime. com

of the most underrated great players in baseball history. That is partially because he was a right fielder who came to the big leagues two years after Henry Aaron and who was never quite as good as Aaron, but also because Roberto Clemente, another great right fielder, was also almost an exact contemporary. Robinson had the better numbers, but Clemente's personal story and tragic death have overshadowed Robinson over the last four decades or so. Most fans today would say that Clemente was the better player, but the numbers do not support that. Robinson was a great slugger and solid defender who is still the only player to win the MVP in both leagues. Robinson spent the first part of his career with the Reds, but was sent to the Orioles before the 1966 season. From 1966-1971, Robinson was the best player on an Orioles team that won four pennants and two World Series.

One reason why Robinson is not always recognized as being the truly great player that he was is because no player in baseball history was a victim of the tyranny of round numbers more than Robinson was. Robinson retired only 57 hits and 14 home runs short of reaching 600 home runs and 3000 hits, something only Willie Mays, Henry Aaron, Albert Pujols, and Alex Rodriguez have done.

Here is a quick and pretty easy trivia question. Frank Robinson was the first African American manager in the American League, serving as skipper of the Cleveland Indians during the 1975 and 1976 seasons. Larry Doby managed the White Sox for the second half of the 1978 season. In 1980, Maury Wills became the third African American manager in the American League, but no National League team would hire an African American manager until the following season. Who was that manager? The answer is Frank Robinson.

Robinson served as manager of the San Francisco Giants from 1981-1984. Over that four-year period, the Giants were good for about a year and a half, from the second half of the 1981 season through the end of the 1982 season, and pretty mediocre the rest of the time. I was a frequent visitor to Candlestick Park in those years and saw Robinson's Giants play about fifty times. Robinson was never a great on field tactician, but we still enjoyed watching him manage. He was only a few years removed from being an active player and seemed to frequently have this look on his face as if he wanted to grab a bat and send himself up to pinch hit. By 1983, most fans, including me, would have enthusiastically supported the idea.

Ironically, one of the reasons Robinson fell short of 600 home runs and 3,000 hits is that during the last two years of his career, when the aging slugger was playing with Cleveland, his manager rarely played him. In 1975 and 1976, he only came to bat 228 times despite a very strong 136 OPS+. The manager responsible for that decision was Robinson himself who was trying to put the team and other players above his personal goals.

It was almost thirty years after Jackie Robinson played his first game with the Dodgers before Frank Robinson managed a big league game. That is evidence of the extent to which racism permeated the thinking of baseball executives. By 1970, or even 1965, there had been dozens of African American players who could have become managers, but for years, teams found reasons to go with the white guy. Unfortunately, little has changed in that regard. Even in 2023, there were only two African American managers in the Major Leagues.

Robinson managed a total of 16 years in the big leagues. After the Giants he managed the Orioles and then the Montreal Expos. He was assigned to manage the Expos when the team, in its last years in Montreal, was run by Major League Baseball. When the Expos moved to Washington, Robinson remained with the team and became the first manager of the Washington Nationals. Robinson also served in the MLB executive office in several capacities between 1999 and 2015.

There are few great players whose career in Major League Baseball spanned almost sixty years. Robinson's length of service alone makes him a key figure in baseball history, but he also was a groundbreaking manager in two leagues and a league executive during the years baseball expanded the playoffs, introduced interleague play, and became much more meaningfully globalized.

Eighty
Jackie Robinson

Jackie Robinson was one of the most important base-ball players in history and was also a truly great player. Jackie Robinson, though, was so significant, that he would have to be included on any list of the most important Americans of the 20th Century. Robinson, as most Americans know, was the first African American to play in the American or National League in the twentieth century. From today's perspective, it may be difficult to comprehend just how significant this was, but in the US in the middle of the twentieth century baseball was a massively important cultural institution. Millions of Americans followed baseball, paid attention at the very least to the World Series and

Photo courtesy of the National Baseball Hall of Fame and Museum (Robinson Jackie 279.71 NBL)

knew the names of big stars.

Another reason Robinson joining the Dodgers was of such significance to the larger civil rights movement was because of when it occurred. In 1947, when Robinson played his first game for Brooklyn, Brown v. Board of Education, the Montgomery Bus Boycott, lunch counter sit-ins, the Civil Rights Act and the Voting Rights Act were still several years in the future. President Truman was still a year away from integrating the military. Martin Luther King Jr. had not yet begun his career at Ebeneezer Baptist Church or even graduated from Morehouse College. Malcolm X was still in jail and known as Malcolm Little. In other words, baseball, and Jackie Robinson, were ahead of much of the rest of the country on the issue of integration.

The horrific racism and extraordinary pressure Robinson encountered during his first year with the Dodgers have become part of baseball, and American, lore. Had he failed on the field or been unable to keep his cool, baseball, and indeed American, history would have been very different. During his rookie season, Robinson played a new position, first base, and hit a very solid .297 with 12 home runs and a league leading 29 stolen bases and won the Rookie of the Year Award. He had a similar year the following season, but then got even better in 1949 when, after moving to second base, he won the National League MVP award. From 1949-1954 Robinson slashed .327/.428/.505 and was an All-Star every year. Robinson played 10 seasons for the Dodgers, retiring after the 1956 season.

In that ten year span from 1947-1956, the Dodgers won six pennants but only one World Series. Robinson was the Dodgers top player over that period, accumulating 61.8 WAR with an OPS+ of 132. Robinson also played great defense at several positions and stole more bases than any other player during those ten years. Only Stan Musial had more WAR among National Leaguers during the years that Robinson was playing, but Robinson was more than just a great player. He brought a style of play back into the National League that included more aggressive baserunning and risk-taking that had fallen out of favor but had remained part of the Negro League game.

Baseball has celebrated Jackie Robinson more than any other player. Since 1997 no player has been allowed to wear Robinson's number 42, although some players, most notably Mariano Rivera, who were already using that number were allowed to continue. Every season on April 15th, the anniversary of Robinson's first game with the Dodgers, every player on every team wears number 42 as a tribute to Robinson. The significance of Robinson's career to the Civil Rights Movement and Major League Baseball was enormous, but baseball has raised it to another level. It is almost as if MLB has deified Robinson and therefore believes it has absolved itself from its original sin of segregation.

The Christian overtones in the language above are hard to miss, but Robinson's story cannot be understood outside of the Christian culture that produced and celebrated Robinson and his career. Branch Rickey, a devout Christian himself, stressed to Robinson the need to not fight back, suffer the slings and arrows of outrageous racism and, in short, to turn the other cheek. This approach was a bit patronizing, but that is the same message that Jesus preached. Robinson himself sometimes is presented as an almost Christ like figure. He suffered for our, that is to say baseball's, sins and in doing that made us all better people. Moreover, he suffered quietly and with dignity. He did not have disciples, but he had teammates, including Pee Wee Reese, who stood by him. The analogy only goes so far. Nobody betrayed Robinson and he was not crucified. However, the Christian themes around Robinson may help explain the enduring resonance of the story of Jackie Robinson in 1947.

Robinson remained a public figure, and civil rights advocate, until his death. As the Civil Rights movement grew and sometimes became more radical, Robinson struggled to remain a central and relevant voice. He was a liberal Republican throughout much of his life. You can still find grainy videos of Robinson at the 1964 Republican Convention cheering for Nelson Rockefeller, the liberal Republican Governor of New York, who Robinson supported, but who ultimately lost that nomination to the right-wing and anti-civil rights candidate, Barry Goldwater.

Robinson passed away in 1972, but a few days before his

death he made one last public appearance and spoke a few words at a ceremony before game two of the World Series celebrating the 25th anniversary of Robinson beginning his career in the National League. His comments were gracious, thanking a number of people and singling out Reese, who was present at the ceremony, but he closed by saying "I'm gonna be tremendously more pleased and more proud when I look at that third base coaching line one day and see a Black face managing in baseball." In doing that Robinson made the point that while baseball was congratulating itself over what happened in 1947, there was still a lot of work to do. Frank Robinson would take over as Cleveland's manager fewer than three years later.

Jackie Robinson is, uniquely among baseball players, a profoundly important American here. His life is a deeply intertwined with the African American struggle for Civil Rights. Robinson was also a great ballplayer who helped revitalize the game with his energy, baserunning and exciting style of play.

Eighty-one
Alex Rodriguez

As a twenty-year-old, Alex Rodriguez slashed .358/ .414/.631 for an OPS+ of 161, hitting 36 home runs and stealing 15 bases while playing excellent defense at shortstop. Only five players in history had a higher OPS+ at that age. Four are in the Hall of Fame. A fifth, Mike Trout, will get there someday. None of them were shortstops. Rodriguez's 9.4 WAR was the most ever by a

Photo 20683509 / Baseball © Scott Anderson | Dreamstime.com

20-year-old until Mike Trout had a 10.5 WAR in 2012.

The young Alex Rodriguez was one of the greatest and most complete players ever. There was nothing he could not do on the field. He could steal bases, draw walks, hit for average, hit for power all while playing fine defense at shortstop. That was unprecedented in baseball history, particularly for a shortstop. He was Ernie Banks with a higher batting average, Cal Ripken Jr., but a better overall hitter with more speed and Honus Wagner with home run power. Through his age 24 season Rodriguez had a 138 OPS+ 189 home runs, 133 stolen bases, and 38.1 WAR. Only Trout, Mantle, and Cobb had more WAR by that age. There are a lot of numbers here, but Rodriguez's place in baseball history is only significant because he was such a great player.

Rodriguez spent the first years of his career with the Seattle Mariners, having cups of coffee in 1994 and 1995, before his rookie season of 1996. The Mariners were a good team during that time, but Rodriguez was overshadowed by teammates like Ken Griffey Jr., Edgar Martinez, and Randy Johnson. While with the Mariners, Rodriguez was a superstar, but was not one of the highest profile players in the game. He was part of a trio of American League shortstops, including Derek Jeter and Nomar Garciaparra who were lumped together and competed with each other, but Rodriguez was the best. He was friendly with Jeter at first, but that soon turned into a pretty intense rivalry.

Following the 2000 season, Rodriguez became a free agent, eventually signing a ten year $250 million contract with the Rangers. That massive contract marked the beginning of Rodriguez's transition to becoming one of baseball's great anti-heroes. Rodriguez spent three years with the Rangers. He continued his extraordinary play, winning the MVP award in 2003, but a different narrative began to emerge around him. His contract was a constant source of media attention. The Rangers were not winning much and were beginning to regret signing Rodriguez, so they tried to trade him after the 2003 season. It didn't help that the Mariners got better after Rodriguez left, winning a record 116 regular season games in 2001.

The early 2000s were the heart of the PED era. Rodriguez was not one of the players, yet, who were widely suspected of PED use, but nobody would have been surprised to hear that the slugging shortstop who seemed to have gotten quite a bit bigger since his rookie year was a PED user. Seeking to get out from under Rodriguez's contract, the Rangers traded him to the Yankees. The Yankees already had a shortstop in Derek Jeter, so Rodriguez moved to third base. Moving to a new position because a teammate, who by most measures was not his equal defensively, did not fit into the emerging narrative of Rodriguez as a selfish player, so it is often overlooked. However, changing positions like that was a very unselfish move by Rodriguez, one that clearly prioritized harmony on his new team over his own ego.

This gesture of moving to a new position was never fully appreciated by Yankees fans or the national baseball media. Rodriguez was resented by some Yankees fans because he somehow was seen as a threat to Jeter, even though Rodriguez had deferred to Jeter. Rodriguez also performed badly in the 2004-2007 post-seasons with the Yankees, so earned a reputation as not being the big game player that Jeter was. In 2009, Rodriguez changed that narrative by staying hot throughout the entire post-season and helping the Yankees win the World Series. He then played poorly in his final four post-seasons.

Rodriguez retired after the 2016 season, having stayed with the Yankees for 12 years. His career numbers were extraordinary. Had he hit four more home runs, Rodriguez would have been the only player other than Henry Aaron with 3,000 hits and 700 home runs. His 117.5 career WAR is second only to Barry Bonds among position players who began their career after 1960.

Unfortunately, all of Rodriguez's accomplishments are tarred by PED use. He was one of the very few prominent players to be formally sanctioned for PED use, having been suspended for the entire 2014 season. Missing the 2014 season cost Rodriguez his chance at 700 home runs. Before that, accusations and rumors of PED use had dogged Rodriguez for years. Unlike Barry Bonds and Roger Clemens who had established themselves as great players before they used PEDs, or Sammy Sosa and Mark McGwire who visibly transformed from good to great players once they started using PEDs, Rodriguez's PED use is more difficult to categorize. That is because we do not know for certain when Rodriguez started using PEDs. He did not get sanctioned until 2014, but many believed he had been using PEDs since his days with the Rangers, possibly earlier and possibly throughout his entire career.

It is easy to see Rodriguez as divisive, but more accurate to describe him as broadly disliked. Rodriguez was not always good with the media and did not have an easy way with fans, but was an historically great player who is one of the two greatest short-stops of the last century and changed positions halfway through his career as a courtesy to a teammate. However, the PED issue will always dog Rodriguez. He was on the Hall of Fame ballot for the first time in 2021 and received only 34.3% of the vote. The following year he improved slightly to 35.7%. How his candidacy plays out over the coming years will be a major part of the next chapter in how baseball reckons with the PED era.

Eighty-two
Pete Rose

If you did not see Pete Rose play, you may not appreciate how big a star he was in the 1970s. Rose was the face of the Big Red Machine. Joe Morgan was the team's best player, but Rose was with the Reds before Morgan and had a much larger public profile. He was a constant in the post-season, playing October baseball in seven post-seasons between 1970-1983, back when only four teams made the playoffs. He played in every All-Star Game from 1965-1982, but that only

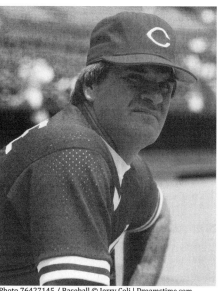

Photo 76427145 / Baseball © Jerry Coli | Dreamstime.com

captures some of his fame. Rose, who had more hits, singles, plate appearances, and appeared in more games than anybody who ever played big league baseball, was Charlie Hustle, a throwback and a winner. The dude ran to first base when he drew a walk.

Rose was also a strange player with a strange skill set. He could hit and get on base, but had little speed or power. Rose is one of three players, along with Paul Waner and Wade Boggs who had more than 3,000 hits, but did not either hit 200 home runs or steal 200 bases. Rose stole twenty or more bases in a season once, but never hit twenty or more home runs in a season. Rose was an extreme singles hitter. Fully 76% of his hits were singles. Despite these shortcomings, Rose's ability to get on base made him a very valuable player. Rose was also unusual because he changed positions frequently throughout his career. He started out as a second baseman, moved to the outfield, then to third and finally first base. He is the only player in baseball history to play 500 or more games at first, second and third base. For good measure he played more than 500 games in both left and right field. Rose was not a great defender at any position, but was willing to play anywhere to help his team.

The last few years of Rose's career changed perceptions around him and reframed his place in baseball history and lore. Early in the 1978 season, shortly after he turned 37 Rose got his 3,000th hit. That was a major milestone for a great player who was showing few signs of slowing down. Rose's last good year was 1981. By the end of that year, he had almost 3,700 hits, a .310 batting average and 124 OPS+ for his career. Those were excellent career numbers, but Rose had other goals in mind. He was aiming for 4,000 hits, which seemed doable, and breaking Ty Cobb's all-time hit record of 4,189, which seemed much more remote.

Over the next five years Rose, who had begun his career in 1963, seemed craven in his attempt to break the record. He was a pretty bad player for that entire period. By then Rose could only play first base, but could not hit enough for that position. He hit five home runs between 1982 and 1986 while compiling and OPS+ of 86, acceptable for a slick fielding shortstop, but not a first baseman. His career batting average dropped to .303 and his OPS+ to 118. Rose spent those years with the Phillies, briefly with the Expos and from mid-1984 through 1986 back with the Reds. In 1985-1986 he also managed the Reds. In that capacity he put himself in the lineup way too frequently until he finally broke Cobb's record.

Rose's 4,256 hits in the big leagues is an extraordinary accomplishment regardless of how he got there, but at the time his pursuit of the record was very off-putting. He reached the finish line by spending five years as a very mediocre player and ultimately by making it tougher for the team he managed to win. Charlie Hustle had become Charlie Selfish. The throwback so widely celebrated in the 1970s became just another symbol of the overpaid athlete who thought only about himself.

That was the good news for Rose in the late 1980s because shortly after breaking Cobb's hit record, word got out that Rose had a gambling problem and may have even bet on baseball. Some speculated whether he'd bet on his own team. After ending his career as an active player, Rose continued to manage the Reds. As reports, and evidence, of his gambling came to light, MLB began to focus more on the question of whether Rose had bet the Reds, specifically in 1987. Rose admitted nothing, so MLB did an investigation that led ultimately to Rose agreeing to accept a lifetime ban, with the possibility of reinstatement after a year in exchange for MLB making no formal declaration of his guilt. The following year, Rose was convicted for tax fraud and spent time in prison, so he was not reinstated. In 1991, the Hall of Fame decided Rose would not appear on the ballot. Thus, the all-time hit leader is still essentially banned from the Hall of Fame. It was an unfortunate coda to the career of one of the most famous players ever.

Since his ban from baseball, Rose has become a sad, but also crass, character. He is still on the periphery of the game and remains a polarizing figure among older fans. He usually signs his autographs "The Hit King." While he has admitted he bet on the Reds, he has clarified that he bet on them to win. Rose continues to see himself as a victim, but there might be something to that. We now know that gambling is an addiction-and Rose was an addict. MLB, for its part, has embraced gambling in recent years so the hypocrisy around Rose is hard to miss. It seems like a sport that gives the over on the number of strikeouts for a playoff game might find room in its heart, and in its Hall of Fame, for a great player who had a gambling addiction, but never threw a game or played anything less than his best.

Eighty-three
Babe Ruth

In the 1980s Yankees star Don Mattingly said "at one time I thought Babe Ruth was a cartoon character. I really did, I mean I wasn't born until 1961 and I grew up in Indiana." At first glance this is just a funny line, but there is something more to it than that. Babe Ruth was not quite a cartoon character, but with the passing of time, he seems almost fictional. In some sense, the more you know about the Babe, the more fictional he sounds.

As a player, Ruth was almost impossibly good. A top young pitcher who switched

Library of Congress, Prints & Photographs Division [Bain News Service - LOC LC-DIG-ggbain-33131]

positions and became the best hitter ever. So much more about the Babe-the called shot, prodigious appetites, humble origins, huge personality and extraordinary skills on the diamond don't seem quite real. He learned to play baseball in a Catholic home for orphans and troubled youth where his family had all but abandoned him when he was a young boy. Ruth did things like visit sick children in the hospital and then hit home runs for them that same day. Ruth was a folk hero like Yogi Berra or Satchel Paige, but even more mythological seeming, perhaps because he was older than both of them. If the Bambino had not existed, some hack 1920s baseball writer would have invented him.

Ruth was real, and because of him modern baseball began to take shape. Ruth was the best player on the best team in the biggest city just as the 20th century media culture was emerging. He achieved a level of fame that would not have been possible on another team, in a previous decade, for a lesser player or if he had a different personality. It all came together for Ruth and for baseball. Babe Ruth's life story taught Americans how to think about their baseball stars and how to turn ballplayers into American celebrities and heroes. Babe Ruth did not just help create baseball fan and celebrity culture but helped American learn how to consume culture and celebrity.

There were other famous ballplayers before Babe Ruth, including Christy Mathewson who, like Ruth, played in New York City, but Ruth was on a completely different level. Matty was good with the media, but Ruth was in a separate class in that regard. He was endlessly entertaining, quotable, and charming. Nobody ever described Ty Cobb that way. Ruth had a fun nickname that suggested that he was a young carefree type. Ruth's drinking and womanizing, while largely kept out of the press, also made him more colorful and entertaining to the media. When he came to the Yankees and completed his switch to the outfield, Ruth, unlike Matty, became an everyday player, making him a more accessible and marketable celebrity.

More than any player in baseball history, Ruth changed how the game is played. Big league baseball today is still largely the game that Ruth created sometime around 1919-1920. Before Ruth, the home run was an oddity around which teams did not build their strategy. From 1900 to 1920, the leader in home runs was Gavvy Cravath with 119. Other than Ruth and Cravath, no other player even had 100 home runs over those twenty years. Only two players other than Ruth, Cravath with 24, and Frank Schulte with 21, even managed more than 20 in a season during the first two decades of the twentieth century.

In 1920, Ruth's first season with the Yankees, he hit 54 home runs. Only one team in either the American or National League hit that many. By the end of the 1920s, the home run had supplanted the stolen base and the deadball style of play as the primary offensive weapon of most teams. Other hitters such as Lou Gehrig, Rogers Hornsby, and a few years after that, Jimmie Foxx, and Mel Ott, began to hit for power after Ruth came to the Yankees, but it began with Ruth.

In the 1920s baseball was deeply intertwined with America and Ruth was deeply intertwined with baseball. Sometime in 2021 my aunt asked me to help digitize some cassette tapes of family interviews. After I got them digitized, I listened to the files. One of them was from the early 1990s and included my beloved grandfather, who was then well into his 80s, telling an old story about a new immigrant going to Yankee Stadium to see a baseball game. The climax of the story was the Babe hitting a long home run, and the immigrant, upon hearing everybody yell "home run," grabbing his sandwiches and running home. It is funnier in my grandfather's Yiddish, but it also shows how the Babe permeated the culture at the time and helped bring immigrants, not just Jewish ones, to that most American of institutions-baseball.

One part of the mythology around Babe Ruth is that he was the league's best pitcher before he moved to the outfield. That isn't quite true because Walter Johnson was the pitcher in the American League during those years. However, Ruth was among the league's best pitchers from 1915-1918. Ruth stopped pitching when he joined the Yankees. Enough has been written about Babe Ruth as a player, but one thing fans may not know is that on the last day of the 1933 season the Yankees beat the Red Sox 6-5. The 38-year-old Ruth hit a solo home run, but he also pitched a complete game in his first time on the mound in two years and only his third since 1921.

The Babe was perhaps the greatest player ever, but in addition he was a larger than life figure who was in the right town at the dawning of the mass media era. Because of that, Babe Ruth, more than any other athlete, helped create the culture of sports and celebrity that still exists today.

Eighty-four
Nolan Ryan

On September 11th, 1966 Mets manager Wes Westrum called upon Nolan Ryan to pitch the top of the 6th inning. Ryan, who was not yet twenty-years-old, was making his first big league appearance. The first batter he faced was opposing pitcher Pat Jarvis. Ryan struck him out. Ryan then got Felipe Alou to fly out to right before striking out future Hall of Famer Eddie Matthews. Twenty-seven years and eleven days after that, Rangers manager Kevin Kennedy removed Ryan from a game in the first inning after he walked Mariners first baseman Dave Magadan. Between those two games, over the course of seven presidential administrations, Nolan Ryan had an extraordinary career, one that has taken greater significance as baseball has changed in the decades since he retired.

Photo 186835107 / Baseball © Jerry Coli | Dreamstime.com

There is nothing in baseball quite like the strikeout; and no player quite like the strikeout pitcher, particularly if that pitcher relies on a fastball to ring up opposing hitters. The strikeout is the primal baseball outcome of the eternal battle between batter and pitcher. Ryan had a pretty good curve, but by far his best pitch was his Linda Ronstadt fastball, as we used to say in the 1970s when Ryan was in his prime, because it Blue Bayou. Ryan was one of the few pitchers of the time to be clocked at over 100

MPH. He was not only the hardest throwing pitcher of his era, but he remained among the very fastest in the game well into his 40s.

There has never been a strikeout pitcher quite like Nolan Ryan. Ryan led his league in strikeouts more times, 11, including when he was 43 years old, than any pitcher in history. He set the single season record for strikeouts since 1900 in 1973 and still holds that record. Ryan's 5,714 career strikeouts are the most ever by a margin of almost 900. Randy Johnson is second with 4,875. Only 19 pitchers in baseball history have even half as many career strikeouts as Ryan.

Ryan threw an astounding seven no-hitters, three more than any other pitcher ever. However, despite his great accomplishments, Ryan was never an inner circle elite pitcher, partially because he couldn't always find the strike zone. He led the league in walks eight times, has the record for most career walks with no other pitcher coming within 900 walks, or two thirds as many as Ryan. He never won a Cy Young award and had very few big moments or games that were not simply personal accomplishments. He pitched well in his only World Series, with the Mets in 1969, but did not have any big post-season moments.

During most of his career Ryan was one of the most recognizable players in baseball, particularly in his home state of Texas where he played for both the Astros and Rangers. He was also good for attendance because of his strikeouts and, by mid-career, the possibility that on any given start he could pitch a no-hitter. This became relevant when Ryan became a free agent after the 1979 season and signed a four year contract with the Astros for a total of $4.5 million, making him the first player in baseball history to make a million dollars a year.

One of the things that made Ryan so unusual is that he had an amazingly long career. Ryan threw 1,271.2 innings and struck out 1,437 batters after his 40th birthday. Only four pitchers threw more innings after their 40th birthday, but they were all either knuckleballers or junkballers. Ryan struck out almost 300 more batters after turning 40 than any pitcher in history.

Late in his career, and particularly since retiring, Ryan has become a symbol of a kind of baseball machismo. This reputation was bolstered by an incident during one of Ryan's last starts when Robin Ventura of the White Sox, then 26-years-old, charged the mound and tried to fight with Ryan. Ryan fought back, got Ventura in a headlock and began punching him in the face. More pertinently, people who look at the game and think the changes are because pitchers are soft or not mentally strong, point to Ryan as an example of somebody who just kept on pitching and would have laughed at pitch counts. This is a comforting idea for many who don't like the changes in the game, but it is also a bit nonsensical.

Nolan Ryan is such an extreme outlier that his career tells us almost nothing about baseball or pitching more generally. At age 43 Ryan could pitch more than 200 innings, average 10.2 strikeouts per nine innings and lead the league in strikeouts not because ballplayers were tougher in the 1990s, but because he was Nolan Ryan. There is also some inherent selection bias here. Ryan was the pitcher who did not get injured due to pitching too much at a young age, but there were many pitchers who might have had longer careers if they had been handled more carefully.

Additionally, pitching has changed an enormous amount since Ryan was playing. Ryan was considered to have the best fastball of any pitcher for almost the entire time he was playing. Today, a pitcher throwing as hard as Ryan with as good a curveball would probably still be effective but would not be the hardest thrower on most teams. When Ryan was pitching, a 100 MPH fastball was newsworthy. Now there are dozens of pitchers who throw that hard. In other words, as good as Ryan was for his time, his physical skills and athletic ability would not make him a top tier pitcher today. That is not meant to take anything away from Ryan, but simply to point out that pitchers today are bigger, stronger, and asked to do more than those of Ryan's era. Ryan remains the archetype against which all fireballing strikeout pitchers are measured. It is unlikely any will ever be able to strike as many batters out, and excel for as many years, as Ryan did.

Eighty-five
Curt Schilling

I've hated Curt Schilling since way before it was cool. As a Yankees fan, I was frustrated by his pitching in both the 2001 World Series and the 2004 ALCS. I thought the bloody sock schtick was a bit much, and for me Schilling always represented the height of Red Sox triumphalism. Nonetheless, Schilling was a great pitcher. While he may not have seemed to be a Hall of Fame caliber pitcher when he was playing, by the time he retired he had

Photo 17976481 / Baseball © Jerry Coli | Dreamstime.com

a strong Hall of Fame case. Schilling had just short of 80 career WAR, is 17th on the all-time strikeout list, had an ERA+ of 127 and a post-season record of 11-2 with a 2.23 ERA. His 216 career wins, on the low side for the Hall of Fame, and no Cy Young awards may have put some voters off at first, but on balance Schilling had a pretty good shot of making it. Mike Mussina, a very similar pitcher who pitched during the same era as Schilling, got elected to the Hall of Fame in 2019, so it seemed like Schilling had the on-field credentials to get in.

Schilling came close to getting to Cooperstown a couple of times, including winning 71.1% of the votes in 2021, but in 2022, his tenth and final year up on the ballot, he came up well short of the 75% needed to make it into the Hall of Fame. Schilling was never associated with PED use or gambling, so that was not the obstacle. Nor did he commit a violent crime or anything like that. Rather, Schilling is being kept out of the Hall of Fame because of his political opinions. For the record, his opinions are pretty much the opposite of mine.

Many ballplayers, including many Hall of Famers, are conservative. On their own, those views would not dissuade voters from supporting a candidate for the Hall of Fame, but Schilling is different. He has been a visible and outspoken supporter of far right causes, an ardent follower of Donald Trump, and an apologist for the insurrectionists who violently stormed the Capitol on January 6th, 2021. Schilling has embraced numerous untruths that permeate the far right media, and is active on Twitter, using his account to promote his political views.

There have been examples of this in the past. In the 1980s, the San Diego Padres had several members of the far right John Birch Society on their pitching staff. Additionally, John Rocker, a one-time top reliever for the Atlanta Braves, had a homophobic, racist, and anti-immigrant rant quoted in *Sports Illustrated*, but none of those players had Hall of Fame credentials.

Schilling seems aware that his politics have hurt his Hall of Fame chances and has often criticized those who have seemingly changed their vote because of those politics. The question of the extent to which a player's politics should be a factor in Hall of Fame voting is subjective. However, Schilling is significant because he is former ballplayer who demonstrates how the politicization and polarization of American life has permeated areas where politics were never previously part of the discourse. There are other retired ballplayers, notably Aubrey Huff, who share Schilling's views and have faced similar controversies in retirement, but Schilling was the best and highest profile player of the bunch.

This raises some big picture questions for the future of baseball and its place in American culture and life. Baseball has never been entirely disconnected from politics, but many fans told themselves it was. For example, it is impossible to think seriously about the American and National League before 1947 without recognizing the racist context in which it existed, but many, mostly white fans, seek to do just that. Labor issues, treatment of minor leaguers and questions around stadium financing have long been part of the politics of baseball, but Schilling represents something different.

As America becomes a country where political divisions are acute and where friendships across political lines become increasingly difficult, how can fans continue not to know or care about the politics of players. For a liberal or progressive baseball fan, rooting for a player, no matter how good he is, who refuses to get vaccinated for Covid or express their support for Trumpism, is difficult. Similarly, some players like Tim Anderson or Mookie Betts have taken clear progressive positions on several issues regarding race in America. Giants manager Gabe Kapler announced in 2022, following yet another mass shooting that he would not stand on the field during the National Anthem. Rooting for these players or manager would be difficult for conservative fans.

Politics are already remaking baseball and baseball historiography. In my view, the election of Minnie Minoso and Tony Oliva to the Hall of Fame in 2022 was a good development because it recognizes the challenges facing many Latino ballplayers in the 1950s and 1960s. I would like to see Felipe Alou join them there someday as well. However, politics, and the need to be more inclusive about baseball history played a role in that. MLB now embraces LGBTQ pride in a way that was unimaginable even at the turn of this century. MLB does this while most team owners continue to give money and otherwise support politicians who would overturn rights and freedoms for LGBTQ people. Baseball is being pulled into the politics of a divided and increasingly angry country. No player encapsulates that more than Curt Schilling.

Eighty-six
Tom Seaver

Tom Seaver is the third, and best, of three consecutive hard-throwing righties in this book. Seaver and Nolan Ryan were teammates on the Mets for a few years before the Mets sent Ryan to the Angels following the 1971 season. Seaver was one of the greatest pitchers ever and is still seventh on the all-time WAR list for pitchers and fifth among pitchers after 1900. He is also sixth on the all-time strikeout list, won over 300 games and had a career ERA+ of 127.

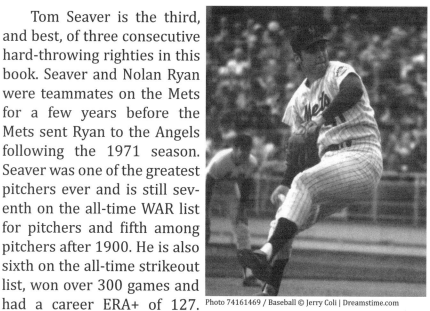

Photo 74161469 / Baseball © Jerry Coli | Dreamstime.com

From 1967-1975 he was the best pitcher in baseball averaging 19 wins, four shutouts, 233 strikeouts and 7.3 WAR with an ERA+ of 143. During that period, he won three Cy Young awards and finished in the top ten in Cy Young voting three other times.

Although Seaver also played for the Reds, Red Sox and White Sox, he had a special relationship with the Mets, and will always be identified with that team. Seaver turned a franchise that had spent five years as a punchline into, at least for a while, a very good team. He was the first great player in Mets history and the face of the team when it won the 1969 World Series and came within one game of doing it again in 1973. Seaver began his career with the Mets in 1967, their sixth year. Over their first five years, the Mets had never had a .400 record—they wouldn't until 1968.

They never had a player with even a 4.5 WAR season. Seaver had a great rookie year in 1967 going 16-13 with a 2.76 ERA and 6 WAR, the most in Mets history up until that time.

Two years later when the Miracle Mets won the World Series, Seaver was again their best player. In that magical Mets year Seaver went 25-7 with a 2.21 ERA, good for an ERA+ of 165 and 7.2 WAR. His post-season performance was unimpressive until when, in the pivotal game four of the World Series, he held a very powerful Orioles lineup to one run over ten innings as the Mets won the game 2-1. Four years later, when a very average Mets team won the National League East by 1.5 games, Seaver had an even better year, going 19-10 with a 2.08 ERA and a 175 ERA+. His 11 WAR easily led the National League, but he finished eighth in the MVP balloting.

There was much more to Seaver than the numbers. He was a hard throwing right-handed pitcher with graceful mechanics and a distinctive drop-and-drive delivery. Seaver was also a good-looking young guy. He was 22-years-old when he pitched his first game for the Mets. The late 1960s were a time of generational change in New York and all of America. The Mets, despite being a new team, had sought to build a fan base by bringing in many past their prime former stars, and one famous manager, Casey Stengel, who would be well known to older fans. Ken Boyer, Richie Ashburn, Bob Friend, Warren Spahn, Gil Hodges and Duke Snider were familiar names to National League fans, but they were all past their prime and, to baby boomers moving into adulthood, players from the past.

Seaver was different. He was the first Baby Boomer Mets star and one of the first of his generation to be a prominent big league ballplayer. On the eve of the 1969 World Series, Seaver made it clear that he opposed the Vietnam War. This helped strengthen ties between Seaver and younger fans, but because he had been in the Marine Reserves, Seaver did not alienate more conservative fans. In addition to his views on the war, Seaver was well liked by the New York media who helped elevate him to becoming a major star, familiar even to New Yorkers with little interest in baseball.

It is a baseball cliché to describe a player as defining a franchise, but that is what Tom Seaver did for the Mets. Seaver was the first Mets player to get national attention not for colorful but poor play on the field or because of something he had done years earlier, but for being a great player for the Mets. Seaver was the best and most visible player on the Mets team that finally not only won more games than they lost, but won the World Series. Seaver is, even now, by far the best player in Mets history. His 78.8 WAR with the Mets is still almost thirty more than any other Met. Accordingly, Seaver's memory is still beloved among Mets fans, even those too young to have seen him play.

By the time Seaver had pitched for the Mets for close to a decade, tension began to arise between Seaver and Mets owner M. Donald Grant. This was in part about money. Free agency was beginning and Seaver wanted to be paid what he was worth, but Grant also had somehow grown tired of the best pitcher of his generation. The Mets were not good and needed to rebuild. In June of 1977, the Mets sent Seaver to the Reds for a package of useful but unremarkable players. It was a terrible trade. Seaver remained one of the best pitchers in the game through the 1981 season while the players the Mets got back never amounted to much. Moreover, the trade was devastating for the Mets fan base. Trading away the team's best player and fan favorite, who was also one of the few remaining links to the pennant winning teams of 1969 and 1973 was a terrible idea. Mets fans never forgave Grant for that. There are a handful of trades in baseball history that makes fans feel like they have been betrayed, but none more so than this one.

The Mets were not quite done with Seaver. The team was smart enough to get Seaver back from the Reds following the 1982 season, but then were foolish enough to leave him unprotected in the free agent compensation pool a year later when Seaver was selected by the White Sox. The Mets are an odd franchise, alternating being very hapless and very good for more than 60 years, but there is nothing more Mets than the way they treated Seaver.

Eighty-seven
Sammy Sosa

There may be no player in baseball history who went through the cycle of good player to nationally recognized and celebrated star to scandal to punch line to obscurity as fast as Sammy Sosa. Sosa began his career with the Rangers as an outfielder with some speed and some power, but was quickly sent to the White Sox for an aging Harold Baines. The Rangers owner at that time, who had some responsibility for that trade, was George W. Bush who soon graduated to making poor decisions on a much larger scale.

Photo 170344321 / Baseball © Jerry Coli | Dreamstime.com

For the next several years, Sosa was a pretty good player for the Cubs and the White Sox, twice hitting thirty home runs and stealing thirty bases in a season. Then, in 1998, Sosa was part of the best feel good duet in baseball history that, at the time, was credited with saving baseball. This, of course, was the 1998 home run race when Sosa and Mark McGwire competed to break Roger Maris's single season home run record. McGwire ended up hitting 70 home runs to Sosa's 66. The race was celebrated in the treacly tones that some fans love and others find downright silly. A home run chase that consisted of not one, but two stars trying to break Roger Maris single season record of 61 home runs, seemed like the perfect antidote to whatever bad feelings were left over from the 1994 strike.

McGwire and Sosa contributed to that feeling not just because of their awesome power, but because they were both so likeable and mingled so easily with fans and even the media. Although they were competing against each other, the two seemed to get along well. There was an uplifting racial component to the chase as well as McGwire was white and Sosa a dark-skinned Latino.

After the season and in the years that followed, there were increasing suspicions that both sluggers had been using PEDs, but even during the season any fan with basic powers of observation could see that both players were juicing. One had to be willfully blind not to see that. Both players were bloated muscular versions of their former selves and were hitting the ball further than they ever had. In case that wasn't evident enough, a reporter literally saw a performance enhancing substance in McGwire's locker.

In the aftermath of the PED issue that was part of baseball for almost a generation, a consensus emerged that MLB's leadership turned a blind eye to PED use because the home runs attracted fans and were therefore good for the game. The 1998 home run chase shows that is not quite the truth. In that particular case, MLB did not turn a blind eye to PED use. MLB actively encouraged it.

It soon became obvious to everybody that both players had been using PEDs in 1998. Sosa, McGwire, and Rafael Palmeiro all had to testify at a 2005 congressional hearing on PED use. Sosa denied all PED use at that hearing, but it seemed implausible. A few years later it was revealed that Sosa had tested positive for PED use in 2003, but there had been no PED testing in baseball in the late 1990s.

Sosa's connection to PED use have helped keep him out of baseball as no team has brought him back as a coach or in any similar capacity. The Cubs, the team for which he had his best seasons, have not celebrated Sosa as part of their long history. Since his playing days ended, Sosa was briefly in the news again because, oddly, his skin color changed, making him much lighter skinned than in his playing days. Sosa claimed this was a side effect from medicine he was taking, but the medical evidence to support that was sparse. Since then, he has faded into obscurity.

That 66 home run season was part of a five year run from 1998-2002 when Sosa hit 292 home runs. No player has ever hit that many over a five year period. Sosa is also the only player to hit 60 home runs in a season three times, but he did not lead the league in home runs in any of those three years. Sosa never got more than 18.5% of the votes on the Hall of Fame ballot. This is in large part due to his PED use, but his candidacy is a strange one in another way as well.

Sosa was an absurdly one-dimensional player. He is ninth on the all-time home run list with 609 home runs. All eight players ahead of him have at least 73.1 WAR and an OPS+ of 136. Sosa career totals were 58.6 WAR and an OPS+ of 128. Those are decent Hall of Fame numbers for an infielder or catcher, but not for a corner outfielder. Sosa played most of his career in Wrigley Field, in a very high offense era while on steroids, so his raw numbers overstate how good he was. Sosa was like David Ortiz, without any significant post-season experience. Moreover, there were a lot of things that Sosa could not do well. He played a corner outfield position and was never a great defender. He had a career high batting average of .273, and for a power hitter, other than during his five year peak, never drew a lot of walks. His home run and RBI numbers always were impressive, but he never led the league in batting average, OBP, slugging percentage, OPS+ or walks. A solid player who put up gaudy power numbers for five years, Sosa was briefly the face of baseball, and is now the face of the absurdity, hypocrisy, and strangeness that was the PED era.

Eighty-eight
Casey Stengel

Here's another easy trivia question. Who is the only person to wear the uniform of all four New York teams, the Dodgers, Giants, Mets and Yankees? The answer is Casey Stengel who played for the Dodgers and Giants and managed the Dodgers, Mets and Yankees. Stengel played in his first big league game on September 17, 1912. His Brooklyn Dodgers were at home against the Pirates. This was even before the Dodgers played in Ebbets Field. Stengel had an excellent debut hitting four singles, driving in two runs and drawing a

Library of Congress, Prints & Photographs Division [LOC LC-USZ62-28945]

walk as Brooklyn won by a score of 7-3. The cleanup hitter for Pittsburgh that day was Honus Wagner. Wagner was one of the greatest players ever, but is almost from baseball's pre-history. More than half a century later, the hapless New York Mets, on their way to their fourth consecutive last place finish dropped a game to the Phillies 5-1. The cleanup hitter for the Phillies that July 24th, the last game Stengel ever managed, was Dick Allen. The distance from Honus Wagner to Dick Allen feels like a baseball eternity, but Stengel was there for all of it. Stengel played for John McGraw and mentored Billy Martin. He batted against Carl Mays and Ernie Shore in his first World Series, but didn't play in game two of that 1916 series when Babe Ruth was the opposing pitcher. Bill Mazeroski and Roberto Clemente were his opponents in the last World Series Stengel managed.

Stengel did not simply have a long career in baseball; he left a big mark on the game. During his playing career, Stengel was a good hitting outfielder slashing .284/.356/.410 over fourteen seasons for the Dodgers, Pirates, Phillies, Giants and Braves. In those years, Stengel began to earn a reputation not just as a good ballplayer, but also as a character. His most well-remembered stunt dates to 1919 when he was playing for the Pirates. During a game he somehow caught a sparrow and stuck it under his cap. He then stepped out of the dugout, tipped his cap and the sparrow flew out. Towards the end of his years as a player, Stengel hit an inside the park home run in the 1923 World Series while playing for the Giants. That home run broke up a 4-4 tie in the 9th inning of game one and was the subject of a wonderful column by Damon Runyon. The theme of that column was that Stengel was an old man desperately trying to beat the throw to home plate. Stengel, at that time, was 33-years-old and would be in baseball for another four decades.

While many portrayed Stengel as kind of funny character, more astute observers already could see he had a keen mind for baseball. Nine years after retiring, Stengel became the manager of the Brooklyn Dodgers. He stayed in that position for three seasons, but never had a .500 team. After a year off, he took over as manager of the Boston Braves from 1938 through 1943. He did not start the 1943 season with the Braves, but took over early in the year The Braves finished two games over .500 in 1938, but did not reach that benchmark again while Stengel was there. Stengel had encountered little success managing, but had begun to innovate with ideas like platooning and using his pitchers differently. After a decade as a big league manager and never even smelling the pennant race, Stengel's career seemed to be winding down.

Unable to find a big league job, Stengel was hired to manage the Oakland Oaks of the PCL in 1946. He stayed there for three years and then got the break that solidified his place in baseball history. In 1949, Stengel was hired to manage the Yankees. There he became the most successful manager in baseball history winning the World Series in his first five seasons with the Yankees. During the twelve years he was there, the Yankees won ten pennants and seven World Series.

As manager of the Yankees Stengel was one of the most visible sports figures in New York and one of the most famous baseball people in the US. By then, he had learned how to keep the reporters on his side and became known as a font of, sometimes barely comprehensible, baseball wisdom. Stengel had an unusual way of speaking and frequently talked in circles and garbled his syntax. This came to be known as Stengelese and was most famously on display in a 1958 senate testimony regarding baseball's anti-trust exemption. What Stengel said made almost no sense, but the senators loved it, and him.

The received wisdom about Stengel's years with the Yankees is that with the talent Stengel had, a bonobo in pinstripes could have won as much, but that is not really the case. Those Yankees teams had three Hall of Famers in the primes of their career, Yogi Berra, Mickey Mantle, and Whitey Ford. However, there were few other real impact stars on those teams after Joe DiMaggio retired in 1951. Stengel won by finding ways for players including Enos Slaughter and Johnny Mize, who were thought by other teams to be too old, to continue to contribute, getting the most out of players like Gene Woodling, handling his pitchers creatively and knowing when his veterans were done. Those Yankees obviously had a lot of talent, but Cleveland also had impressive front line talent and better pitching for most of those years. Stengel's Yankees played the Dodgers in five World Series and won four of them. The Dodgers had a much deeper team, regularly putting five future Hall of Famers in their starting lineup, and better pitching, but Stengel found a way to consistently beat them.

After being fired from the Yankees following an unexpected loss to the Pirates in the 1960 World Series, Stengel became the first manager of the New York Mets in 1962 and held that position for almost four seasons. Stengel lent some name recognition to the new franchise, but he quickly fell back to his losing ways. Those Mets teams were terrible. Stengel himself seemed more interested in schmoozing with the media than with turning the Mets into a winner.

Casey Stengel's career in baseball spanned from Honus Wagner to Dick Allen. He was the manager of famously great, and famously terrible teams, and is one of the players who best connects baseball history over the decades.

Eighty-nine
Ichiro Suzuki

Baseball fans have had a lot of tsuris in the 21st century—the PED scandal, the shortened Covid season, the lockout during the 2021-2022 offseason, tanking, the Astros cheating scandal, Curt Schilling, pace of play and length of game issues, shifts and the evolution of the game into the three true outcomes style of play, but if there is one player who during much of that time captured what was still great about the game, it is Ichiro Suzuki. Ichiro was a

Photo 44202141 / Baseball © Jerry Coli | Dreamstime.com

very special player for all the right reasons. He was a wonderful player who played hard, was respected by his teammates and his opponents, never dabbled in PEDs and was always a joy to watch.

Many people, including several players, have had integral roles in the globalization of baseball and in building links between MLB and Asia. Ichiro was not the first player from Japan in the US. By the time he made it to the Mariners in 2001, Japanese players in MLB were no longer such an oddity. However, Ichiro was the first Japanese player to be recognized as a top tier star in the US and will soon be the first Japanese player elected to the Hall of Fame in Cooperstown.

After Ichiro announced his interest in playing in the US in the 2000-2001 offseason, several teams competed to sign him, but Ichiro chose Seattle. He arrived there at an interesting moment. Over the previous three years, the Mariners had traded away, or lost to free agency, Randy Johnson, Ken Griffey Jr. and Alex Rodriguez. The 2001 Mariners were without a superstar for the first time in a decade. Many expected the Mariners to struggle without Rodriguez, who left as a free agent after the 2000 season. Instead, the Mariners won a record 116 game, tying the 1906 Chicago Cubs for the most ever.

A big part of the Mariners success in 2001 was Ichiro. Few players have had a rookie year comparable to Ichiro's. Ichiro batted .350. His 242 hits were the most since 1930. Additionally, he led the league with 56 stolen bases and won a Gold Glove. At the end of the year Ichiro won the MVP and Rookie of the Year awards, becoming only the second player in baseball history—the other was Fred Lynn in 1975—to win both awards in the same season.

Ichiro was an unusual player with a very unusual skill set for his era. He hit for average, stole bases and played excellent defense in right field, but had very little power and did not walk much. There are not a lot of players like that in the modern game. In the age of power and patience Ichiro had neither and, accordingly, modern metrics are not kind to him. His OPS+ of 107 and 60 WAR do not place him among the greats.

Ichiro's greatest skill was his ability to get hits. His ten seasons of 200 or more hits are tied with Rose for the most ever. Ichiro set the all-time single season hit record with 262 in 2004. He and Wade Boggs are the only players since 1930 to have 240 or more hits in a season. Boggs did it once, Suzuki twice. Ichiro also missed doing it a third time by only two hits. Ichiro amassed 3,089 hits between 2001-2019. However, he did not begin playing in the US until he was 27. Before coming to the US, he had another 1,287 hits in Japan, bringing his overall total to 4,367. Just as a case can be made that Sadaharu Oh is the real home run leader, a similar case can be made that Ichiro, not Pete Rose, is the real all-time hit leader.

In addition to being a great player, Ichiro was one of those players who had a style and enthusiasm that drew fans' attention. Largely because he was playing essentially deadball era baseball in the early 21st century, and excelling at it, he was a compellingly fun player to watch. I remember watching an All-Star game a few years back when Ichiro came to bat and got a hit. The person with me was not a baseball fan but noticed Ichiro and commented on how cool he seemed. After playing in the big leagues for several years Ichiro began to learn Spanish, in part so he could trash talk opposing players. Ichiro's love of the game is legendary in Japan and in the US making him one of the faces of globalized baseball today.

Like Ken Griffey Jr., Ichiro's career had a long decline phase. From 2001-2010 Ichiro had a .331 batting average and a 117 OPS+. He played nine more years and managed to hit only .268 with an OPS+ of 83 while going from Seattle to the Yankees and Marlins and then back to finish his career with the Mariners. Although other than his first half-season with the Yankees he was never a good player after 2010, Ichiro remained well liked and respected around baseball. His love for the game was clear. Even into his retirement, stories about him doing things like going to his old high school to take a little batting practice would appear every now then.

During his years playing in the US, Ichiro emerged as the face of the new global game. He was a Japanese man speaking Spanish while playing America's national pastime with tremendous skill, joy and enthusiasm. It is tough to think of a better symbol for the positive side of MLB in this century.

Ninety
Bobby Thomson

On Opening Day of the 1951 season Bobby Thomson was the starting centerfielder for the New York Giants. Within a few months, a rookie named Willie Mays took over in center where he would stay for more than twenty years, so by the final game of the season Thomson was the Giants third baseman. After 1951, Thomson spent the next two years playing a little third, but mostly in the outfield for the Giants, including some time in centerfield when Mays was in the military. Thomson

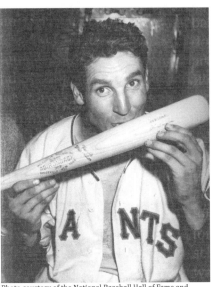

Photo courtesy of the National Baseball Hall of Fame and Museum (Thomson Bobby 3744.68WT1G)

was then traded to the Milwaukee Braves following the 1953 season because the Braves were looking for a power hitting outfielder. However, Thomson injured himself and did not play in a game for the Braves until July. His injury opened up a spot in the outfield for Henry Aaron. So, in a four-year span Thomson lost his job to two of the greatest players ever, and in between he hit the most famous home run in baseball history.

Many people who know of Thomson's famous home run may not know that he was a very good player. He was not a light-hitting infielder who came up big in a dramatic situation like Bucky Dent or Bill Mazeroski, but a slugging outfielder who hit 264 big league home runs. Thomson was one of the Giants best hitters in 1951, leading the team in home runs, slugging percentage and

OPS. With the pennant on the line, Bobby Thomson would have been one of perhaps two Giants, the other was Monte Irvin, who most fans of the team would have wanted to see at the plate. The on deck hitter when Thomson hit the home run, Willie Mays, was better than both of them, but he was still a rookie.

Thomson's big moment arose when the Giants and Dodgers ended the 1951 regular season in a tie and found themselves in a best of three playoff series against each other. The Dodgers had led for most of the early part of the season, but the Giants had clawed their way back, likely with the help of a sign stealing scheme, from being thirteen games back on August 11th. By the early 1950s New York had emerged as the unequivocal center of the baseball world; and this was the ultimate in New York City baseball. Two New York teams were competing for the opportunity to play the third New York team in the World Series. There were 13 future Hall of Famers playing for New York teams that year including four of the greatest centerfielders ever, Mays, Mickey Mantle, Joe DiMaggio and Duke Snider.

The two teams split the first games. Game three was played at the Polo Grounds. After the first seven innings, the score was 1-1, but the Dodgers scored three runs in the top of the eighth to go ahead 4-1, which remained the score going into the bottom of the ninth. Two singles and a one out double made the score 4-2 with two runners on and Thomson at the plate. What happened next may still be the most famous play in baseball history. Thomson hit a three-run home run and the Giants won the pennant.

Thomson's home run was dramatic, but it has taken on a degree of fame and importance that is much bigger than that. After all, the Giants did not win the World Series that year, losing to the Yankees in six games. In those days, there were no playoffs so the series between the Dodgers and the Giants was an oddity that drew a lot more attention than the NLCS would today. The dramatic nature of the home run, the great New York backdrop to the story and even the footnote that the on deck hitter was none other than Willie Mays gave the home run something of a life of its own. The home run found its way into American letters as Dom DeLillo wrote a short story, which later became the first section of his 1997 novel *Underworld* about that game and what may have happened to the ball after it left the yard.

Thomson's home run came to be known as the "Shot Heard 'Round the World." One of the reasons for that was that the game was broadcast on television and radio, including armed service radio, so American military personnel could hear it almost wherever they were stationed. About fifteen years ago, I went to a museum exhibit in New York about baseball in the 1950s. I found myself looking at a picture of Thomson's home run, while standing next to a man in his seventies. After about thirty seconds, he turned to me and said "I lost a month's pay on that home run. I was in Korea and I'm from Brooklyn, so I bet on the Dodgers." He seemed to have gotten over the loss of the money, but not of that pennant.

Because 1951 was the beginning of the television age, Thomson's home run is also the first major baseball event for which we still have video. However, the film most fans have scene includes an audio of Giants radio announcer Russ Hodgers repeating "The Giants win the pennant!" Most fans have seen that film which has helped sear this event into the collective baseball consciousness.

Thomson's home run was a dramatic baseball moment that media and context made even more significant. It now exists at the intersection of baseball, mythology, literature, and Americana.

Ninety-one
Jim Thorpe

Jim Thorpe had a short and not very impressive big league career. Some people may be surprised to learn that Thorpe played baseball at all, but he spent parts of six different seasons with the Giants, Reds, and Braves between 1913 and 1919. Over the course of those years, he came to the plate 751 times and slashed .252/.286/.362. He was an outfielder and first baseman, so needed to hit a lot better than that to remain in the league.

Despite his struggles on the ballfield, Thorpe was one of the greatest American athletes of the first decades of the twentieth century. He was a star Olympian who also excelled on the football field and basketball court. Thorpe was a standout football player in college and with the Canton Bulldogs of the American

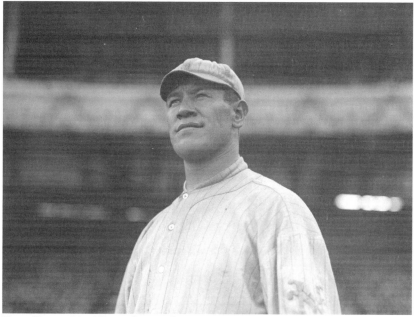

Library of Congress, Prints & Photographs Division [Bain News Service LOC LC-DIG-ggbain-14466]

Professional Football Association, an antecedent of the NFL. Thorpe is best known for his performance at the 1912 Olympics in Stockholm where he won gold medals in the pentathlon and decathlon. Those accomplishments led Swedish King Gustav V. to tell Thorpe "You, sir, are the greatest athlete in the world." However, a year later the Amateur Athletic Union took back the medals because they learned Thorpe had played professional baseball, at the minor league level and for very little money, for a few games before the 1912 Olympics. This was done despite the time allotted for those kinds of protests to be lodged having already lapsed. Thorpe's medals were finally restored in 1983, 71 years after Thorpe won them and almost thirty years after his death.

Thorpe is not the only fantastic athlete to struggle as a baseball player. Almost eighty years after Thorpe stopped playing baseball, Michael Jordan interrupted his basketball career to try his hand at baseball. Jordan never even made it to the big leagues. A better comparison to Thorpe would be Bo Jackson who was one of the best athletes of his generation. Jackson was a better baseball player than Thorpe, but if Thorpe had lived in a different media era, he would have been just as marketable as Bo Jackson.

One of the reasons the Olympic incident is still remembered is because Thorpe was Native American. The decision to take away his medals has always had a bit of the stench of racism around it. The relationship between baseball and Native Americans has been complex. Until 2021, there was a team called the Cleveland Indians whose mascot was a Native American caricature knowns as Chief Wahoo. The Atlanta Braves had a mascot called Chief Noc-A-Homa for twenty years. Braves fans still engage in what they call the Tomahawk Chop. The fans make a chopping movement with their arms while humming a tune that is, I think, supposed to suggest Native Americans preparing to attack. The racism of that gesture is in danger of being overshadowed by how annoying it is.

In addition to these racist team names, there has been a relatively small number of Native Americans in the big leagues. One way we know that is from the racist practice, in the first half of the twentieth century, of nicknaming almost all Native Americans Chief, including Charles Bender and John Meyers. Bender won over 200 big league games, mostly for the Philadelphia Athletics between 1903 and 1917 and is the only Native American in the Hall of Fame. More recent Native Americans in the big leagues include Jacoby Ellsbury and Joba Chamberlain.

After his baseball career ended, Thorpe spent much of the 1920s playing professional football and even a little professional basketball, but by the early 1930s his athletic career was winding down. For the rest of his life, Thorpe worked odd jobs while also acting in many movies. Among his acting credits are *They Died With Their Boots On, Knute Rockne All American, Sutter's Gold* and *King Kong*. In those films, and the total of 71 in which he appeared, Thorpe generally had minor roles. Thorpe was also the subject of a 1951 film called *Jim Thorpe-All American* about his Olympic accomplishments and having his medals taken away. In that film, Thorpe was played by Burt Lancaster.

Thorpe was born in Oklahoma and lived the final years of his life in Southern California, but he attended a special high school for Native Americans called Carlisle Indian School, the same school Charles Bender attended, in Pennsylvania. The school was for high school and college age youth, so Thorpe played college football there as well. After Thorpe died the town of Mauch Chunk, Pennsylvania, located about 100 miles from Carlisle, renamed itself Jim Thorpe. Thorpe is probably the only baseball player in the US to have a town named in his honor.

Thorpe's baseball career is almost a footnote to his broader athletic career. However, in the first half of the twentieth century he was extremely famous and important part of both Hollywood, albeit not as a leading man, and sports where his reputation lasted long after he stopped playing. In 1950 the Associated Press voted Thorpe, not Cobb, Ruth, Knute Rockne, Red Grange, Jesse Owens, Jack Dempsey, or anybody else, the athlete of the half century.

Today Thorpe is largely forgotten. Jim Thorpe, Pennsylvania is a tiny town of only about 5,000. The Burt Lancaster film of Thorpe's life is not exactly blowing up on Netflix; and Thorpe's acting oeuvre is not particularly well known today. However, his career, life and struggles are very much part of baseball's relationship with Native Americans and the broader racial politics of the game.

Ninety-two
Joe Torre

On November 2, 1995, the Yankees announced that Joe Torre would be their new manager replacing the recently fired Buck Showalter. The back page of the *Daily News* the next day featured a photo of Torre with the headline "Clueless Joe." The headline suggested that Torre did not know how to manage in the big leagues, but in fairness to the *Daily News,* they were also saying that Torre was clueless for willingly going to work for George Steinbrenner, who was known for mistreating and firing managers. A few weeks later when Don Zimmer was hired to be the bench coach, I remember thinking that the Yankees had been turned over to two hacks. Torre ended up managing the Yankees for 12 years, winning six pennants and four World Series.

Photo 46409584 / Baseball © Jerry Coli | Dreamstime.com

Torre's last year with the Yankees was 2007, but he then managed the Dodgers from 2008-2010. By the time he was done Torre had managed for 29 years. Only five men had managed more games. Torre is also only one of five managers who have won four or more World Series. Torre's time as a manager was preceded by 18 years as a player and followed by another decade or so in the MLB front office. Torre has been around baseball a very long time. In Torre's first big league appearance he singled pinch-hitting for Warren Spahn. Henry Aaron, and Eddie Mathews were also in the Braves lineup that day in September of 1960. The starting pitcher in one of the last games Torre ever managed was Clayton Kershaw. In between, he managed or played with Derek Jeter, Mariano Rivera, Ozzie Smith, Dale Murphy, Lou Brock, Bob Gibson, and Tom Seaver among others.

As a manager, Torre was never a great tactician. He was predictable, rarely innovated and was given to overusing his relievers. However, he was extremely good at media relations, working with the difficult and demanding George Steinbrenner and shielding his players from the owner's frequent irrational tantrums. Torre's calm personality set the tone for the Yankees and helped the team focus on winning on the field. The manager of the Yankees is a high profile position because of the New York media, but Torre became a media presence of a different kind. Over the course of his tenure managing the Yankees he became kind of a wise man of the baseball community in New York.

To some extent, Torre redefined the role of big league managers. When he took over the Yankees, managers were still evaluated on their in game strategic decisions. Today, most managers work closely with the front office and have much less control of the team than in the 20th century. Torre was part of that transition. He understood that with the Yankees in particular, in-game strategy was not the primary role of the manager. It is easy to evaluate Torre's bullpen use, but more difficult to determine how many controversies and fights between the players and the owners he prevented through his communication skills.

Torre's thirty years as a manager ultimately overshadowed his playing career, but he was a very good player. Torre was elected to the Hall of Fame by the Veterans Committee in 2014 largely because of his work as a manager, but he had close to a Hall of Fame career as a player as well. Torre was a slugging catcher and corner infielder who made nine All-Star teams. Torre slashed .297/.365/.452 for a career OPS+ of 129 and 57.5 WAR. Torre's best year was 1971 when he hit .363 with 24 home runs for the Cardinals and won the National League MVP Award. Torre began his career as a catcher with the Milwaukee Braves in 1960, but was never a great defender behind the plate By the late 1960s, Torre was playing mostly first and third base.

Like Lou Gehrig, Whitey Ford and a small handful of other players, Torre grew up in New York and went on to make a big impact on New York baseball. Torre was born in 1940, so was a star young ballplayer when New York baseball was at its apex. Torre grew up in Brooklyn, but was a New York Giants fan. He spent the last three years of his playing career with the Mets. After he retired midway through the 1977 season, he took over as the team's manager and stayed in that position through the 1981 season. Fifteen years later, he became the Yankees manager.

While managing the Yankees Torre was a link back to New York's past even beyond baseball. He told stories about growing up in Brooklyn, had a sister who was a nun in Queens and even spoke with a New York accent. Many Yankees fans well into middle age by 1996 grew up in the same New York as Torre. The connection was made even stronger when Torre became the most successful Yankees manager since Casey Stengel.

Before he got to the Yankees, only one Joe Torre managed team, the 1982 Atlanta Braves, had ever made the playoffs. That team got swept out of the NLCS by the Cardinals. Had Torre retired after he was fired as the manager of the Cardinals midway through the 1995 season his reputation would have been as an affable guy and pretty good player who was not a good manager and wasn't a winner-thus the "Clueless Joe" headline. By the time Torre left the Yankees, his reputation had changed substantially. By then he had won four World Series and, thanks to the expanded playoffs, still has more post-season wins than any manager in baseball history.

Ninety-three
Cristóbal Torriente

Unless you are Cuban or Cuban American, Cristóbal Torriente may strike you as one of the most obscure players in this book. That is unfortunate, because Torriente was an extremely good player. Babe Ruth is generally considered the greatest ballplayer of the first half of the twentieth century, but in addition to one or two other white players like Ty Cobb and Honus Wagner, there are a few players who were excluded from the big leagues during those years who should be part of that conversation. Torriente is one of those players.

Known sometimes as the Cuban Babe Ruth, Torriente was a slugging outfielder who played in the Caribbean and in the Negro Leagues in the US, but was not allowed to play in the American or National Leagues because he was Black. Torriente was born in 1893 in Cuba and died in New York in 1938 when he was only 44-years-old. He was reportedly

Public Domain Photo

impoverished and alone at the time of his death. Like many great

Negro League players, Torriente did not live a long life and died in relative obscurity. Eventually, he was elected to the Hall of Fame but not until 2006.

Torriente was primarily a centerfielder who, like Ruth, also was a pitcher. Unlike Ruth who was a pitcher and then a hitter, Torriente was a hitter throughout his career. However, due in part to the smaller size of Negro League rosters, Torriente was an occasional pitcher.

The statistical records of Torriente's career are from 1920-1928 and two games in 1932 with Negro League teams including the Chicago American Giants, the Kansas City Monarchs, the Detroit Stars and the Louisville Black Caps. Like all players who were excluded from the American and National Leagues, Torriente's statistical record is incomplete and does not capture the fullness of his baseball abilities and accomplishments. Torriente was 26-years-old when he played in the inaugural season of the Negro National League for the Chicago American Giants. He had a pretty good year leading his team to the pennant. Torriente slashed .411/.479/.606, leading the league in all three categories for an OPS+ of 223.

Over the course of parts of ten years in the Negro Leagues, Torriente played in 646 games and came to bat 2,613 times. During those years, and in the years preceding 1920, Torriente played in countless other games in a mix of barnstorming, undocumented and short-lived leagues, tournaments and exhibitions, so his Negro League record is better understood as a sample of his play rather than a full record of all his baseball accomplishments. The statistics from those years show Torriente slashing .340/.427/.523 for an OPS+ of 158. His 25.9 career WAR seems low, but on a per game basis is about the same as Frank Robinson.

One of the most famous, and fascinating, descriptions of Torriente was from Frankie Frisch who said of the great Cuban star "I think I was playing third base at the time, and he hit a ground ball by me... It dug a hole about a foot deep on its way to left field... In those days Torriente was a hell of a ballplayer. Christ, I'd like to whitewash him and bring him up." That comment provides a sense of what kind of hitter Torriente was. He was not the kind of slugger, like the Babe, who hit soaring home runs. Rather, the right-handed hitting Torriente was a line drive hitter who always hit a lot of doubles. Obviously, the drive to which Frisch refers did not actually dig a hole, but the image is a good one.

There is more to Frisch's quote than him simply lauding Torriente's hitting ability. The next line about wishing to white-wash Torriente is strange and revealing. First, it is cruel and humiliating to even suggesting painting another human being. Second, it speaks to how strong the institutionalized racism in baseball, which Frisch at the very least reflected, was at the time. Rather than saying he wished baseball was less racist, Frisch suggested essentially changing Torriente's race. Lastly, Frisch became enormously influential in the Hall of Fame veterans com-mittee. In that capacity, he worked to enshrine teammates from the Cardinals and Giants who were good, but clearly not up to Hall of Fame caliber. However, he did nothing to help Torriente who made it into the Hall of Fame decades after Frisch's death. The point here is not that Frisch was particularly bigoted, but that baseball for much of its history, completely overlooked the Negro Leagues.

Torriente's career is a reminder that baseball has been an international game for a long time. Other than Dolf Luque, there were no Cuban players making an impact on the American or National League until the1950s, but that is because of the seg-regationist policies of those leagues. Luque and Torriente were born in the same country a few years apart, but in the US, and for the purpose of their baseball careers, one was Spanish and the other was Black and treated very differently. That is one way to understand the bizarre and cruel nature of American racism, both inside and outside of baseball. Great Black Cubans like Torriente, Martin Dihigo and others had been playing alongside top American players for years by then, just not white ones. The limited information we have about Torriente's career, or for that matter his life, underscores this problem of baseball history. We know a lot about one corner of the baseball world before 1950, but have very limited knowledge about other parts of that world.

Ninety-four
Mike Trout

Mike Trout has been the best player in baseball for over a decade and is one of the greatest in the history of the game. Trout turned 31 late in the 2022 season, so 2022 was technically his age 30 season. Among position players, only Ty Cobb, Rogers Hornsby, Mickey Mantle and Alex Rodriguez had more WAR than Trout's 82.4 through their age 30 season. This does not include Negro League stars and several players like Willie Mays and Ted Williams who would be in that group if not

Creative Commons - Keith Allison KeithAllisonPhoto.com

for military service early in their career. However, Trout lost two thirds of a season in 2020 as that season was shortened due to Covid. Another indicator of Trout's greatness is his OPS+ of 176 through 2022, tying him with Mickey Mantle for seventh highest ever of any player through his age 30 season.

In 2012, Trout's first full year with the Angels, Trout had a 168 OPS+, while stealing 49 bases and accumulating 10.5 WAR. He easily won the Rookie of the Year Award and narrowly missed winning the Most Valuable Player Award as well. Since then, he has continued to hit, but he is no longer a base stealing threat and has not stolen as many as ten bases since 2019. Injuries have also begun to take a toll on Trout as he has not played in 150 games in a season since 2016.

Baseball has never been as competitive as it is today when players come from all over the world to play in the US. Moreover, training, coaching, modern medicine, relief pitching and roster maneuverability have made hitting tougher than ever. Trout has dominated in a modern game in a way that, at first cut, does not seem entirely possible.

It is a cliché that statistics do not fully reflect a career of any one player, but Trout may be the exception to that. Trout is a wonderful player, but there is something workmanlike and unglamorous about him. When healthy he just goes out every year hits over .300, draws over 100 walks, wallops 35-45 home runs and plays solid defense in centerfield. However, it is tough to think of any one great moment in Trout's career. For a player who has been an All-Star ten times and has won three MVP awards, he has a very light footprint in the collective baseball memory. It doesn't help that Trout has only appeared in one post-season series during his career. Beginning in 2021, Trout was overshadowed by his teammate Shohei Ohtani who is more exciting and fun to watch. In fact, the most memorable moment of Trout's career may be striking out against Ohtani for the final out of the 2023 World Baseball Classic.

There is something else extraordinary about Trout that helps explain baseball in the 21st century. Trout is the best player in the game and has spent his entire career with the Angels, who play in the country's second largest media market. However, he is almost completely unknown outside of the baseball world. It is not an exaggeration to say that few Americans who are not big baseball fans would recognize Trout if he were standing behind them in line at the grocery store.

Some of this can be attributed to Trout who has kept a low profile, avoided controversy and seemed reluctant to embrace any kind of spotlight, but that only somewhat explains Trout's relative anonymity. Trout reflects an important aspect of baseball over the last twenty years or so. The game has become a much less important in the context of American culture. Stars of a previous era were often recognizable by ordinary American well into their old age, but if Mike Trout came into my local café, which is only about five subway stops from Yankee Stadium, I would be surprised if anybody knew who he was.

The changing role in the culture has occurred as baseball has become a much bigger and more lucrative business. In March of 2019 Trout became the highest paid player in baseball history signing a 12-year contract for a total of $426.5 million. Trout makes about $37 million a year, but is nowhere near as famous as players of 50 or 100 years ago, who made a fraction of the money Trout does, ago were during their playing days. That is the paradox of 21st century baseball.

Ninety-five
Fernando Valenzuela

Today we think of Los Angeles having a huge Mexican American population that has helped form the character and culture of that city. If you go to a Giants-Dodgers game in either San Francisco or Los Angeles, you will see that baseball's best and oldest rivalry now occurs substantially in Spanish. This was not always the case. When the Dodgers moved to Los Angeles from Brooklyn, little thought was given to the possibility of becoming a favorite team among Mexican Americans. That is understandable as back then Los Angeles County was only about ten percent Latino. Today about half the population of that county is Latino.

The Dodgers relationship with Mexican American Los

Angeles was difficult from the beginning as the team displaced an old Mexican American community to build Dodgers Stadium. During the 1960s and 1970s, despite some very good Dodgers teams, Mexican Americans never warmed to the Dodgers.

Fernando Valenzuela was a Mexican pitcher who changed all that. As a 20-year-old rookie in 1981, Fernando Valenzuela was the biggest thing in baseball. He was called up late in the 1980 season and threw 17.2 scoreless innings for the Dodgers. The Dodgers ended that season in a tie for the National League West title and had to play a one game playoff against the Astros. There was some talk that the Dodgers would start Fernando, but manager Tommy Lasorda opted for the struggling veteran Dave Goltz instead. Goltz pitched poorly and the Dodgers lost that game 7-1.

The Dodgers opponent on Opening Day 1981 was the Astros again. This time Valenzuela got the start and threw a shutout. He made a total of five starts that April of 1981 giving up only one run. That run came at Candlestick Park in his second start of the season. I remember because I was at that game and commented to my friend that we had seen Fernando give up his first run. He went on to win the Cy Young and Rookie of the Year award that year as his Dodgers won the World Series.

In 1981, Fernandomania swept the baseball world. Every one of his starts, particularly before the strike, was a major event in two countries. Fernando was only 20-years-old, 5'11, a little on the pudgy side and the best pitcher in baseball. His windup was unusual as at the midpoint of his delivery he would look upward as if summoning help from the heavens. Fernando did not speak great English so he was not very quotable, but stories of him trying to navigate celebrity and a new country provided a bit of levity as baseball careened towards a strike that would take away the middle third of the season. In 1981, Fernando was not just a great pitcher, but a huge and culturally significant celebrity.

At the time of the strike, with just over a third of the season over, Fernando was 9-4 with a 2.45 ERA. The strike may have cost Fernando a few wins, but it also saved some stress on his arm and limited him to 192.1 innings in his rookie year. After the strike, Fernando slowed down a little, but was still the best story in baseball and helped melt some of the anger fans felt towards both players and ownership.

Beginning in 1981, Fernando was also an important person to the Mexican American community throughout the country, but specifically in Los Angeles. Valenzuela became a prominent celebrity in both Mexico and the US. Valenzuela was the first Mexican ballplayer to become a major star in the US and one of the first prominent Mexican celebrities in any field. Valenzuela was the key person in reversing the Dodgers' standing in the eyes of many Mexican Americans. In doing that he helped the Dodgers access a huge fan base. Even today, he is known in Los Angeles, where he has been part of the Dodgers Spanish language broadcast team for twenty years, simply as Fernando.

Valenzuela's best year was 1981, but he remained one of the top pitchers in the National League through 1986. In the six-year span from 1981-1986, Fernando was an all-star every season and finished in the top five in Cy Young voting four times. However, following the 1987 season, Fernando began to encounter injury problems, in no small part because he had thrown 1,800 innings before his 27th birthday. Fernando remained in the big leagues through the 1997 season, with one year off to play in Mexico and retired with 173 wins and 41.4 WAR.

Despite having credentials that are very comparable to his contemporary Jack Morris, who became a kind of cause celebre of the curmudgeonly sportswriter crowd, Fernando received little support for the Hall of Fame. He never even got ten percent of the vote and fell off the ballot after only two years. However, this lifelong Giants fan thinks Fernando should be in the Hall of Fame. His career numbers, like those of Morris are a little bit light for a Hall of Famer, but he was an essential part of the history of baseball and was one of the few Mexican players who had real star power. For the first six years of his career, when you watched Fernando pitch, you felt you were watching a Hall of Famer. That should count for something too.

Ninety-six
Honus Wagner

There is a good case to be made that Honus Wagner was the greatest player ever. In my view he is fourth among those who played in the National or American Leagues behind Babe Ruth, Willie Mays and Barry Bonds, but that is to some extent because he played in the deadball era so his home run numbers are not great. However, Wagner hit a lot of doubles and triples and led his league in slugging percentage six times. Only Rogers Hornsby,

Library of Congress, Prints & Photographs Division [LOC - LC-USZ62-28926]

Stan Musial, Barry Bonds, Ty Cobb, Ted Williams, and Babe Ruth have equaled or exceeded that. Wagner also led his league in WAR for non-pitchers 11 times, something only Mays, Hornsby, Bonds, and Ruth have done. Wagner was a great hitter who stole bases and, in his era, was a powerful hitter and run producer, but he was also a standout defensive shortstop. If you took Jeff Bagwell's offensive value and maybe not Ozzie Smith, but perhaps somebody like Omar Vizquel's glove, you would get Honus Wagner. That is a very valuable player.

Wagner had doubles and triples power at the plate and stole 723 bases during his career. Wagner is still, by far, the greatest shortstop ever. A couple of data points make this clear. Alex Rodriguez has the second most seasons with an OPS+ of 150 or better while playing shortstop. Rodriguez did it four times;

Wagner had eleven such seasons. Wagner also had more seasons with seven or more WAR and more career WAR than any other shortstop.

Wagner is one of the very best players from baseball's very early days. He began his career in 1897 and retired following the 1917 season, spending all but his first three years with the Pittsburgh Pirates. However, that is not what makes Wagner an extremely impactful player. To understand what makes Wagner different, we have to talk about baseball cards. For fans of a certain age, baseball cards represent an almost Proustian connection to baseball, and their own past. Baseball cards are fun, sometimes valuable, and as much a part of the lore and feel of the game as bleacher seats, the crack of the bat or labor strife. For decades no card was more famous or valuable than Wagner's.

In my home office where I wrote most of this book, I have a display of 80 of my favorite baseball cards from roughly 1965-1982. Some of those cards were purchased at corner stores in San Francisco, some were acquired in trades with friends and a handful of them were purchased at baseball card stores or conventions. I stopped avidly collecting around the time I graduated from high school, but when I look at each of those cards I can not only think of specific memories of most of the players, but can remember the feel of opening the pack of cards or perusing the collection at the card shop in Berkeley I used to frequent. For me baseball cards were a tangible expression of my love for the game. The statistics on the back were central to my baseball education and the photos on the front to my baseball imagination.

Not all collectors are in it just for the memories and love of the game. There is a cliché of the middle-aged man bemoaning the valuable baseball card collection that his mother threw away when he grew up and left home. I was fortunate my mother never threw out any of my cards. Many of those baseball card collections that got thrown away would not be worth all that much today. Many cards from the last thirty years are all but worthless. Complete sets in mint condition have some value, but for the most part baseball cards are not the best investment.

The exception is that a handful of cards, for different reasons, are extremely valuable. For many years the most valuable baseball card was a Honus Wagner card from the years 1909-1911 issued by the American Tobacco Company. The card is known as the T206 Honus Wagner Card. There are fewer than 50 of these cards in existence. In 2022 one of them was sold for $7.25 million. The Wagner card was eclipsed in August of 2022 when a collector paid $12.6 million for a 1952 Mickey Mantle card.

The reason the Wagner card is worth so much is not just because Wagner was a great player, but because the card is extremely rare. In those days, tobacco companies sponsored cards and they were packaged with tobacco products. Wagner did not smoke and thought smoking was harmful, particularly for young people, so did not want to be associated with tobacco products. However, the American Tobacco Company had already made a very small number of those cards before Wagner was able to make them stop producing them.

The story of the T206 also affirms Wagner's reputation as a decent affable man who cared about things like young people's health habits. Ty Cobb and Honus Wagner were two of the biggest baseball stars of the deadball era and were archetypes of two different kinds of baseball stars. Cobb was the angry unpleasant star who the media never liked. Wagner was different. He was a well-liked and decent man who got along well with media and fans and by doing that was a key player in the development of baseball card collecting.

Ninety-seven
Hoyt Wilhelm

There is something strange, offbeat, tantalizing and funny about the knuckleball. The fastball is still the primary way pitchers are evaluated and measured, but the knuckleball is like the anti-fastball. It is thrown slowly and moves unpredictably. A good knuckleball is just as tough to hit as a good fastball, but for completely different reasons. Because it is not thrown hard, the knuckleball seems like a pitch anybody can throw, almost like a ticket to the big leagues through a side door.

Photo courtesy of the National Baseball Hall of Fame and Museum (Wilhelm_Hoyt_BL-4066-69_HS_NBL)

However, although the knuckleball looks easy very few pitchers have mastered it.

The knuckleball adds an unusual dimension to the game. A good knuckleball pitcher can make even very good hitters look silly as they flail at a slow pitch that is moving completely unpredictably. Because of its movement, the pitch is hard to catch, so the catcher sometimes looks foolish too. The knuckleball may have fallen victim to baseball's new emphasis on speed and athleticism in general. In 2021 there was only one pitcher in the big leagues who threw the knuckleball, but there were none in 2022. Nonetheless, the knuckleball is a strange and important part of the game and deserves some representation in this book.

Hoyt Wilhelm is one of two knuckleballers in the Hall of

Fame. The other is Phil Niekro who was Wilhelm's teammate in 1969-1971. Niekro was the better pitcher, but Wilhelm had a bigger impact on the game because he was one of the key people in the creation of the modern relief pitcher. There had been pitchers before Wilhelm who pitched mostly in relief, but none for as long or as effectively. Players like Firpo Marberry, Wilcy Moore, and Joe Page had a few good years out of the bullpen. Wilhelm was different. He was a reliever from the time he arrived in the big leagues with the New York Giants in 1952. It is true that he started a total of 52 games in his career, but he relieved in 1,018 games. Moreover, Wilhelm pitched in 363 games in relief before he started a game.

When Wilhelm began his career, there were no relief specialists in the game. The year before he began his career, Ted Wilks, a player who almost nobody remembers, led the National League with 13 saves, but saves were not even an official statistic at the time. The best known reliever in the game was probably Ellis Kinder, who had 16 saves for the Red Sox in 1951. By the time Wilhelm retired following the 1972 season, relief pitchers like Roy Face, Lindy McDaniel, Ron Perranoski, Phil Regan, Rollie Fingers, John Hiller and Sparky Lyle had either become or were about to become stars.

The emergence of relief specialists and the bullpen as an important part of the game is one of the biggest changes in baseball over the last seventy years and has changed everything from the pace of the game to almost all elements of baseball strategy. The evolution has been gradual, but in today's game, starting pitchers rarely go through the lineup three times or throw more than 110 pitches. It is no longer unusual to see a team use five or more pitchers in a game. One result of this is that rarely are starting pitchers the protagonists of each game as they were in the twentieth century. Additionally, as the bullpen becomes more important teams carry 12 or 13 pitchers, which means they frequently only have four or even three position players on the bench. This changes strategy because managers can pinch hit and use defensive replacements less than in the past.

These changes were gradual and have accelerated in the last

ten years or so. However, during the course of Wilhelm's career, relief pitchers became much more important to the game. Some of that was due to how Wilhelm was changing baseball. Wilhelm was not a closer, but more of a fireman who would enter the game when his team needed him most. Because of how he was used, Wilhelm never collected saves the way later relievers would. His career total of 228 saves is currently 43rd on the all-time list. However, when he retired Wilhelm had by far the most saves ever. He held that record until Rollie Fingers passed him in 1980.

Wilhelm was unlike any other pitcher in baseball history. He was 29-years-old when he first made it to the big leagues and pitched until he was two weeks short of turning 50. Because the knuckleball stresses the arm so much less than other pitches, knuckleballers can pitch much longer than most. Wilhelm pitched in almost 500 games after he turned 40. No other pitcher came within even 100 games of that record. In his rookie year eight National League teams, playing 154 games each, combined for 443 complete games or 36% of all games. In 1972, his last year in the league, twelve teams playing 144 games each (the start of the season was delayed in 1972 due to a strike) combined for 507 complete games, for a total of only 29% of all games.

As a knuckleballer who didn't make it to the big leagues until he was almost thirty and then stayed for twenty years, and who all but invented a new position, Wilhelm was a very unusual, even quirky player, but there is one more story about Wilhelm. It doesn't have much to do with his impact on the game, but captures the gestalt of his unusual career.

Wilhelm was a very bad hitter, even for a pitcher. Over the course of his career, he came to the plate 493 times and slashed only .088/.131/.106. Wilhelm's career at a batter started on a more positive note. In his first big league at bat, he homered off of Boston Braves pitcher Dick Hoover. Wilhelm never hit another one.

Ninety-eight
Ted Williams

It is sometimes difficult to understand just how good a hitter Ted Williams was. A lot has been written about that topic, so I will make two points that are sometimes overlooked. First, John Updike wrote a famous essay about Williams's last game at Fenway Park and the home run he hit that day. It is a wonderful piece of prose that captures something special about Williams. However, there is more to Williams's last season, 1960, than what Updike wrote. The AL MVP that year was Roger Maris. Maris

Photo courtesy of the National Baseball Hall of Fame and Museum (Williams Ted 17.54_Bat_NBL)

was, like Williams, a slugging corner outfielder. Age and injuries limited Williams to only 113 games and 390 plate appearances in 1960, so he did not quite play a full season. However, during 1960 Williams had a higher batting average, slugging percentage, and on base percentage than Maris. Williams's OPS+ was a full thirty points higher than Maris's in 1960.

Second, most people know that Williams missed a lot of playing time due to military service, but that deserves some more attention. Williams missed three years in his prime and about one and three quarters more in his early thirties. If he had managed 79 home runs, 600 hits and 500 walks during those seasons, all conservative estimates, Williams would have retired with more than 600 home runs, more than 3,000 hits and the second most walks of any player ever. His rate statistics would be higher too. Instead, he hit 521 home runs, more than 2,600 hits and has the fourth most walks ever. Williams has the highest on base percentage of any player in baseball history and is second only to Babe Ruth in slugging percentage and OPS+. Batting average is no longer seen as the most important statistic, but his .344 batting average is higher than any other American or National League player who began his career after 1920.

Williams was one of the greatest hitters ever, but was also an intriguing player. Williams was not well liked by the media when he was playing and was frequently described as surly or disagreeable. He was neither a player like Babe Ruth or Willie Mays who had an easy and enthusiastic rapport with fans, nor a star like Joe DiMaggio who had some intangible characteristic that made him untouchable.

I have long believed there is more to Williams than that. Part of this goes to baseball's very complex racial history and policies. Williams, who spent his whole career with the Red Sox, the last team to have an African American player, occupies a fascinating role in baseball's racial history. During his Hall of Fame induction speech in 1966, Williams encouraged the Hall to recognize the great Negro League players who had been excluded and is credited for helping open the doors to Cooperstown to many of those players. Williams did not single handedly bring Negro Leaguers into the Hall of Fame, but he was the first prominent white player to point out this substantial oversight by the Hall of Fame. Williams helped start a process that led to inducting Satchel Paige into the Hall of Fame in 1971, and Josh Gibson and Buck Leonard in 1972. Today there are almost forty Hall of Famers who played primarily in the Negro Leagues.

Williams was not outspoken on race issues as a player, so his Hall of Fame speech was something of surprise. One explanation for why Williams chose to advocate for Negro Leaguers may have to do with his own background. Williams, who grew up in San Diego, was Mexican American on his mother's side. Williams began playing with the Red Sox when segregation was still strong in baseball, particularly with the Red Sox. Given his skin pigment and last name, Williams was able to pass. However, he more or less concealed his Mexican background throughout his career, suggesting he was, at the very least, concerned about racism he might confront in baseball. Had Williams been Ted Venzor, his mother's maiden name, and forthright about his background, he might still have had a career in baseball, but he would have been treated very differently. Williams can perhaps be criticized for largely concealing his background, but it is more appropriate to see his experience as evidence of the racism in baseball. Williams was American by birth and citizenship, but it is still relevant that by 1939, when Williams began his career in Boston, there had only been two Mexican players in the American or National Leagues. The exclusion of Black players, from the US and the Caribbean during the years from about 1890-1947, was an enormous blemish on the American and National Leagues, but the racial policies around Latinos were also very damaging, but much more complex. Williams is evidence of that.

Williams may not have gotten along well with the media and fans, but he was perhaps the most macho big star to play the game, almost baseball's John Wayne. In addition to his baseball stardom, Williams was an avid and highly accomplished fisherman and was elected to the Fishing Hall of Fame in 2000. He was a bomber pilot who served his country in two wars, in the Navy in World War II and the Marines in Korea. He cultivated the image of a tough guy who didn't say much. For a certain kind of mid-century American man, Williams was a role model more than even Joe DiMaggio.

Ted Williams was one of the very best hitters ever and the greatest player in the history of one of baseball's most famous franchises. He was an important advocate for celebrating the Negro Leagues and is a largely unrecognized link in the history of Latinos in baseball.

Ninety-nine
Connie Wisniewski

Connie Wisniewski was an AAGPBL player for the Milwaukee, and then the Grand Rapids, Chicks. Wisniewski was probably the best pitcher in the history of the AAGPBL, but then, because of a rule change, decided to move to the outfield where she became a very good hitter. During her first three years, from 1944-1946, she was a combined 88-30 with a 1.52 ERA. Wisniewski pitched for two more years, but was no longer among the very best pitchers in the league. When the AAGPBL started, pitchers were required

Photo courtesy of the National Baseball Hall of Fame and Museum (AAG Wisniewski Connie 228-2007-14_FL_NBL)

to throw underhand, more or less in a submarine style. In 1946, that was expanded to allow pitchers to throw sidearm as well, but beginning in 1947 pitchers were required to throw overhand. Wisniewski was the best pitcher during the AAGPBL's early years because she was a great sidearm pitcher, but she had trouble adapting to the new overhand requirements.

Although, she continued to pitch overhand for two years, by 1948 Wisniewski was primarily an outfielder. She had always hit well for a pitcher and soon became one of the league's best hitters. The AAGPBL was a pitcher's league, so Wisniewski's .272/.362/.349 slash line does not look as impressive as it is. However, she was among the league leaders in hits and batting average after moving to the outfield full time. Wisniewski was not a power hitter. She only hit seven home runs in her career, all in 1947. However, she had decent doubles and triples power. The AAGPBL did not have an All-Star team until 1946, but Wisniewski was named an All-Star as a pitcher in 1946 and then twice more as an outfielder. Wisniewski was the best pitcher in the league for several years and then was among the best hitters for a few years, so she may have been the best player in AAGPBL history.

The AAGPBL was the only baseball league that gave women a chance to play professionally and to make some money doing it. The significance of this is underscored by the fact that since the league disbanded 70 years ago, there has no women's baseball league that was as successful as the AAGPBL. Additionally, the AAGPBL was the last league in the US to exist alongside what is now MLB. By the time the AAGPBL started, the Negro Leagues were beginning to struggle. Integration of the National and American Leagues beginning in 1947 accelerated the decline of the Negro Leagues, but that process was already underway by the time Jackie Robinson made it to the Dodgers. The Continental League was never much more than an idea in the late 1950s and the late 1960s. Since then, the hegemony of MLB has been almost complete. There are a few independent teams and leagues, but they have all struggled simply to make it from year to year.

One of the results of this hegemony is that MLB is now almost solely responsible for the changes and evolution of the game. It is true that MLB usually tests rule changes in the minors before bringing them to the big leagues, but the ideas come from MLB rather than rising organically. One exception to this is the ghost runner on second base at the beginning of every extra inning. This rule was implemented in the 2020 Covid season and has remained. It was originally a rule from youth baseball and should have stayed there.

Before 1950, the American and National Leagues were influenced by other forms of baseball. Jackie Robinson, Willie Mays, Minnie Minoso and other early African American players brought the Negro League style of aggressive base running back to the rest of baseball. In the late 19th and early 20th century, rules changed frequently, in many cases because the game was played differently in different regions of the US.

The AAGPBL also innovated and changed rules in an effort to get the best product on the field. The style of pitching changed twice, but also things like the distance from the pitcher to home plate, the distance between bases and even the size of the ball changed, in some cases several times, during the life of the AAGPBL. This made life difficult for some players, but it also made the game interesting for fans. Today, MLB struggles to address pace of play related issues. This challenge is greater because MLB cannot point to another league, at least in the US, to see what works there and try to copy it.

Wisniewski was unusual because she was able to adapt to the rule change and reinvent herself as a player. Because she was a successful two-way player, Wisniewski is sometimes compared to Babe Ruth. That seems like an unfair comparison because Ruth was such a singular player. Whereas Wisniewski changed her game to adapt to a rule change, Ruth changed the game and forced the rest of the baseball to adapt. Wisniewski's accomplishments are still very significant. Over the last decades, there have been countless outfielders whose careers were cut short because they couldn't learn to play first base. Many hitters today have seen their statistics plummet because they have been unable to adapt to the shift. While almost no pitchers can switch mid-career to the outfield, it seems like some relievers trying to hold on to a big league job might be able to make themselves more valuable if they could pinch run or play passable outfield defense.

Connie Wisniewski was more than just a very adaptable player. She was the best player in the only league in the US that ever gave women a real chance to play the game.

One Hundred
Cy Young

One last easy trivia question: who threw the first pitch in the first World Series? The answer is Cy Young. The first World Series was in 1903 when Young's Boston Pilgrims, who later became the Red Sox, faced off against Honus Wagner's Pittsburgh Pirates. Young, coming off a season in which he went 28-9 with a 2.08 ERA got the start in game one. He did not pitch well giving up seven runs, three earned, in a complete game 7-3 loss. Young ended up going 2-1 over four games and 34 innings in that series, which the Pilgrims won five games to three.

Library of Congress, Prints & Photographs Division [LOC - LC-DIG-ppmsca-18460]

Today, Cy Young is best known for the award named after him. Cy Young's name has become synonymous with pitching excellence. There are many baseball fans today who know the Cy Young Award and have strong feelings about who should get it every year, but know very little about Cy Young the pitcher. There are probably some fans who do not even know he was a real player. It is striking that Cy Young's name has stuck to the award. The award for the best rookie is named after Jackie Robinson, but nobody calls it that. The Henry Aaron Award goes to the best overall offensive player in each league, but nobody pays much attention to that award. Until 2020, the MVP award was named after Kenesaw Mountain Landis, but almost no fans even knew that. The Cy Young award is different. In the baseball world, everybody knows what the Cy Young Award is, and cares about who wins it ever year. Cy Young, like Tommy John, has become a baseball term that is more well known than the player himself, but Young was also a great, and important player.

Cy Young's career started in the baseball pre-history of the 19th century, but he played until 1911. The baseball he played in the 1890s was different even from the deadball era of the early twentieth century. This makes Young seem almost mythical. Walter Johnson and Christy Mathewson were great pitchers from another era, but their accomplishments are accessible to a baseball fan today. Young's are less so. For example, seven times in the 1890s, Young threw forty or more complete games in a season. In five of those years he pitched over 400 innings. Young's best year was probably 1892 when he started 49 games and completed 48. Over his 453 innings that year he went 36-12 with a 1.93 ERA. Today, those are the kinds of numbers we might expect from a great pitcher over his first two or three years in the big leagues.

Young holds career records for wins, losses, games started, complete games, hits allowed, earned runs allowed and batters faced. The margins, for example, almost 100 more wins and complete games and 40 more starts, than any other pitcher, are also astounding. During his career, Young faced 25,565 batters. Today a team might send 4,000 batters to the plate in a season. Young pitched to the equivalent of every batter for six teams over the course of a full season. Because his numbers are so freakish, it is tough to determine just how good Young was. For this reason, he is frequently left out of the conversation about who was the greatest pitcher ever. However, if we don't penalize him for playing a very different game, then he should at the very least be part of the discussion. Modern analytics also demonstrate that as well. His 163.6 WAR is second only to Walter Johnson's 164.8-meaning they are essentially tied. His 138 ERA+ is excellent, but behind that of Pedro Martinez, Walter Johnson, Lefty Grove and a few others.

To some extent, Cy Young is now an award, not a former

ballplayer. However, he is one of the few names from baseball's pre-history that most fans recognize. Baseball today is a totally different game than it was back when Young was throwing forty complete games a year, but baseball is also a game that almost obsessively celebrates, with varying degrees of honesty and sensitivity, its history. Cy Young, and the award named for him, is one of the ways that baseball keeps that connection to its distant past strong.

Young lived until 1955, so was able to see Ruth, DiMaggio, Robinson and Willie Mays play the game that was so different than the one he played in the 1890s. The Cy Young Award was created by Commissioner Ford Frick in 1956 following Young's death. It was meant to elevate the role of pitchers because hitters dominated the MVP voting. Through 1966 the award was only given to one pitcher, rather than to one in each league. On balance, the Cy Young Award has made it tougher for pitchers to win the MVP award because some sportswriters refuse to vote for pitchers for MVP on the grounds that they already have the Cy Young Award.

Ironically, while Cy Young is still one of the most famous names in the baseball world, Cy was a nickname. It was not a shortened from of Cyrus or perhaps even Simon as some might think. Rather it is a short form of cyclone which is not really a name at all. Young was nicknamed "Cyclone" because of how hard he threw as a young man. His full name was Denton True Young, but somehow the Denton Young award wouldn't sound quite the same.

Conclusion

Baseball is fascinating as both a unique American, and increasingly global, sport, but also because of the ways in which it helps us understand broader histories, politics, and culture. It is my hope that by briefly exploring the lives and careers of the players in this book, I have contributed to that understanding.

Babe Ruth, Willie Mays, Jackie Robinson, and a very few others have been central figures in American history. No true cultural history of the US would be complete without addressing these three men and the impact they made on sports, celebrity and, in the case of Robinson, civil rights. Similarly, the stories of race and racism are inseparable from the American story itself. The careers of Robinson, Jim Thorpe, Cristóbal Torriente, Dolf Luque, Josh Gibson, Juan Marichal, and Dick Allen are among the players who help us explore those questions in more depth.

In the third decade of the 21st century baseball reflects the increasingly globalized world in which we live. Recent and contemporary players like Shohei Ohtani, Miguel Cabrera, Pedro Martinez and Chan Ho Park are evidence of that, but they are standing on the shoulders of Masanori Murakami, Felipe Alou, Orestes Minoso, Roberto Clemente and others.

Players including Andy Messersmith, Catfish Hunter and Curt Flood were integral to baseball becoming the huge multi-billion dollar industry it is today. Absent their willingness to take chances, and in the case of Flood, make real sacrifices, baseball would be a very different game, and industry, today.

One of the things that makes baseball magical is the way it travels across generations. John McGraw, whose team won the 1922 World Series managed Casey Stengel who in turn managed Roger Craig for whom Dusty Baker, whose team won it all in 2022, coached. McGraw, Stengel and Baker are among baseball's great connectors whose careers span across decades and baseball generations.

The multi-generational nature of baseball leads to the question of how baseball developed into its current form. The careers of players such as Cy Young, Ty Cobb, Honus Wagner the Babe, Robinson, Hoyt Wilhelm, Mariano Rivera, Mike Trout and many others profiled in this work, help us see how the game is played and managed differently than it was 120 years ago.

The history of baseball goes back for well over a century and, in many respects, feels infinite. There are thousands of players, millions of games, several important leagues and countless connections that can be made. Narrowing that history down to one hundred players was a challenging, but very fun, task. There are many players who just missed. Helen Callaghan-Candaele, Martin Dihigo, Leo Durocher, Elmer Gedeon, Bob Gibson, Eddie Grant, Harry O'Neill and Albert Pujols are among the players who could easily have been part of this book.

Given how difficult it was for me to assemble this list and make the final cuts, I do not expect everybody to agree with this list. If I have helped provide more insight into the special American institution that is baseball, then I have achieved my primary goal for *The One Hundred Most Important Players in Baseball History*, and if it leads to a few good baseball arguments and discussions, that is great too.

Acknowledgements

Many baseball books, including this one, rely heavily on statistics. The statistics in this book are drawn from the excellent, thorough and way too addictive, website baseballreference.com. I used on that site, along with the Society for American Baseball Research (SABR) player biography project, to check many of the numbers and details in this book.

This work, like all my baseball books, is a product of a lifetime thinking obsessively about baseball. There are also many people with whom I have been conducting years-long, in some cases, decades-long baseball conversations. Some of those people include Corey Busch, Joseph D'Anna, Charles A. Fracchia, Jr, Dave Gluck, Adam Iarussi, Charles Karren, Mark Klitgaard, Alan Metrick, Andrew Shear, Geoff Silver and The Baseball Freaks. Those conversations have not only helped shape some of the ideas in this book, but have been sources of great enjoyment and meaning for me.

My colleagues from the now defunct "Say It Ain't Contagious" webinar series and podcast which later became the "Left of Baseball," have been instrumental in my thinking about baseball and society in recent years, so a big thanks to Adrian Burgos Jr., Craig Calcaterra, Steven Goldman, Frank Guridy and Tova Wang.

I first got the idea for this book while watching old World Series games from the 1970s on YouTube with John Maschino. I am grateful for John's friendship in baseball and life for more than forty years. After that discussion, I proposed writing a kind of annotated list of the 100 most important players ever to Paul Semendinger who runs the great Yankees website "Start Spreading the News," where I had been writing for a few years. It was winter of 2022 and there was a paucity of baseball news due to the lockout, Paul encouraged me, and put a very early, and much abridged, version of the book on the site. Paul also offered extensive and extremely helpful comments on a draft of this book. *The One Hundred Most Important Players in Baseball History* exists, and is a better book, because of Paul. It was also a great pleasure working with Geoff Habiger at Artemesia Publishing. Geoff was tireless and supportive and helped make this book possible.

My wife Marta Sanders and sons Asher and Reuben do not share my passion for baseball history, although my sons were much better players than I ever was. Nonetheless, they have patiently listened to far more of my baseball stories than I would have liked. My research assistant, Penny Lane, slept on the job a lot and has never learned to use a computer, but was by my side when most of the writing of this book occurred.

About the Author

Lincoln Mitchell teaches at Columbia University's School of International and Public Affairs. In addition to his books on topics ranging from foreign policy to the history of San Francisco to baseball, Lincoln's writing has appeared at CNN, NBC, the *New York Times,* the *San Francisco Examiner* and numerous other publications.